MEXICAN WOMEN AND THE OTHER SIDE OF IMMIGRATION

***Chicana Matters: Deena J. González and Antonia Castañeda,
series editors***

*Chicana Matters Series focuses on one of the largest population groups in
the United States today, documenting the lives, values, philosophies, and
artistry of contemporary Chicanas. Books in this series may be richly diverse,
reflecting the experiences of Chicanas themselves and incorporating a broad
spectrum of topics and fields of inquiry. Cumulatively, the books represent
the leading knowledge and scholarship in a significant and growing field of
research and, along with the literary works, art, and activism of Chicanas,
underscore their significance in the history and culture of the United States.*

MEXICAN WOMEN AND THE OTHER SIDE OF IMMIGRATION

Engendering Transnational Ties

LUZ MARÍA GORDILLO

UNIVERSITY OF TEXAS PRESS
Austin

Requests for permission to reproduce material from this work should
be sent to:
    Permissions
    University of Texas Press
    P.O. Box 7819
    Austin, TX 78713-7819
    www.utexas.edu/utpress/about/bpermission.html

⊗ The paper used in this book meets the minimum requirements of
ANSI/NISO Z39.48-1992 (R1997) (Permanence of Paper).

LIBRARY OF CONGRESS CATALOGING-IN-PUBLICATION DATA

Gordillo, Luz María, 1962–
    Mexican women and the other side of immigration : engendering
transnational ties / by Luz María Gordillo. — 1st ed.
        p.   cm. — (Chicana matters series)
    Includes bibliographical references and index.
    ISBN 978-0-292-72203-3 (cl. : alk. paper)
    1. Mexican American women—Michigan—Detroit—Social
conditions—20th century.   2. Mexican American women—Identity—
Michigan—Detroit.   3. Mexican American women—Cultural
assimilation—Michigan—Detroit.   4. Immigrants—Michigan—
Detroit—Social conditions—20th century.   5. Women—Mexico—San
Ignacio (Jalisco)—Social conditions—20th century.   6. Women—
Identity—Mexico—San Ignacio (Jalisco)   7. Transnationalism.
8. Detroit (Mich.)—Emigration and immigration.   9. San Ignacio
(Jalisco, Mexico)—Emigration and immigration.   I. Title.
F574.D49M514   2010
305.48′868077434—dc22
                                                        2010007678

Para mi mamá, Luz María de los Cobos Torres.

CONTENTS

ACKNOWLEDGMENTS

Writing this book has been a long and enlightening journey. I am deeply grateful to all the San Ignacians and Detroiters who generously shared their memories, their homes, and their lives with me. Among other things, they reminded me that as a Mexicana immigrant I have had similar experiences that are full of contradictory feelings—both painful and rewarding—and that it is all right to recognize and acknowledge these as part of a successful immigrant narrative.

Gracias to Juan Javier Pescador, who opened up the fascinating discipline of history and offered his friendship and guidance. His cutting-edge research on transnational studies and his eagerness to share it with me have enriched my research and made me a better educator. I deeply thank him for his intellectual integrity and creativity. I thank many scholars at Michigan State University for teaching me how to become a strong feminist historian: Lisa Fine, Dagmar Herzog, who shared her passion on sexuality studies, and Leslie Moch. I am grateful to David W. Walker (1948–2001), *que en paz descanse*, who spent time sharing his experiences as a Mexicanist. Thanks also to my dear friend Jolee Blackbear, who read the manuscript in its beginning stages.

Staff members of the various archives where I did primary research were helpful in many ways. I particularly want to thank the archivists in the Secretaría de Relaciones Exteriores and the National Archives in Mexico City, the Immigration and Naturalization Service office in Detroit, and the National Archives regional branch in Chicago for sharing their knowledge with me.

Financial support for this project came from several sources. From Washington State University Vancouver I received a Faculty Seed Grant, Diversity Council mini-grant, and College of Liberal Arts Research Grant. The American Association for University Women (AAUW) Educational Foundation awarded me an American Fellow Summer/Short-Term Research Publication Grant. All of this helped make the publication of this book possible.

I am grateful to my *compañeras* and insightful scholars at Washington

State University who have read this manuscript at one point or another and have gently offered comments and suggestions: Linda Heidenreich, Pavithra Narayanan, and Noël Sturgeon. Special thanks to Candice Goucher and Laurie Mercier, who read the manuscript more than once and kindly provided critical perspective and meticulous comments on style and form. Their suggestions made this manuscript much stronger. Mexican historians and sociologists offered guidance and aid. Jorge Durand kindly made interesting comments. Basilia Valenzuela Varela opened up her personal archives and shared her research on San Ignacio with me. Having said that, I take full responsibility for this study and its findings.

I presented excerpts of this book at various academic conferences and received invaluable suggestions from several scholars. In particular, I would like to thank my *compañeras* from MALCS (Mujeres Activas en Letras y Cambio Social) and all my queer *amigas* from NACCS (National Association for Chicanas and Chicanos Studies) for providing comments and sharing great humor.

Editors have contributed their wisdom and expertise. I am grateful to Antonia I. Castañeda and Deena González, the Chicana Matters Series editors, and to the anonymous reviewer, who offered incredible bibliographical references. I am indebted to Antonia Castañeda for supporting this very important study from the beginning and for her invaluable critical analysis. Thanks to Kandy Robertson at Washington State University Vancouver. I appreciate Kathy Sunshine's delightful narrative and wonderful disposition. I also extend my gratitude to the editors at the University of Texas Press for their guidance throughout this process: Theresa May, assistant director and editor-in-chief; Leslie Doyle Tingle, managing editor; Kathy Lewis, copyeditor; and Kaila Wyllys.

Gracias a mi familia. To Gangue, whose strength and resilience kept our family afloat. To my *hermano* Ricardo, for bringing home the difficult emotional process of what it is to become a Mexican immigrant in the United States. Thanks to my nephews, Bruno and Bernardo, for sharing with me the pains of transnational familial dislocation. To my *mami*, the best feminist role model anyone could ask for. I am eternally grateful to her for the many hours she spent working on this project: researching, translating, transcribing, videotaping, and living with me in San Ignacio—and, most importantly, helping me see working-class Mexicanas through a different lens. And finally, *mil gracias* to my partner Kevin Díaz, who not only patiently and kindly fed me and provided emotional stability but also offered insightful comments.

MEXICAN WOMEN AND THE
OTHER SIDE OF IMMIGRATION

INTRODUCTION

Afternoon sunlight lit the main avenue of San Ignacio Cerro Gordo as Carmen waited for the sign to begin the procession. She was wearing a formal black dress trimmed with delicate white lace along the plunging neckline. Her hair, perfectly done, was held up with an ornate black hairpin. Standing next to Carmen was her fiancé, Roberto, wearing a dark gray suit. Together they held a magnificent painting of the Virgin of Guadalupe, their family's contribution to the local Catholic church. Immediately behind Carmen and Roberto stood a young woman, also dressed in formal attire, proudly holding aloft a sign proclaiming "DETROIT." Hundreds of immigrants lined up behind the sign to participate in the celebration they had been awaiting all year.

The purpose of the procession was twofold: to honor the Virgin of Guadalupe, patron saint of Mexico and of San Ignacio, and to celebrate the return of the town's immigrants, making their yearly visits from the United States. The town of San Ignacio celebrates its *fiestas patronales* (patron saint festivities) each year during the last week of January. Traditionally a religious ceremony, the festivities now also serve as an elaborate welcome for *los hijos ausentes*—the town's "absent sons and daughters," most of whom are members of the large working-class San Ignacian colony in Detroit.

The regional bishop joined forces with several local priests to orchestrate the week-long celebrations. There were several processions each day, celebrating the Virgin of Guadalupe and the many patron saints of nearby towns. They included special parades for young people, children, business owners, beauty queens, married couples, and even single women and single men. Father Ignacio Ramos Puga, the local priest and main organizer of the festivities, had carefully selected most of the participants who took on significant roles in the parades. Being chosen to be a character in one of the biblical scenarios represented on the intricately decorated custom-built trucks was an honor.

The celebration also served as a reminder of the economic and social importance of immigration. Returnees displayed their immigrant success by flaunting clothing and jewelry purchased stateside. Children were dressed in the latest Detroit styles and wore gold bracelets and necklaces, from which dangled medals of the Virgin of Guadalupe. Some children wore medals honoring San Toribio, to whom immigrants pray for protection during risky border crossings. Young women from Detroit took the opportunity to transgress forbidden spaces by wearing revealing dresses and blouses that drew disapproving glances from the town's older women.

For the celebration of 2003, Father Ignacio Ramos Puga chose Carmen and Roberto to lead the procession of *los hijos ausentes.* The parade would end at the town's church, where a special mass had been planned for the visitors. As the opening procession got underway, *charros* and *charras* (traditional cowboys and cowgirls) mounted on their magnificent thoroughbreds were followed by antique cars, beauty queens, Aztec dancers, and the truck-borne floats. Carmen stood proud, representing her own transnational family and the larger family of San Ignacian youth, who experience both Detroit and San Ignacio as their home.

This vibrant celebration, held every year in San Ignacio, symbolizes the enduring connections between members of a working-class single natal community that now straddles two contested geographic sites thousands of miles apart. The communities of San Ignacians in San Ignacio, Mexico, and Detroit, Michigan, are not separate entities but one transnational community that navigates in two nation-states and that is continuously shaped and reshaped by back-and-forth migration and by complex family, social, and economic ties.

MEXICANS IN THE MIDWEST

Scholarly work on Mexicans in the Midwest appeared in the 1930s, written by sociologists and economists who thoroughly recorded the growth and composition of the Mexican population there. One of the most notable works, and directly relevant to this study, was Paul S. Taylor's in-depth sociological analysis of Mexican immigrants from Arandas, Jalisco. The small town of San Ignacio Cerro Gordo in Los Altos de Jalisco (the case study presented in this book) belonged to the municipality of Arandas until 2003, when it was approved to become an independent municipality.[1] Along with Taylor, who also wrote on Mexican immigrants in Chicago and the Calumet region, sociologist Norman Daymond Humphrey recorded the lives of Mexicans in Detroit, starting in the 1930s. Their work

MAP I.I.   *Map of Mexico with Jalisco and San Ignacio highlighted.*

provides a narrow window into Mexican immigrants' lives in the Midwest and tells us more about the academic approach to the study of people of color—including assumptions and stereotypes about Mexicans and Mexican Americans—than it does about Mexicans' experiences as immigrants. Nonetheless, these scholars left thorough statistics and numerous interviews that have enriched the work of later historians of Mexicans in the Midwest.

It was not until the 1990s, however, that Chicana/o historians turned their attention to the Midwest and produced monographs that revealed new circumstances surrounding the lives of Mexicans in the Midwest. Dionicio Nodín Valdés, Juan R. García, and Zaragosa Vargas mapped out social and labor experiences that differed from the experiences of Mexicans in the Southwest.[2] Vargas focused on Mexicans in Detroit, providing a detailed account of labor relations and labor experiences that set the stage for community formation in Detroit during the first three decades of the twentieth century. Building on Vargas's work, which ends in the

Great Depression years, this book seeks to provide a sense of historical continuity by analyzing the postwar experiences of Mexicans in Detroit. Moreover, it integrates gender as an inherent component of the study of Mexicans in the United States and more specifically in Detroit.

This book holds a specific conversation with Chicana historians who contributed a gendered historical analysis emphasizing the lives of Mexican women and women of Mexican descent in the United States. These Chicana historians focused on the Southwest, where Euro-American conquest and violence underscored the history of Mexican Americans in the United States. They recorded how, after many Mexicans were dispossessed and marginalized by hegemonic Euro-American conquest, struggles of resistance began to map out Mexican American history.

Vicky Ruiz challenged not only Euro-American mainstream historians but also Chicano historians who left women outside of their narratives. Her narrative emphasized the lives, experiences, and struggles of Mexicanas in the Southwest. Ruiz demonstrated strategies such as "cultural coalescence" that Mexicanas appropriated in order to navigate Euro-Americans' stratified society, which privileges some while marginalizing others. Mexicanas, according to Ruiz, appropriated cultural capital from the United States that they felt most appropriately covered their needs.[3] Historian Deena González contested Eurocentric discourses of the Southwest that erased Mexican and Mexican American women's agency. González emphasized the strategies of resistance applied by Mexicanas to contest and challenge colonization while their social organization was severely disrupted.[4] Antonia Castañeda's work centered on contestations of Euro-American historical narratives, underlining the importance of social constructions that historically devalue women of color and justify narratives of conquest. Enriching the field of history, Castañeda proposed a social constructionist approach that is now integral across disciplines and inherent in the recent field of transnational studies.[5]

TRANSNATIONAL STUDIES ON MEXICANS IN THE UNITED STATES

Several researchers have attempted to redefine the historiography and literature on Mexican immigration to the United States. Of particular note is the innovative work by Jorge Durand and Douglas S. Massey, who began their study of immigration in the early 1980s and continue to supply us with invaluable statistics and information on Mexican immigration to the United States.[6] Most recently, however, Gabriela Arredondo has provided a notable gendered study on Mexicans in Chicago, contributing not only to the history of Mexicans in the Midwest but also to transnational studies.[7] Arredondo proposes the innovative term *mujeridades* for what she considers to be a collection of experiences that Mexican women undergo while experiencing movement in their nation-state. *Mujeridades* are Mexican (and often nationalist) ideals of social expectations of and about women—notions of "womanhood" that are far from representing working-class Mexican women's realities. Arredondo not only frames gender as central but also begins to look at the complexities of gender relations within Mexican immigrants' social networks during the interwar years in Chicago. My study expands on gendered literature of working-class Mexicans in the Midwest and also begins to interrogate the way transnational studies have approached the study of working-class Mexicanas in the United States.

Starting in the 1990s, feminists and other scholars have opened up the dialogue focusing on gender as a category of analysis while investigating Mexican immigration to the United States and framing their argument within a transnational context.[8] Pierrette Hondagneu-Sotelo and Saskia Sassen offer a socioeconomic and political analysis of how the capitalist global economy has interlocked transnational corporations and labor forces in underdeveloped countries, triggering large diasporas. They suggest that the global economy creates a tier of low-wage labor that for the past three decades has been filled mostly by women.[9] While I largely agree with their approach to the study of social institutions and their effects on transnational subjects, I focus on an in-depth examination of the everyday processes within the migratory experiences of Mexican immigrants.

This book contends, first, that the experience of working-class immigrants is not fragmented into two different spaces—their community of origin and the receiving community. My research shows that both spaces are integral to their everyday lives and should be considered as parts of a whole. The collection of experiences while migrating from one nation-state to another is what I refer to as the immigrant experience. Moreover, the immigrant experience is gender specific and affects and influences San Ignacian working-class men and women differently.

Second, I introduce the concept of "transnational sexualities," which emphasizes the social construction of working-class sexuality informed by experience in both the sending and receiving communities. This process shapes and reshapes meanings and understandings of different social realities that apply to working-class Mexicanas' and Mexicanos' experiences in San Ignacio and in Detroit. In tandem with recent literature focused on constructions of sexualities in transnational spaces, I argue that transnational studies should attend to the ways in which gender meanings operate and are reconstructed in these transnational spaces. In addition to offering a gendered feminist analysis of migration, however, I maintain that many San Ignacian working-class women take the first step toward fragmenting gender stereotypes and transgressing traditionally male roles while they are still in their community of origin, often while their husbands or other family members are living abroad as immigrants. These transgressions facilitate the later migration of the women themselves and their adaptation and accommodation to the new environment in Detroit.

Some feminists and academics of transnational studies (like Pierrette Hondagneu-Sotelo in her work on Mexican domestic workers in Los Angeles) have suggested that Mexican immigrant women achieve semi-emancipation from patriarchal roles first by immigrating and later by joining the paid labor force.[10] I contend, however, that these processes of emancipation are complex: they begin in the community of origin and later provide Mexicanas with certain tools while they are experiencing immigration to the United States. Mexicans in both San Ignacio and Detroit have expanded their understandings of femininity and masculinity and their constructions of gender and gender roles.

A third goal of this monograph is to deconstruct the social networks that support and sustain immigration to understand the contributions made by the reproductive and productive labor of Mexicanas. The concept of "social networks" contributes to our understanding of the construction of transnational communities. Although we have grown accustomed to reading about social networks that sustain immigration, as researchers we have failed to explore the meanings that working-class Mexicanas and Mexicanos themselves attach to these networks. In this analysis I deconstruct these support systems in order to understand how working-class Mexican women built upon the bracero generation's first attempts to initiate the movement of San Ignacians to Detroit. Within the gender dynamics of these social networks we can observe how immigration is stimulated and sustained. It is particularly important to recognize that the immigrant experience is full of contradictions, and these shape the lives of working-class Mexicanas and Mexicanos as they contribute to the building of transnational networks.

In *Servants of Globalization: Women, Migration, and Domestic Work* Rhacel Salazar-Parreñas argues that "the experience of migration is embodied in dislocations."[11] These dislocations include first and foremost familial separation but also dislocation from one's accustomed place in the socio-economic structure. Salazar-Parreñas documents the downward social mobility experienced by many Filipina immigrants in Los Angeles and Rome, who have had some formal education yet have to work as domestics. Her work focuses on four institutions (the nation-state, the family, the labor force, and the migrant community) and underscores the dehumanization or commoditization of labor in the context of the global economy. This study contends that these dislocations—transnational dislocations—are embedded in the immigrant experience. Moreover, it adds that transnational studies must integrate these dislocations as an inherent variable in studying "diasporic subjects," as Chicana feminist Emma Pérez calls the global mobilization of labor from developing countries to industrialized world powers.[12]

Finally, this book shows clearly that the immigrant experience has transformed both the sending and receiving communities and has created an innovative and dynamic gendered culture that supports what I call transnational citizenship, grounded in "membership" in two or more nation-states. In the process, contradictions and tensions continuously arise, challenging working-class Mexicanas and Mexicanos constantly to re-create, adapt, accommodate, shape, contest, and create new meanings for the environment in which they live. Many of these contradictions are gender specific to the transnational experience. Thus this study examines the impact of migratory movements on the gendered politics of movement within the larger context of globalization.

MEXICAN IMMIGRANTS AND TRANSNATIONAL SPACES

I began my work with working-class Mexican immigrants in Detroit by visiting Patton Park, where Mexican immigrants play soccer every Sunday. After numerous visits I became aware of the large numbers who hailed from the state of Jalisco and from the town of San Ignacio in particular. I attended soccer games in Patton Park over a period of three years. Every Sunday afternoon large numbers of Mexican immigrants would gather in the park to watch the soccer matches and enjoy each other's company. While the men took the field, women set up vending booths and sold the favorite foods and products of Mexico—*chicharrón con chile y limón* (pork rind with chile and lemon), *tacos de carnitas* (braised pork tacos), cowboy boots and sombreros, T-shirts emblazoned with the Virgin of Guadalupe and the Mexican flag. As Mexicanas gathered in small bunches to exchange the latest news and gossip, the public park was transformed into

Working-class Mexican women at Patton Park were relaxing and enjoying the soccer games. Mexican women appropriate this very public space to talk about their priorities in life and to share their immigrant experience.

an intimate, familial space that attested to the importance of leisure time in Mexican women's lives.

Historians of Mexicans in the United States like José Alamillo and Juan Javier Pescador have documented the importance of leisure in shaping political activism and identities within Mexican and Mexican American communities. Pescador's work focuses on the soccer fields as transnational spaces of leisure where men explore notions of "masculinity" while sharing the immigrant experience.[13] Moreover, his gendered analysis of immigration, documenting experiences from the Oiartzun Valley and its inhabitants' immigration to the New World from 1550 to 1800, has influenced transnational studies as well as contributing to the conceptualization of the "immigrant experience" as an analytical tool.[14] Alamillo reconstructs leisure sites as political and civic platforms for Mexican Americans to build sociopolitical resistance.[15] Patton Park, very much like Alamillo's pool halls and Pescador's soccer fields, provided a forum for working-class Mexicanas to explore, contend, and contest their social, political, and economic realities while making a home in the United States. Thus they appropriated and Mexicanized this public space in Patton Park, Detroit.

Spending time in the park on Sundays, I met many women from San

Ignacio. They shared their collective experiences with me, recounting how they had adapted to their new surroundings and how they navigated the frequently hostile and racist environment of Detroit. Topics of conversation ranged from health to marriage, child rearing, and jobs in the paid workforce, as women compared their lives in Detroit and San Ignacio. San Ignacian women reclaimed this public space where they constructed their social positioning in the United States. In the process, they continuously shaped and reshaped notions of womanhood, motherhood, and domesticity. Moreover, this public space became the center stage where women made important decisions in their everyday lives about their well-being and their families.

Traditionally patriarchal structures, both religious and civil, and most notably the Roman Catholic Church, have influenced the lives of the people who emigrated from San Ignacio.[16] But the migrants' transnational experience in turn has influenced and changed these institutions. San Ignacians in both Detroit and San Ignacio have continuously challenged the conventional constructions and understandings of womanhood and manhood and of gender relations, thus extending the parameters and complicating the meanings of immigrant experience. Viewing transnationalism in such personal terms introduces us to contradictions and harsh encounters, but it also emphasizes the creations of new meanings embedded in gendered processes that force us to understand transnational communities without romanticizing, criminalizing, victimizing, or demonizing the migrants who live in them.

SAN IGNACIO AND DETROIT

San Ignacio Cerro Gordo is a small town in the state of Jalisco, in western Mexico. It belonged to the *delegación* of Cerro Gordo (part of the *municipio* of Arandas) until 2003, when it was approved to become a separate municipality (put into effect in 2005). The town's population was approximately 17,500 in 2000. Its economy is based on the cultivation of corn and agave, the plant used to make tequila; other activities include cattle ranching, dairy farming, and brick making. In the last fifteen years San Ignacio has seen the rapid expansion of small businesses, financed partly by immigrants' remittances. Construction companies are booming, due to the demand for new houses paid for with Detroit dollars. Bars, restaurants, and small retail businesses have sprung up.

Both the town and the state have a long tradition of migration to the United States. People have been journeying north from Jalisco since the last decade of the nineteenth century. In the first quarter of the twentieth century some Mexican men and women migrated to midwestern states, including Michigan, where they worked in beet fields or on railway construction crews. Mexican immigrants from the states of Michoacán, Guanajuato, and Jalisco were reported to be in the majority in this early migration flow.[17]

In stark contrast to San Ignacio's rural landscape, Detroit's urban setting surrounded San Ignacians' transnational experiences. Its highways, the main arteries of the city's grid, cut across poor neighborhoods in the late 1960s and early 1970s in the name of urban development. One of these fragmented neighborhoods was the barrio in southwest Detroit known as Mexican Town. Postwar Detroit attracted many immigrants from Mexico and migrants from Texas to the booming economy of America's "arsenal of democracy." This economic mirage lasted but a few years, however, before the city's economy plummeted due to deindustrialization, worsened by white flight to the suburbs. By the 1950s Detroit looked like a skeleton: "Whole sections of the city [were] eerily apocalyptic."[18] Adding to this image of a city where institutionalized racist practices such as redlining (lending that discriminated against neighborhoods viewed as high-risk areas) were a regular practice, the racial tensions that had been simmering on the back burner culminated in the Detroit Race Riots of 1967.

San Ignacians settling in Detroit in the late 1960s and early 1970s experienced the bizarre and serious implications of the historical racial tensions plaguing the city. Racist real estate and banking institutions pushed minorities to what they considered "appropriate" urban spaces for these already marginalized groups. This housing segregation allowed San Ignacian immigrants to purchase homes at very reasonable prices, however, even though the neighborhood had the look of a war zone, with burned-down houses next to the houses that they purchased. Segregation went hand in hand with lack of public services such as garbage collection, street lighting, and access to health and education in the poor barrios. Nevertheless, the Mexican transnational community of San Ignacio grew, facilitated first by Latinas' social networks, followed by the first bracero San Ignacians (like Don Chuy, who is believed to be the first San Ignacian to settle in Detroit in the late 1960s). The community was later reshaped by the arrival of San Ignacian women in southwest Detroit.

Mexican Town, the part of southwest Detroit where Mexican immigrants are concentrated, offers a prime example of how a transnational community functions culturally, economically, and politically. The direct connection to Jalisco and San Ignacio can be seen and felt everywhere in

Mexican Town. The names of local businesses, many owned by Mexican entrepreneurs, refer to the region, from Jalisco's Auto Sales to Aranda's Low Rider to Los Altos Restaurant (Los Altos de Jalisco is the geographic area where San Ignacio is located). After several visits to Patton Park, where I developed friendships with San Ignacian women, I decided to conduct my investigation in San Ignacio and Detroit. My work aims to provide a more complex and substantial picture of the Mexican immigrant experience in the United States and in Mexico.

In the first three decades of the twentieth century there was already a small but steady flow of Mexican migrants to the Midwest, attracted by jobs in the beet industry and work on the railroad. They were also attracted to Detroit by the growing auto industry. Thus many became industrial workers in the "Motor City"; as early as 1930, however, the Mexican consul in Detroit reported to his embassy in Washington, D.C., on the deplorable conditions of Mexicans in Detroit due to stagnation in the automotive industry. The letter emphasized that Mexican families had to depend on public services but that the U.S. government gave U.S. citizens preferential access to these services. Because of this situation, many Mexican families were forced to work in the beet fields for extremely low pay. The consul asked the Secretaría de Relaciones Exteriores (Ministry of Foreign Relations) to stop the flow of Mexican immigrants to the United States.[19] Working-class Mexicans had been imported through labor agreements between Mexico and the United States. The numbers of Mexicans entering the Midwest were low in relation to the numbers of Mexicans who were entering the United States through California and Texas during the first three decades of the twentieth century. Many were experiencing rural dislocation; others were fleeing the Mexican Revolution. The vast majority were male immigrants participating in more informal gendered-male labor agreements that predated the Bracero Program implemented in 1942.

The numbers of migrants surged in the Midwest during the 1940s and 1950s, when the gendered-male Bracero Program, one of the first official state-sponsored and state-managed bilateral labor agreements between Mexico and the United States, began bringing thousands of working-class Mexican men to work in the agricultural fields of California and Texas and on the railroads in the Midwest. Some of these braceros eventually made their way to the cities of the Midwest, enticed by better-paying job opportunities in industry. In the early 1960s a handful of working-class Jaliscans from San Ignacio who had been hired initially as braceros in Texas and California arrived in Detroit, becoming the nucleus of a future San Ignacian transnational community. In the late 1960s Delfino Hernández, who had worked as a bracero in California, moved with his brothers into Don Chuy's apartment in Detroit. In 1970 his wife, Doña Tita, arrived in Detroit with all of her children. A woman from Chihuahua informed Doña Tita where to purchase necessities as well as how to go about enrolling her children in school in Detroit. Doña Tita began to nurture a future transnational community by receiving large numbers of San Ignacians into her home in Detroit, while they settled and found jobs. She and her family marked the beginning of a San Ignacian transnational history of community formation, full of complexities that are not only gender specific but also inherent in the immigrant experience.

A GENDERED APPROACH TO TRANSNATIONAL STUDIES

Although the current literature on transnational studies enriches our understandings of transnational subjects, feminist narratives that represent and highlight Mexicanas' everyday experiences are still few. I support Edna A. Viruell-Fuentes's contention that "our knowledge of 'the emotional lives and subjective experiences of those embedded in transnational social fields' remains limited."[20] Contributing to this much-needed literature, my study relies primarily on oral histories. Oral narratives, much like pictorial narratives, provide an important tool for the historian to trace women's experiences and the media through which they chose to narrate their transnational lives. *Exvotos* (votive offerings), for example, left a historical visual account of rural Mexican women's social and cultural anxieties while providing degrees of resistance (albeit small: prayers and promises of payment for miracles) to situations over which they could otherwise have no direct control. Scholars such as Olga Nájera-Ramírez have considered the impact of popular culture on transnational subjects through musical genres like the *ranchera* (mariachi-style music). They have analyzed "the long history of labor migration within greater Mexico, which has caused the fragmentation of families," and argued that "for many listeners such songs may apply as much to parent-child separations as they do to separations experienced by two lovers."[21]

Popular culture is understood and readapted to fit a transnational reality. Diversity of resources such as cultural forms of expression should be a common denominator for researchers of diasporic and gendered transnational studies. Women have different ways of expressing their (dis)content and carving their own socioeconomic and political discursive space(s): "that interstitial space where differential politics and social dilemmas are negotiated."[22] Moreover, as Emma Pérez notes, "the historian's political project, then, is to write a history that decolonizes otherness."[23] This study highlights Mexican immigrant women's narratives, thus challenging hegemonic male-dominated narratives on transnational subjects. San Ignacian women's narratives offer a close-up examination of how these gender-specific relationships unfold in a transnational space.[24]

My first interview in San Ignacio was with Doña Luna, whose daughter and son-in-law I had met in Patton Park in Detroit. The son-in-law, Francisco, was the owner of the Detroit soccer team representing San Ignacio, Las Chivas de Guadalajara. My interview with Doña Luna led to others, and my contacts snowballed as each person I spoke with suggested talking to his or her family members and friends. I was touched by people's willingness to invite me into their homes and to share their lives with me.[25]

ABOUT THE BOOK

This book is divided into four chapters, followed by brief Conclusions. Chapter 1 maps out the relational changes in the religious festivities in San Ignacio and the principal influences that have brought about this evolution. Because of large-scale emigration from the town, small, local pious celebrations were transformed into an elaborately choreographed production to welcome *los hijos ausentes* upon their return. The starting point for this story is the migration of young men from San Ignacio to Texas to work in agriculture in the 1940s. Over the next two decades many continued on to Detroit, where industrial jobs beckoned. The San Ignacian women who arrived in Detroit beginning in the 1970s greatly expanded the economic, social, and cultural ties between Detroit and their hometown. This chapter analyzes the ways in which Mexican immigrant women and men became agents of demographic, social, cultural, economic, and political changes in their own histories as they constructed their transnational community in San Ignacio and Detroit.

Migration opened social and cultural spaces that allowed women to contest and negotiate traditional gender roles. Chapter 2 challenges the common assumption that immigrants' experiences can be cleaved in two—one set of experiences, values, and practices in their community of origin and another in their adopted community. Instead I use the term "transnational sexualities" to refer to a single set of constructed notions shaped by experiences in both San Ignacio and Detroit. In this chapter Mexicanas from different generations explain their understandings of femininity, womanhood, and motherhood and how these have been affected by migration. They discuss appropriate behavior in relation to courtship, marriage, sex, contraceptive use, and childbearing, weighing various economic and social imperatives against the influence of church teachings.

Chapter 3 turns to the development of the San Ignacian community in Detroit as the small Mexican Town of the 1960s burgeoned into a bustling immigrant community continually replenished by new arrivals. As more and more women came to Detroit, they played crucial roles in creating and sustaining the networks that supported the immigrant community's social and cultural life. Women performed productive labor in the paid workforce as well as reproductive labor, caring for extended families and for new immigrants arriving from Mexico. These new roles for women have given rise to a number of conflicts and ambiguities, especially in the realm of marriage and family life.

Chapter 4 examines the politics of transnational identity and citizenship that come into play when immigrants feel a sense of belonging to more than one place. San Ignacians living in Detroit play an important role in the economic, social, and political life of San Ignacio. For example, San Ignacio had tried to become a municipality in the state of Jalisco since the 1970s; it finally succeeded in 2003, thanks in large part to economic contributions from Detroit-based San Ignacians in support of the cause. This chapter explores Mexican immigrants' conflicted feelings about the prospect of living permanently in the diaspora. Economic success in the United States is a compelling goal, and most want to stay long enough to achieve it. Yet pernicious stereotyping of Mexican immigrants and their exclusion from full participation in U.S. society—even as their low-wage labor is in demand—shape immigrants' feelings about living out their lives in *el norte* (the north). Many older immigrants nurture the romantic dream of a permanent return to Mexico, though few will achieve it. Younger people tend to see their future in Detroit, yet they have a clear-eyed view of institutional racism and the need to fight against it.

Finally, Conclusions offers some final thoughts on the creation and sustainability of a very complex transnational community in San Ignacio Cerro Gordo, Jalisco, and Detroit, Michigan. It reiterates the need to reshape transnational studies to integrate all the transnational processes experienced by diasporic subjects. More importantly, it confirms that the migratory process is gender specific: it is in fact women who continue to supplement and support the migratory flows that sustain Mexican immigration to the United States.

Moreover, this book begins to integrate legislative processes such as immigration policies—often detrimental to the well-being of immigrants—into the study of transnational subjects. The militarization of the Mexico–U.S. borderlands has created a whole set of complex circumstances surrounding Mexican immigration to the United States. These gendered circumstances are experienced differently by Mexican immigrants seeking a better future for their families while joining the global mobilization of labor in the twenty-first century.

The patron saint of the town is San Ignacio de Loyola, but curiously it's like we don't love him. It's as if the Virgin of Guadalupe told him, "Get out of the way because here I come." We don't even make an effort to celebrate December 12; it's as if the Virgin of Guadalupe said, "I'm going to wait until January so that they celebrate my day with all the festivities." And that's when we have all the peregrinations, and we sing happy birthday and throw firecrackers and celebrate first communions, and the bishop also comes in January.[1]

—FATHER IGNACIO RAMOS PUGA, INTERVIEW IN SAN IGNACIO, NOVEMBER 2001

Waking up in 2003 in San Ignacio Cerro Gordo was like being in an old Mexican musical with Silvia Pinal singing in the background, a male voice intoning *gas Noel, gas Noel, gas Noel, el gas que te da más* (gas Noel, the gas that gives you more), the tinkle of bells from the ice cream cart, the ringing of the water truck announcing its rounds, and the whisking sound of women sweeping and mopping the sidewalks beginning around five in the morning. San Ignacio is the land of *la tierra colorada*, red earth that continuously blows into people's houses and across their sidewalks. Colorful tiles adorn the houses' facades, and their living room floors extend onto the sidewalks: when people walk down the street they are literally stepping on parts of private living quarters, a stretch of personalized street that they carefully keep clean. Thus public space in the town has an intimate feel.

The melodies and rhythms continue into the night, becoming deeper and louder. A constant *bum, bum, bum* shakes the glass of apartment windows as *música ranchera* (mariachi-style music) and hip-hop blast from the stereos of decked-out *trokas* (trucks) and cars (Mustangs and Toyotas are preferred) with Detroit license plates. It is January, the time of *las fiestas patronales* in San Ignacio, and San Ignacians living in Detroit

Carmen, Roberto, and their son Junior were selected to lead the parade in 2003. Her family stood proud while representing their transnational family and success. As they marched down the main avenue this transnational family represented the present and the future of the San Ignacian/Detroit transnational community. The Virgin of Guadalupe as the main protagonist of the religious festivities continued to represent a national figure for San Ignacians.

and in San Ignacio have been preparing all year for this grand event. La Fiesta de los Ausentes—the fiesta celebrating the immigrants' return—has evolved over the decades from a small, private, family-oriented affair into an extravagant public ritual that is emblematic of what migration to the United States means culturally, socially, politically, and economically to San Ignacio.

The celebration honors both the patron saint of San Ignacio, the Virgin of Guadalupe, and the contemporary heroes and heroines of San Ignacio, *los hijos ausentes*—the town's absent sons and daughters who have returned from abroad to visit. *Los hijos ausentes* is understood to mean townspeople who have immigrated to the United States, but it also includes those who have moved to big cities in Mexico like Guadalajara, Jalisco, or Mexico City. The festivities for the immigrants have become so important in the town's religious and civic life that the celebration of the Mexican national holiday—the birthday of the Virgin of Guadalupe, normally observed on December 12—has been moved in San Ignacio to the last week of January to coincide with the time when most immigrants return. The centerpiece of the festivities is the grand procession of immigrants. The Virgin of Guadalupe is everywhere, in the costumes that the participants are wearing, in the flags they hold, in the beautifully framed paintings and posters, and in the *relicarios* (reliquaries) and medals that people wear around their necks, close to their hearts. The celebrations take on a surreal, magical aspect when the local priest, Father Ignacio Ramos Puga, clad in immaculate white regalia, steps from a billowing cloud of gray smoke and firecrackers begin to burst. Once the noise and smoke dissipate, the regional bishop, clothed in black with a fuchsia pileolus on his head, steps forward, followed by six priests dressed in white tunics imprinted with the image of the Virgin of Guadalupe. They make their way slowly down the avenue, shaking hands with the ecstatic townspeople. Having the highest diocesan authority visit during the fiestas is a great honor for the town. Behind the garbed priests, a group of Aztec dancers moves to the rhythm of the drums, ankle bells jingling.

This grandiose religious, cultural, and social spectacle highlights, among other things, the temporal dialectic of immigrants' "presence" and "absence" in their community of origin. The ritualistic procession cele-

The procession of the hijos ausentes *in January of 2003. This grand event represented the successful return of the immigrants living abroad. The celebrations began at the town's main entrance (the arches) and proceeded down the main avenue, finishing at the church for a special mass organized by the local priests and the regional bishop.*

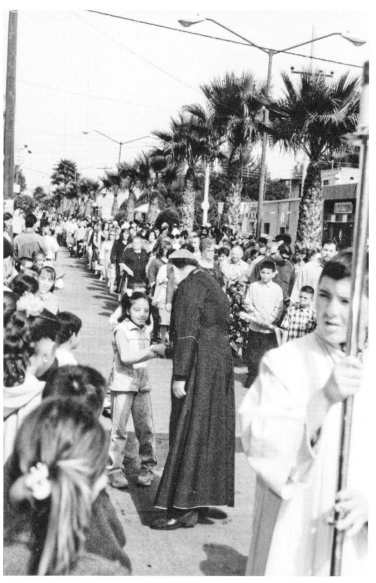

The regional bishop welcomed all the townspeople to the hijos ausentes *celebrations in 2003. San Ignacians wait impatiently throughout the year for these yearly celebrations, when their co-nationals living abroad return to take part in their religious festivities.*

brates both their return to San Ignacio and their financial contributions via remittances when they reside in Detroit. This temporal contradiction of being present while absent, I argue, becomes a medium through which Mexican immigrants continue to construct their identities as transnational subjects. Furthermore, this third space between presence and absence provides Mexican immigrants with an imagined and participatory transnational citizenship that contributes to the development of a cultural and economic life in San Ignacio and in Detroit.

Immigration studies have done much good in demarcating gendered systems of inequality embedded in transnational fields, but they have yet to extend the conversation to include what I refer to as the "immigrant experience": the way working-class Mexican immigrants experience immigration through gendered prisms that shape how they situate themselves in relation to their community of origin, the receiving site, and each other. Transnationalism as a conceptual tool of analysis has triggered a plethora of academic and cultural productions underscoring the importance of integrating a broader analytical framework for the study of immigration. This book defines transnationalism as a collection of experiences that represent the immigrants' multiple social locations and processes during movement from their community of origin to the United States. In recent popular cultural production, a hagiographic view of working-class Mexican immigrants has reinscribed their positions as (divine) heroes and heroines in the transnational visual framework. In a complex mixed-media installation entitled *Las/Los Héroes del Domingo* (The Sunday Heroes) that included photographic images, a clothesline with soccer jerseys hung to dry, a food stand with plastic imitations of edible food, and a *carro de paletas heladas* (ice cream cart), Juan Javier Pescador and I represented Mexican men and women as Sunday heroes appropriating a public space—Patton Park—in Detroit. The images portray Mexican men and women performing their transnational experiences while attending soccer games on Sunday in Detroit. Among other things, women appropriate this public space to sell a packaged, commoditized transnational Mexicanness. Women from several regions in Mexico sold Mexican food like shrimp ceviche from Guerrero and *tacos de carnitas* from Jalisco. Apparel featuring the Virgin of Guadalupe was among the most popular commodities for sale that represented Mexicanness in Detroit. Moreover, in the midst of this procession of cultural signifiers, the spectator discovered that this public space included intimate portraits: women sitting on portable chairs around the food booths, some rocking a baby stroller back and forth, almost as if they were gathering around their living rooms at home.

In her photographic series "Superheroes," visual artist Dulce Pinzón makes a similar statement by turning working-class Mexican immigrants' everyday lives in the United States into heroic deeds that demand special attention—the viewer is forced to stop short and carefully peruse the familiar but dissonant images. In the photographic frames, both immigrant men and women are portrayed in the outfits of Mexican and Euro-American superheroes while performing their daily labor routines. In this form of representation, the Mexican immigrant woman working at the laundromat becomes the superhero Wonder Woman, who sends $150 a week home. In her battle to overcome transnational dislocations that enable her to "make a home" in the receiving site, she is also an imagined and a tangible superhero—through remittances—in her community of origin. Remittances thus become symbols of the heroic contributions that not only enhance their relatives' lifestyles but also facilitate social mobility for the absent-present immigrants in their communities of origin.

Immigration from Mexico has been a gendered process facilitating the mobility of men—like the Bracero Program—but also the mobility of large numbers of Mexican women who initially might have traveled with their husbands as well as many who ventured alone or with other siblings and relatives. Mexican women have historically been migrating, working, and "making a home" in the United States as men have—albeit in dissimilar numbers. While programs like the Bracero Program were gendered male, since they exclusively hired Mexican men, women in Mexico both contributed to and were affected by them. Moreover, the creation of a transnational San Ignacian network is accredited to Don Chuy, the man believed to have been the first San Ignacian to arrive in Detroit. It was a Cuban immigrant woman (along with her husband), however, who introduced Don Chuy to his new transnational network. Through this Cuban immigrant couple Don Chuy underwent his transition from an agricultural bracero in Texas to an industrial worker in the Motor City.

The women of the Bracero Program generation underline the current need to analyze gender in immigration studies. Their voices, narratives, memories, and immigrant experiences have been underrepresented and absent from academic narratives, making immigration discussions on this particular gendered program one-dimensional and androcentric and thereby supporting patriarchal and homogeneous narratives. These narratives more often than not misrepresent the immigrant experience as strictly gendered male, thus neglecting its dynamic and contested gendered nature. The immigrant experience is a set of gendered experiences that shape the way Mexican immigrants construct their transnational lives in San Ignacio and in Detroit.

Working-class San Ignacian women join the migratory experience whether present in, or absent from, their community of origin. This makes them active participants in their heroic transnational constructions when "making a home" in Detroit and "preserving a home" in San Ignacio. This continual proxy membership—being absent from the community of origin yet sending remittances—is continually refurbished by their yearly return and import of cultural remittances. In this way the procession for the *hijos ausentes* and the yearly festivities become epistemological symbols of this transnational network. These celebrations bring to the foreground the historicity of gendered migratory patterns and the formation of a transnational field supporting and maintaining a San Ignacian community in Detroit and San Ignacio.

The January religious festivities in San Ignacio have been transformed by steadily increasing emigration and by the emergence of a transnational community of San Ignacians in San Ignacio and Detroit. This chapter traces the recent history of immigration from San Ignacio, beginning with the men who migrated as braceros to the agricultural fields of California, Texas, and other states in the middle of the last century. Gravitating later to Detroit for industrial jobs, the men built upon Latinas' incipient social and economic networks, which expanded rapidly once women from San Ignacio began arriving in Detroit. These processes of emigration brought about new gendered social roles for both working-class Mexican men and women experiencing transnational dislocations. San Ignacian men migrating to Detroit found themselves becoming part of a vibrant transnational network dating back to the late nineteenth century. The San Ignacian transnational network unfolds as more and more San Ignacian women join the flow north: some to reunite with their husbands, but also single women looking for alternative ways to make a living—or escape parental or community supervision.

With a slow but steady influx of San Ignacian women in Detroit in the 1970s, the social networks initiated by the Latina/o community and continued by San Ignacian men were expanded and maintained by San Ignacian women. In the process these social networks continued to grow and delineate their collective and individual transnational subjectivity. The immigrants' yearly return to San Ignacio in January is the time when these networks are renewed and strengthened and the transnational nature of the San Ignacio–Detroit nexus is on full display. These celebrations, however, have historically changed as immigration patterns were consistently replenished and solidified. The image of the Mexican immigrant as a hero or heroine develops from familial recognition and admiration to a collective celebration of transnational capitalist success. Implicit in their success is earning better wages while navigating hostile sociopolitical realities that surround the life of Mexican immigrants in the United States.

THE BRACERO PROGRAM

On a sunny morning in 1948 Don Jesús Mercado, known as Don Chuy, crossed the U.S.-Mexico border for the first time. He was not alone: Don Chuy was one of thousands of Mexican men who were hired under the Bracero Program that began in 1942. He was hired initially to work in California (the main entry point for Mexican workers), picking tomatoes, onions, and citrus fruits. Like many other men from San Ignacio, Don Chuy traveled back and forth between the United States and Mexico for several years under the program. "We would go from here to Tijuana and from there we would be hired and they would move us inside [the United States]."[2] Don Chuy did not know his ultimate destination then, but he would later become the first San Ignacian to settle in Detroit, where he became the link to the creation of an emerging San Ignacian transnational community.

The Bracero Program was one of the first official bilateral labor agreements between Mexico and the United States. There had been several earlier labor agreements. In the nineteenth century presidents William Howard Taft and Porfirio Díaz entered into an agreement for Mexican laborers to work on railroad construction in the United States. During World War I Mexico and the United States again entered into an agreement allowing Mexicans to work in the United States. Neither of these agreements set out a systematic structure for the incorporation of Mexican labor into the U.S. workforce, however; nor did the accord provide for specific governmental agencies in both Mexico and the United States to take responsibility for the arrangement (as did the later Bracero Program). Moreover, these early agreements were essentially unilateral, in that the United States delineated the economic and political contours of both programs. The Bracero Program recruited Mexican laborers to work in agricultural fields and on railroads in the United States on a temporary basis. During the early years of the program thousands of Mexicans left their hometowns to travel north in order to satisfy the labor demand ini-

TABLE I.I. PERSONS OF SPANISH LANGUAGE IN DETROIT

Year	Total Population	People of Spanish Language	Mexican
1970[a]	1,511,482	27,038	N/A
1980	1,203,339	28,466	N/A
1990[b]	1,012,427	28,280	17,650
2000	951,270	47,167	33,143

Source: U.S. Department of Commerce, Bureau of the Census, *United States Census of Population, 1970–2000* (Washington, D.C.: U.S. Government Printing Office, 2000).

[a]For the 1970 and 1980 census information, Mexicans were not classified separately; the census lists them as part of "General Characteristics of Persons of Spanish Language for Areas and Places."

[b]In 1990 the census began to classify Mexicans separately.

TABLE I.2. PERSONS OF SPANISH LANGUAGE IN DETROIT: MEN AND WOMEN

Year	People of Spanish Language	Women	Men
1970[a]	27,038	13,726	13,312
1980	28,466	14,567	13,899
1990[b]	28,280	14,189	14,091
2000	47,167	23,280	23,887

Source: U.S. Department of Commerce, Bureau of the Census, *United States Census of Population, 1970–2000* (Washington, D.C.: U.S. Government Printing Office, 2000).

[a]For the 1970 and 1980 census information, Mexicans were not classified separately; the census lists them as part of "General Characteristics of Persons of Spanish Language for Areas and Places."

[b]In 1990 the census began to classify Mexicans separately.

tially brought on by the war in Europe. By the end of the war, however, the U.S. agricultural economy had become dependent on Mexican labor; more braceros were hired every year after World War II than during all the war years combined. Approximately 168,000 braceros were hired in total in 1942–1945; according to some scholars, the numbers after the war were between 400,000 and 450,000 annually.

Douglas S. Massey, Jorge Durand, and Nolan J. Malone state: "Nearly 5 million Mexicans entered the United States during the program's twenty-two-year history—a figure that dwarfs the combined total of legal and contract labor between 1900 and 1929—but this massive movement remained out of the public eye."[3] This statement questions the politics of immigration during the period of the Bracero Program, particularly during Operation Wetback in 1954, when thousands of Mexican immigrants were deported to satisfy the political forces of McCarthyism.[4]

World War II demanded Euro-American as well as African American, Native American, and Mexican American soldiers on the front lines in Europe. At home, the United States needed Mexican labor to survive economically during the war and to rise as a world power in the postwar years. But unlike the soldiers who were acclaimed as heroes and martyrs of democracy in their fight against enemies on the other side of the ocean, Mexicanos originally recruited through the Bracero Program to help with the war effort endured discrimination in the United States. The terms of their contracts were systematically violated, depriving them of basic civil and labor rights to which they were legally entitled under the program's guidelines. In a letter to the Secretaría de Relaciones Exteriores (Ministry of Foreign Relations) dated June 5, 1952, the vice-consul of Mexico, Humberto Martínez, warned of labor violations taking place in the reception centers in California where braceros initially arrived and were hired: "Continued violations of the workers' contracts and irregularities by the agents from USES [United States Employment Services] are the main complaints that our Mexican laborers are filing. An example is how our workers are being forced under threats by a 'tyrannical' government representative to sign contracts with specific companies. This is a violation of their contracts that stipulate that our workers are free to choose their employers."[5]

Even though the Bracero Program was referred to as a "guest worker" program, with the United States designated as the "host" country, the process created an open and vulnerable space where Mexicanos were subject to mistreatment, forced to work under deplorable conditions, and paid meager wages—exploitable guests, as it were. Both governments tolerated the overt exploitation of Mexican laborers as well as corruption within the institutions that were charged with administration of the Bracero Program, especially between 1942 and 1954.[6]

The Bracero Program was controversial in its time, causing economic, political, and cultural dislocations in both Mexico and the United States. During the first fourteen years of the program's existence both nations sought to negotiate and shape the outlines of the international agreement. Resistance came from all sides. Mexican nationalists believed that the loss of hundreds of thousands of urban and agricultural laborers would hold back Mexico's progress. They were also well aware of the massive deportations of Mexican immigrants from the United States during the Depression years and of the civil rights violations against Mexican immigrants and Mexican Americans by U.S. authorities. Thus Mexican politicians, artists, and business leaders interceded, albeit in vain, to stop the exportation of Mexican laborers.[7]

There was opposition in the United States as well, but the reasons were different. U.S. nativists argued that Mexican immigrants would depress wages, take jobs away, contaminate cultural life, and tear the social fabric of the United States. Euro-Americans on both sides of the Mexican immigration debate had socially constructed racist images for several years. In 1928, while introducing legislation in Congress to deport Mexican immigrants, congressman John Box commented: "Every reason which calls for the exclusion of the most wretched, ignorant, dirty, diseased, and degraded people of Europe or Asia demands that the illiterate, unclean, peonized masses moving this way from Mexico be stopped at the border." During congressional hearings on naturalization in 1930 a prominent Pasadena, California, medical doctor testified: "The Mexican is a quiet, inoffensive necessity in that he performs the big majority of our rough work, agriculture, building and street labor. They have no effect on the American standard of living because they are not much more than a group of fairly intelligent collie dogs."[8] Nativist and xenophobic sentiments inflamed by the Cold War gave rise to legislation tailored to keep out "undesirable immigrants." Meanwhile, the United States engaged in an aggressive campaign to recruit Mexican laborers under the Bracero Program, which included being more flexible or lax in enforcing immigration restrictions when documenting Mexican workers. The U.S. attitude was schizophrenic: the demonization of Mexican immigrants went hand in hand with continuing recruitment of Mexican workers.

In 1951 some braceros who came from the states of San Luis Potosí, Jalisco, Hidalgo, and Mexico City to work in Arkansas wrote a letter to the

Mexican Ministry of Foreign Relations (Secretaría de Relaciones Exteriores), describing the conditions they had endured.[9] Their journey began on October 10, 1951, when approximately four hundred braceros were signed up in Monterrey, Nuevo León, Mexico. They were assembled at a military base, assigned numbers, and interrogated by U.S. immigration officials. In their letter the braceros claimed that the U.S. officials (some of whom, they believed, were of Mexican origin) mistreated them. After questioning, they were told to undress for a medical examination that they described as *muy riguroso* (very rigorous). They were vaccinated, and all of their personal data, including their fingerprints, were filed. Afterward they were taken to a large dining room where dinner was provided by the U.S. government: *chilaquiles* (pieces of tortilla with tomato sauce), beans, and bread. The braceros were then transported by bus to a recruitment camp at Harlingen, Texas. Upon their arrival, they were told to settle for the night on the floor without blankets or sleeping mats.

The next day the braceros realized that they were among approximately three thousand other braceros in the recruitment camp, waiting to be hired. After breakfast the farmers, supervised by immigration officials, chose the laborers they wanted, leaving until the end those who appeared older and weaker. Some of the latter had been in the camp for more than eight days and complained of intimidation by U.S. soldiers with machine guns who patrolled at night. The letter also described how a few braceros were forced to eat their supper naked, as punishment for some unknown transgression.

The letter writers were hired on contract to work on a ranch in Arkansas for forty days. They were paid low wages, and the employer docked their paychecks ninety cents a day for food. Whenever it rained, there was no work and consequently no pay. When their contracts expired, the employer went to the Mexican consulate in Memphis along with the braceros to renew them. One of the employees in the consulate, according to the letter, asked for a bribe of $100 per contract. The braceros were sent back to Mexico, having earned only $60 to $75 in the forty days.

The stigma attached to working-class Mexican immigrants was embedded in all sectors of both Mexican and Euro-American societies. Mexican officials often used very paternalistic language when referring to Mexican immigrants: "Outside my office hours, I have dedicated my time to visiting families, places of work, in order to acquaint myself with the working class, our masses. I want to learn what their aspirations and ideals are, and also to find out what they need from our offices."[10] The Mexican consul in Yuma, Arizona, Ascensión G. Lerma, wrote a letter to the Ministry of Foreign Relations in 1912. Three decades later (in 1946) sociologist Norman Daymond Humphrey commented on Mexican immigrants in Detroit: "Thus early in the process of change, one segment of the Mexican population is found living in basement apartments which, in being lightless and airless, approximate the adobe huts of the peasant village."[11] Some current scholars who refute Chicana/o stereotypes nonetheless continue to depict Mexican immigrants—in particular braceros— as faceless and passive laborers lacking agency and aspirations: "Daily life [for Mexican immigrants] was consumed by making a living, and their aspirations rarely reached beyond the four walls of their houses."[12] The experiences of the San Ignacian men I met refute these stereotypes. Archival documentation and oral history sources also contest the image of the passive bracero. Braceros constantly challenged and negotiated with authorities to obtain fair wages and better working and living conditions. They wrote letters of complaint to the Ministry of Foreign Relations in Mexico City and appealed to the Mexican consulates to intercede for them. In 1959 a letter addressed to "Sr. Presidente de la República Mexicana" (President of the Mexican Republic) and signed "un grupo de trabajadores" (a group of workers) read:

> And this is the reason why we fervently ask you, Mr. President, that when you renegotiate the new *convenio* [guidelines for the Bracero Program] you remedy our pathetic situation in relation to our meager wages and horrible living conditions. Health services are also far from efficient because they treat all sorts of illnesses with pills rather than providing treatment for those who require more than just pills.[13]

The consulates were designated as the main supervisors of the Bracero Program and were empowered to file complaints on behalf of the braceros for contract violations; because of the magnitude of the program, the number of braceros, and the pervasive corruption within the consulates, however, they seldom did so effectively.[14] In addition to filing official complaints against cancellation of contracts, dire working conditions, and meager wages, "Mexican workers deserted because of their living conditions."[15] Braceros walked off the agricultural fields and either returned to Mexico or changed to work sites where they hoped that employers would treat them better.[16] Many such actions were organized by word of mouth through immigrants' networks. In 1949 the Mexican consul in Detroit provided a list of names of braceros who "abandoned" the fields, leaving behind their paychecks.[17]

Despite the many strategies of resistance that working-class Mexican immigrants implemented in their struggle to construct a transnational life, the negative image surrounding contract farm labor permeated the Mexican imagination and influenced the construction of new transnational identities. Labor hierarchies placed agricultural back-breaking labor at the bottom, while new industrial jobs in Detroit generated a sense of pride. During the interwar years Mexican workers had "the desire to disassociate themselves from farm labor [which] became widespread because Midwestern Mexicans recognized its lowly rank in the emerging hierarchy of obtainable labor that was an integral part of the social order they created in the North."[18] Like their predecessors, San Ignacians in Detroit who made the transition into industrial jobs in the 1960s disassociated themselves from agricultural work.

Nonetheless, working conditions for industrial workers were substandard and unsafe. Doña Chavelita remembered visiting the auto factory where her husband, Jesús Hernández, worked: "He took me where he worked when I went [to Detroit] the first time. I don't know how he could bear the noise, it was so loud, and they wouldn't wear any protection for their ears. . . . The steel factory was really big and very dirty, full of oil everywhere. The car pieces would come in a conveyor belt."[19]

Work hazards as well as unsafe and risky conditions often accompanied the immigrant experience. Doña Luna's son fell prey to such labor risks: "[When] we were in Detroit, we had a very painful experience because one of my sons cut off his hand. In a machine. It happened to Gerardo in a machine."[20] Accidents while operating heavy machinery were not the only casualties suffered by Mexican immigrants. In July 1952 the Ministry of Foreign Relations in Mexico City received the following telegram from the Mexican Consulate in Los Angeles: "I am informing you that sixty braceros contracted by Citrus Growers Incorporated suffered food poisoning from meals prepared in the fields."[21] Unsafe and risky labor conditions thus were caused not only by "job casualties" but also by the capitalist growers' irresponsible and inhumane attitudes toward working-class Mexicans.

CIRCULAR MIGRATION: NEW ROLES FOR WOMEN AND MEN

Although many Mexicanos during the Bracero Program were aware of the hardships that awaited them across the border, Mexicanos continued to travel back and forth between the United States and Mexico on tourist visas or as undocumented immigrants. Don Antonio left San Ignacio to go north for the first time in 1943 with his brother, who had been hired as a bracero in California. Don Antonio began a circular migration that was to last many years before he moved to Detroit. "One time, after I had crossed through the barbed wire in 1951 [undocumented], I signed up as a bracero, but they only hired for forty days and I didn't like it."[22] For years Mexican immigrants hired under the Bracero Program—or traveling on their own—followed a pattern of migration laid out by Mexican immigrants and Chicana/o migrant field workers since the late nineteenth century. In the second half of the nineteenth century developments in irrigation technology turned California into the "garden" of the United States. Patriarchal institutional racism and imperialist expansionism carried out via the Mexican-American War created a troupe of migrant workers both domestic (Chicanas/os and Mexican Americans) and foreign (Chinese, Filipino, Japanese, and Mexican). Mexican and Mexican Americans dispossessed of their lands through this geopolitical conflict found work as migrant field-workers. These nomadic workers would follow the citrus belt harvests up the Pacific Northwest rim and return home to California and Texas and Mexico during the winter. This circular migration continued into the second half of the twentieth century, until anti-immigrant legislation disrupted these migratory patterns by enforcing tougher immigration laws at the end of the twentieth century and into the new millennium.

Initially directed mostly to California and Texas, the flow of migrants slowly began to branch out to different states, depending on the needs of the workers, the opportunities available to them, and the choices they made in their effort to secure better futures. For many, California and Texas became a stepping-stone to destinations in the Midwest. During the dislocations that immigration brings about, Mexican men often began to experience changes in their roles as family members as well as laborers. Many working-class San Ignacians experienced transnational familial dislocations that placed them in precarious situations vis-à-vis the family. Fatherhood and the authority that this position entailed in a patriarchal system frequently became linked to capitalist consumerism. Material accumulation not only served as a sociocultural symbol of success and thus represented a certain acquisition of power but also took on a more intimate meaning: San Ignacian men displayed warmth and deployed familial affection via the amount of material capital they contributed to the household. Transnational ideologies about working-class manhood and masculinity worked in correlation with the material experience and success of the immigrant. Transitioning from an agricultural worker to an industrial worker also represented a successful immigrant experience and helped build transnational urban subjectivities.

Like Don Antonio, Don Chuy traveled back and forth for years between San Ignacio and California. But one day, he recounts, a man in Laredo, Texas, with whom he was chatting advised him to go to Detroit. According to this man, a worker could make twice as much in Detroit ($3.00 an hour) as working in the fields ($1.25 or less). According to Don Chuy, "I thought, I'm already far away from my parents and my family, so I might as well go. And I made the decision and I went to Detroit."[23] Don Chuy left Texas for Detroit in 1962. He returned to Mexico for a short period, only to be back in Detroit by 1965. The Bracero Program had ended the previous year, but many bracero contracts expired a year later.

At twenty-four, Jesús Hernández left San Ignacio in 1953 to work in Salinas, California, under the Bracero Program. His father was a well-known Mexican *arriero* (muleteer) who bought and sold manufactured goods from town to town in the Altos de Jalisco region. Jesús signed up for the Bracero Program to help his father support the family. After two years of going back and forth he was hired as a cook to feed the large groups of bracero field-workers. His wife, Doña Chavelita, remembers:

> Some men from here [San Ignacio] were going to Ciudad Juárez to get passports. So my husband [Jesús] came and said: "I have everything in order, I'm leaving again." . . . The first time he went to Stockton and then he went to Salinas, where he became a cook for the braceros. He worked first in the fields and then this man came and said: "You know how to cook, right? So come with me to the kitchen."[24]

With a couple of years of experience under his belt, Jesús stopped working under the bracero contracts and obtained a letter of recommendation from one of his employers, which he used to become a legal immigrant and eventually an industrial worker.

Roles for men continued to change as their immigrant experience shaped the way they constructed their transnational identities. For Jesús, working in the fields was a new experience and cooking for several hundred braceros represented a 360-degree turn in his life. Unlike many of his San Ignacian counterparts, Jesús received a higher degree of education. Performing manual labor in the fields or cooking—associated with domestic tasks—was not a reality that Jesús was familiar with. His wife, Doña Chavelita, commented:

He [Jesús] used to come and visit me. He went to Guadalajara and was in the Seminary for about four years. However, within his second year that he was there, we saw each other again. He wanted us to get together again but I told him: "No, because you are in the Seminary and I don't want to be blamed for taking your life-vocation away." But he said, "I don't want to be in the Seminary," and we went back and forth like that until he left the Seminary.[25]

After seven years of traveling between Mexico and California, Jesús submitted the documentation necessary to ask for his brothers' residencies. The first to join him was Don Gabriel, who crossed the border on May 23, 1960. Don Gabriel worked for five years with his brother as an assistant cook in the agricultural fields, cooking for crowds of braceros. A year after Don Gabriel arrived in California, their brother Delfino joined them, and a year later their younger brother Rubén followed. Although Delfino and Rubén worked in different fields, they all joined forces and began to run a small business in Salinas. The brothers bought a car and would go to the nearest town to buy everyday necessities then go back to the fields and sell them to the braceros. It was a ready market, as lack of transportation, long work hours, and the language barrier meant that most braceros seldom strayed far from the fields. "When he [Jesús] was working he was making fairly good wages. And aside from his job, they would let him sell items to the braceros. He [and his brothers] would sell them razors, cigarettes, things that they needed like soap. The brothers would go into town to purchase the stuff and would make a small profit."[26]

As the Hernández brothers and other San Ignacians traveled back and forth over more than a decade, they formed families in San Ignacio that depended on their wages. These families became tied to the United States economically, culturally, and emotionally, experiencing a form of transnationalism even without leaving Mexico. The early male migrants and their families thus laid down the path for what would eventually become a dynamic transnational community in San Ignacio and Detroit.

The wives of the Hernández brothers, along with many other women of the bracero generation, recalled their experiences raising families in San Ignacio while their husbands were away in the United States. The 2,000-mile geopolitical border between Mexico and the United States divided the families; coincidentally, the distance between San Ignacio and Detroit is also approximately 2,000 miles. Nonetheless, as long as the men continued to return periodically, their families continued to grow.

San Ignacio is a very Catholic town in the Cristero region of western Mexico. While working-class San Ignacian women have historically contested religious oppression in several ways, childbearing in San Ignacio was then, and continues to be, influenced by the church's prohibition against contraceptives and by the lack of health education. Doña Chavelita had thirteen children while her husband, Jesús Hernández, followed a circular migration path over fourteen years. She and her sisters-in-law— Doña Tita, Doña Ana, and Doña Elodia (married to Delfino, Rubén, and Gabriel Hernández, respectively)—shared a precarious position as the wives of immigrants. Their husbands' paychecks could be delayed, lost in the mail, or not sent at all. Worse, their migrant husbands could abandon them, suffer injuries, or even die. The Hernández women and other migrants' wives in San Ignacio developed familial systems of support as strategies to sustain their families in their husbands' absence, such as by caring for each other's children while they worked.

Rhetoric about the Bracero Program in both Mexico and the United States often put forth the notion that the program provided financial opportunities that would improve life for rural campesinos in Mexico. In reality, many migrants' wives were left alone in Mexican towns and villages to fend for themselves and their children. When Rubén Hernández decided to join his brothers in California, for example, Doña Ana was left with four children and twenty pigs to take care of while he tried his luck in *el norte*. The couple ultimately had eight children. Doña Ana recalled how she managed:

> He would send money almost every month. First he sent $40, then it went up to $80, but in the meantime I took care of raising twenty pigs here. I was pregnant and I did everything in the house [including raising the children]. I did laundry, I ironed . . . I tell you being young is amazing. You don't get as tired, you rest at night and then you get up with a lot of energy and ready to take care of the children. While I fed one the others needed clean diapers, and back then there were no disposable diapers; we had to wash and iron them. We were so silly we even ironed the diapers. Now young women complain when they have only two children.[27]

Like many other migrants' wives, Doña Ana became a de facto head of household, taking control of the finances and making all the decisions concerning the family's well-being. While women continued to care for their children and homes, the threat of economic destitution forced many of them into new roles, running small businesses or taking care of farm animals. The traditional working-class male-female division of labor thus became blurred, as women performed tasks associated with both reproductive and productive labor and transgressed the boundaries of male gender roles. In the absence of adult males, many women became breadwinners and even primary providers for their families. Still, they continued to allocate their absent husbands a certain degree of authority despite the distance between them. "[When he wasn't here] I took care of my daughter. It was hard, believe me, doing it by myself. I had to do it alone and educate them; I had to have a strong hand [*mano dura*, a phrase normally associated with males] and I sent them to school."[28]

Some Mexicanas took charge of small businesses that their husbands financed with money earned in the United States. Doña Chavelita ran a *tortillería* (tortilla-making shop) in San Ignacio while Jesús worked in the United States. Some of Doña Chavelita's thirteen children later migrated to the United States and joined her husband. Doña Minerva took care of a small locksmith shop that her husband, Luis Mercado, opened just eight years after he began his immigration cycle in 1960. She and her oldest daughters ran the business from 1968 until 1974, when the whole family left for Detroit.

Although the Bracero Program dislocated Mexican families, causing women and men to realign themselves vis-à-vis the household's economy and emotional care-giving, for them the economic benefits undoubtedly superseded these transnational disparities. Many poor Mexican women appealed to the Mexican government's paternalist nationalistic attitude toward civil society and wrote letters to the Mexican president in order to receive the Bracero Program's economic benefits. On April 4, 1948, fifteen-year-old Josefina González Flores, originally from Pátzcuaro, Michoacán, wrote a letter to Mexican president Miguel Alemán:

> I Josefina González Flores with all due respect wrote a letter a few days ago asking you to please let me have a sewing machine. I said that even if it is a very old sewing machine I would take it. I would like to help my parents, who are very anguished. My father is making very little money and it's not enough to support all of us. All my brothers and sisters are small and I am fifteen, and I already know how to sew; but I don't have a sewing machine. . . . People know that you will be granting more bracero contracts to work in the United States. For the love of God if you could please grant my father, Zacarías González Flores, a *tarjeta* [documentation] so that he can go and work and make money. Then he could buy me a sewing machine and pay my brother's debts.[29]

In her letter González Flores not only indicates her willingness and need to contribute to the economy but uses patriarchal ideologies about women and labor to underscore her father's need to enter the bracero economy in order to fulfill his duty as the breadwinner and grant her the opportunity to work. Once her family enters the transnational field, then her father can provide the commodity that she so desires: a sewing machine. Within this discourse, she designates her labor contribution as supporting income rather than primary income, which would come from her father, the appropriate head of the household.

Women had to also deploy all their coping skills when a migrant husband died abroad. In March 1949 José Santos Gálvez died in a truck accident while working as a bracero for the Fitzgerald and Litrov company in California. The family was originally from Zacatecas. Six months after his death, his widow, Eloisa Ortega de Gálvez, asked her daughter to write a letter to the Mexican consul, requesting his help to get the insurance money that her husband's labor contract provided in case of accident or death. The Mexican consul wrote to the Ministry of Foreign Relations, asking for permission to act as arbiter in the dispute. Nine months later the consul wrote to Fitzgerald and Litrov, petitioning for the death benefits owed to the Gálvez family under the company's insurance policies. The company, after a long delay, claimed that it had sent papers for compensation of $3,200 to Señora Gálvez, who should sign and return them.

In June 1950 Señora Gálvez again wrote to the Mexican consul, letting him know that she had never received the company's papers. Instead, she had received an ultimatum, stating that if she did not return the documentation the company would no longer be responsible for payment of compensation. The last letter filed in the archive is dated January 20, 1951: in it Señora Gálvez implored the Ministry of Foreign Relations in Mexico City to intercede on her behalf, since she was unable to travel to California and her family desperately needed the compensation money for their survival.

The Gálvez case apparently remained unresolved: there is no further trace of legal action in the available documentation. But Señora Gálvez's situation demonstrates some of the difficulties that immigrants and their families experienced as they constructed their lives in both the United States and Mexico. The case also shows the transnational resilience that Señora Gálvez demonstrated by continuing to write letters to the consulate and to demand that her rights as the wife of a bracero be respected and honored.[30]

Women also appealed to kinship in order to take on all the responsibilities left behind by their bracero counterparts. Doña Ana notes: "Sometimes my brother-in-law, Nacho, would come and stay with me to help out. Other times my sister-in-law Celia or one of my other sisters-in-law. But other than that I raised my children by myself [while my husband was working in the United States]."[31] Relying on familial ties to engage in a feminine network of support in the community of origin was usually the rule rather than the exception.

Working-class women in San Ignacio transgressed gendered local border crossings when they had to take on their male counterparts' labor while they took the trip north. These border crossings went against the grain of prescribed gendered divisions of labor and also against familial expectations of appropriate behavior for women. While crossing this gendered border in their community of origin, many women developed strategies of resistance that allowed them to survive a transnational network that dislocated traditional social identity formations. Women who became heads of households resisted gendered designations, and many participated in new ways of working toward supporting their familial economies. Some women took initiative and "demanded" participation in the bracero program's economy by asking for resources and accessibility; and others persevered to get insurance money owed to them, usually from the loss of a loved one. Women took on the challenges associated with transnational households and made the best of their experience in order to exercise some form of control over their lives and those of their children. Mexican women wrote letters to the president of Mexico and to authority figures at the Office of Foreign Affairs, communicated with consuls in the United States, wrote letters to the U.S. Department of Labor, and relied on extended familial kin to help them survive and be effective as these transnational networks began to disrupt and change many Mexicanas' perceptions of the world around them.

Some women who later joined the migratory flow to Detroit, like Doña Minerva, also began to use their access to their transnational experience to challenge traditional patriarchal oppressive male roles. Doña Minerva commented:

I said that the young men help their wives; Jorge and Raúl [her sons-in-law] are very good cooks. When Raúl didn't work, Nena [her daughter] had to work all day; when she came back he had all the food ready. Yes, they learned because they were in the United States for a while by themselves. I think it's great [that they help with domestic chores]! My other son also helps Ana [his wife]; and he makes tortillas in the machine, but he helps. In the past there was a lot of machismo, but now I see that men help women more and more over there [in the United States]. Here we still have a lot of machismo in San Ignacio. I don't see men helping their wives.[32]

Doña Minerva appealed to her transnational access in order to condemn, in front of her husband, what she perceived to be machismo, which meant men who did not help women with their domestic chores. Her point of comparison is the United States and her younger sons-in-law. She advocates for a more equal marriage where men "help" women with domestic chores. It is not important whether it is true that younger male generations in Detroit are helping more with domestic chores. What is important to underline is Doña Minerva's appeal to her transnational experience to comment on masculinity and femininity as she condemns her husband: "Here we still have a lot of machismo in San Ignacio [she looks at her husband]. I don't see men helping their wives."

The new responsibilities thrust upon women while their spouses, male siblings, or parents migrated to the United States enabled them to deploy strategies of resistance while they acquired skills that, for many, facilitated their own later migration. Much of the literature on immigrant women focuses on how their experiences as immigrants and workers in the United States have empowered them to challenge traditional gender roles. For San Ignacian women this transformation began even before emigration, while the families of male migrants were still in their community of origin. As the wives of migrants from San Ignacio took charge of household decision making and small businesses, in some cases serving as their families' main providers, they developed strategies for survival as well as transnational skills that they could later transfer to the labor market in Detroit. These transnational experiences, sometimes spanning more than ten years, equipped women to cope with many challenges that they would confront in adapting to life in the United States.

Both San Ignacian women and men underwent a process of transnationalism that disrupted the traditional gender division of labor and, more importantly, dislocated constructions of femininity and masculinity. San Ignacians had to realign themselves to fit this new social reality that transnationalism brought about: men's long commuting to find better job opportunities while women transgressed assigned roles by crossing gendered male social borders.

PIONEERS OF THE SAN IGNACIAN DETROIT COMMUNITY: GENDER AND THE BEGINNINGS OF SOCIAL NETWORKS

Migration north to the Midwest began in the late nineteenth century and beginning of the twentieth century with aggressive recruitment by the beet industry and railroad industry. Southwestern farmers were overprotective of their access to cheap Mexican labor, thus curtailing recruitment from the Midwest. Nevertheless, the recruitment efforts by midwestern contractors paid off when seasonal migration from Texas to the Midwest became self-perpetuating. Mexicans and Tejanas/os usually worked for the sugar beet industry and the railroads before they entered factory work. Many worked by following the sugar beet harvest and then worked in factories during the cold months.[33]

Working-class Latinas had historically built social networks that had supported the migration of Hispanics into the Midwest since the late nineteenth century. Mexicanas and Tejanas worked alongside each other to support their families and communities. Mexican women and Chicanas increased their income by running *casas de asistencia* (renting rooms to tenants). This strategy for survival underlines not only women's integration into the labor force through reproductive labor but also their sustainability and maintenance of social networks that supported the migratory flow into midwestern cities.

> In 1928, Mrs. Joseph Pino augmented her husband's autoworker income by renting furnished rooms and cooking meals for her tenants at their house on East Columbia Avenue. From 1926 to 1929, Detroiter Jennie Godina rented furnished rooms and offered board to workers at a house on East Congress Street, where she lived with her two brothers, who worked in the car plants. The widow Mrs. González supported herself and three children by operating a boardinghouse after her husband died from tuberculosis in 1927.[34]

Not only did these earlier pioneers support and maintain social networks, but they also continued to link cultural symbols that sustained and developed cultural capital lending to identification with a Latin American transnational network. The comfort of familiar cultural symbols such as language, music, and food brought comfort to people of Mexican descent and provided a sense of trust and national identification that allowed Latina/o intragroup relationships to flourish, albeit not without a degree of conflict. Don Chuy narrates his experience with the Cuban woman, who deployed her cultural capital through food:

I worked in construction. I was so lucky. I arrived [in Detroit] on a Sunday, the twenty-first was a Sunday. I was sitting at Clark Park; I just sat there on a bench for about two hours. Back then things were so quiet and peaceful; one could sleep in the park. It was already about three in the afternoon, so I asked myself: "Where can I go?" So that woman spoke Spanish, she was Cuban and she had a small grocery store across the street from where I was. She said, "Hey, who are you looking for?" "No one," I said, "but you speak Spanish." "My husband and I are Cubans and we own that store. Are you hungry?" "Yes, I have some money for food but I don't know where to go. I am a bit lost because I don't know anyone here in this town . . . in this city." Then she said, "Come with me." And she took me to her store, and I remember she brought me *un plato de cocido* [a dish of stew]. Very kind those people [the Cuban wife and husband].[35]

While the relationship with the Cuban woman who opened her arms and thus entry to her social networks to Don Chuy was fairly new, the familiarity of language and food made Don Chuy feel not only welcomed by these "kind people" but also safe.

Don Chuy left Texas in 1962, to seek better wages in Detroit. After returning to Mexico for a short period, he went back to Detroit in 1965. Two years later he asked his brother Luis to join him. Luis Mercado had been in Texas in 1960 as a bracero but returned to San Ignacio the same year. He joined his brother in Detroit in 1965, entering on a tourist visa, and was later deported. By 1967 Luis had become a legal resident through Don Chuy's sponsorship. According to local tradition in San Ignacio and Detroit, Don Chuy and Luis Mercado were the first San Ignacians to settle in Detroit.

Don Chuy was hired by the couple to expand the grocery store since he had experience in construction. In San Ignacio he had helped his father expand their house. While Don Chuy was working on the expansion of the grocery store, the Cuban couple introduced him to Arturo Barry, an African American who worked as a *mayordomo* (foreman) for a construction company. Don Chuy was able to process his immigration papers and become a legal resident through the construction company. Like those of many immigrants in Detroit, his labor patterns vary at different periods but are consistent with holding multiple jobs at the same time and during different months of the year. After Don Chuy finished the renovations for the Cuban couple, a friend of theirs took him to the steel company where he worked for eighteen years.

Don Chuy's experience as a first-time Detroit worker resembled a pattern that San Ignacians would follow after the Mercado brothers settled and began to facilitate the migration of several San Ignacians: Don Chuy tapped into the existing social networks that Latinas and Latinos had been developing while migrating to the Midwest in the late nineteenth and early twentieth centuries. The sugar beet industry and the railroad industry in the Midwest became the main champions of employment of a substantial labor force that initiated a migratory pattern from Texas and Mexico into the Midwest. Although the number of Hispanic laborers in the Midwest is much lower in comparison to the number of Hispanic laborers in the Southwest, "over 58,000 Mexicans settled in the cities of the Midwest during the fifteen-year period from the end of World War I to the first years of the Great Depression."[36] By 1929 there were 15,000 Mexicans living in Detroit.[37]

After the Great Depression of the 1930s migratory patterns changed. Mexican migration was severely curtailed by the massive repatriation and deportation programs carried out in full force in midwestern cities and all over the United States; as a result, a new Hispanic migration emerged in the Midwest: "in late 1937 and early 1938, the emigration process triggered by the events of 1929 began to reverse itself. This time, however, many of those who traveled to the Midwest were Mexican Americans from Texas and other southwestern states. Also on the increase were Hispanics from other regions such as Puerto Rico, Cuba, and Central and South America."[38]

While Tejana/o migration tended to accumulate in industrial suburban areas "among recent arrivals from the Southern United States and the children of European immigrants," Mexicans who were hired initially as braceros and Mexicanas who migrated in the postwar years tended to look for "established Mexican neighborhoods in the largest industrial cities, particularly Chicago, Detroit, and Milwaukee, where the Mexican population and related cultural and business activities were most densely concentrated."[39] It is no coincidence that Don Chuy had immediate access to inter-Latina/o social networking in Detroit. While he found accessible resources, including a place to stay, access to meals, and incorporation into the labor force, his Cuban benefactor was cashing in on room and board but also on access to cheap labor in order to expand her store. This mutually dependent and reciprocal relationship between Latina/o and sometimes Chicana/o groups laid the foundation for a future San Ignacian transnational community. Almost five years after Don Chuy's arrival Doña Tita, who is believed to be the first San Ignacian woman to reside in Detroit, would also benefit from these cross-Latina intergroup relationships, when a Mexican woman from Chihuahua introduced Doña Tita to her social transnational network.

Unlike their Mexican predecessors, who were more scattered in Michigan due to the diverse locations of auto factories, auto part plants, and foundries, San Ignacians arriving in the late 1960s were welcomed by a growing Hispanic population that had gradually been establishing itself in southwest Detroit and what later became known as Mexican Town.[40]

After Don Chuy became a legal resident (thanks to Latina/o intergroup relations), he sponsored his brother Luis's permanent residency; Luis Mercado then arranged for his family to join him in Detroit in 1974. The brothers worked as mariachi musicians in San Ignacio before leaving for the United States, and after Don Chuy arrived in Detroit he decided to continue his musical career. Later he and his brother played with a group called El Carretero, which also included a few other young Latino men. Initially the group had very little business, as they were the first to introduce mariachi music to Detroit. After two years, however, they got gigs in cantinas, and people also hired them to play for weddings, baptisms, and funerals.

Supported by the growing Detroit Mexican community of the late 1960s and early 1970s, the mariachi group did well, but not well enough for the men to be able to support their families and the small businesses they had already opened in San Ignacio. They continued to work and seek better-paid jobs. Don Chuy kept on working in the steel plant while pursuing his musical career. But music served as another anchor for the growing cultural production of this latent Hispanic community in Detroit.

Once the Mercado brothers established themselves in Detroit (with Don Chuy's job in the steel industry and Luis's in the construction industry), they encouraged other San Ignacians to head east from Texas and north from Mexico to cash in on better labor opportunities. Through access to established Latina/o social networks, the Mercado brothers thus became the pioneers of the newly formed San Ignacian transnational community. Many San Ignacians began their journeys to Detroit, where they found jobs in the auto, steel, construction, and meat-packing industries.

In 1967 Don Chuy and his brother Luis contacted the Hernández brothers in California and told them of the higher wages and better working conditions in the Midwest. They emphasized the self-respect that came from holding respectable jobs in industry rather than doing back-breaking stoop labor in the fields. In 1969 Jesús, Rubén, Gabriel, and Delfino Hernández moved to Detroit and lived with the Mercado brothers until one by one they began to rent or buy their own homes. Doña Ana Hernández remembered: "My husband [Rubén Hernández] lived in a house with his brothers and Chuy and Luis Mercado. The men would get together to pay for all the bills. But the one that worked hardest was my husband, because he was the clean one. He would tell them: '*Cabrones huevones* [lazy fuckers], I come home and the dirty dishes are still there.' He would then clean the kitchen, leaving it very clean."[41]

The Hernández brothers were the first ones to live with the Mercado brothers after their arrival but not the last. Some of the Hernández brothers brought their families to Detroit, as did Luis Mercado. This was the beginning of the social networks that encouraged many more San Ignacians to move to Detroit. Most made their first stop at the Mercados', where they were provided with much more than just a place to stay. They were privy to labor availability and working conditions as well as cultural disseminations through *parrandas* (parties) with the mariachis and participation in *partidos de football* (soccer matches).

Almost a decade after the Mercado and Hernández brothers' extended network arrived in Detroit, large numbers of working-class San Ignacian women began to migrate to the city. These arrivals changed the dynamics established previously by Latinas' networks and consequently those of San Ignacian men living in Detroit. The initial contact by Don Chuy with these already settled social networks established and sustained by Latinas not only facilitated his transition from an agricultural worker to an industrial worker but also enabled Don Chuy to lay the foundations for a San Ignacian transnational community. These cross-Mexican/cross-Latina affiliations that unfolded in Detroit when the first San Ignacians began to have contact with other Latinas/os point to the historical presence and importance of Latinas and Chicanas in the United States already participating in socioeconomic transnational sites.

THE ARRIVAL OF SAN IGNACIAN WOMEN
AND EXPANSION OF SOCIAL NETWORKS

Mexican and Mexican American women had been migrating to and within the United States since the late nineteenth century. A dislocated mobilization of Mexicans en masse after the Mexican-American War in 1848 changed the ethnic landscape not only in the Southwest but also in many other regions where labor was desperately needed. After the United States tightened its immigration policies to curtail Chinese immigration (first by implementing the Page Law in 1875, which excluded Chinese women, and a few years later through the Chinese Exclusion Act of 1882, which excluded male laborers), Mexican and Mexican American labor became a premier commodity. Many states in Mexico contributed to the increase of Mexican immigrants going north, especially to the Midwest. Jalisco in particular has been sending immigrants to the Midwest since the nineteenth century and into the twenty-first. Urban industrialization in the Midwest also brought with it large numbers of laborers from the Southwest, particularly Texas.

In 1930 sociologist Paul Taylor reported that 73.7 percent of Mexican migration to Chicago came from the Central Plateau, which he defined as consisting of Aguascalientes, the Distrito Federal, Guanajuato, Jalisco, Michoacán, and Zacatecas. More specifically, the 1930 census reported that the resident Mexican population of Michigan was 86.8 percent urban. The census undercounted Mexican dependence on agricultural labor during the beet industry's harvest, however (since the census was conducted in April before sugar beet workers migrated from Texas, Mexico, and midwestern cities). Sugar beet farmers coerced their employees to settle in urban areas while awaiting the sugar beet migratory pattern of harvesting instead of going back home.[42]

The depression of the early 1920s and then the Great Depression in the 1930s were two moments in U.S. history that Mexicans and Chicanas/os will never forget. During the Great Migration approximately 1 million Mexicans and many Mexican Americans were deported. Despite these social blows, both Mexican and Chicana/o communities flourished in the Midwest. Contrary to postwar national rhetoric on domesticity, working-class Mexican and Mexican American women continued to carry the double-shift day, thus participating in a gendered formal economy that devalued their work. "In 1947, entry-level wages for men at Swift in St. Paul were 96 cents per hour, but for women only 85.5 cents."[43] At the same time they continued to engage in reproductive labor.

Unlike many of her Mexican predecessors who found housing in separate localities due to job distribution, in 1971 Doña Tita came to her own home, in a neighborhood that already housed a semidiverse Latin American population. Her husband, Delfino Hernández, and his brothers had purchased a house in what is currently known as Mexican Town in southwest Detroit.

For San Ignacian women, traveling almost 2,000 miles to Detroit in the 1970s was not an easy venture. Many had traveled locally and some as far as Mexico City: "On my honeymoon [in the 1950s] we went to Mexico City and to Tulancingo, Hidalgo, where my husband had an aunt. . . .

Then we went to Guadalajara and stayed with another aunt that he had and from there we came back [to San Ignacio]."[44] But going north and consequently crossing the border, making their journey international, was an entirely new experience. Their lives had been transnationalized in San Ignacio by virtue of contributing to the sustainability of their families and via their male counterparts who worked and lived in the United States but returned often to their community of origin. These recurrent visits, infused with transnational transformations, ideologies, and material culture, exposed San Ignacian families to a transnational immigrant experience. Physical mobility entailed a whole new set of transnational challenges, however, which affected women in every step of the process from moving to settling and "making a home" in a new geographical location.

> The first time I went [to Detroit in 1970] I traveled by bus to Laredo, Texas. Then I didn't take another bus; instead I took a van. Those vans would do trips from Laredo to Chicago. The driver took pity on us, because the van just went to Chicago. So after Chicago I had to take another bus all the way to Detroit. There was another man riding the van that was also going to Detroit, and with me were my two sons Pepe Luis and Javier and two of my youngest ones as well. So Pepe Luis asked the driver: "How much to take us all the way to Detroit so that we don't have to transfer?" I think he charged $40; and he took us all the way to Detroit. Very early in the morning we arrived at the house. Well, actually no, I didn't like it [Detroit] and the little house I didn't like either. But I was happy because I had all my family and my husband. So I am happy, now that I have experienced [being in Detroit]. I was happy because we also had my brothers-in-law and two other friends [the Mercados].[45]

Despite the dislocation of moving to a new geographical locality and into a new nation-state, Doña Tita began to feel at home through the emotional support and consolation of having all of her family together in Detroit. Although women in San Ignacio raised their children, did household chores, worked in the fields, tended cattle and pigs, and sometimes managed a small business, their community clung to the idea that without a male presence the family was unprotected and vulnerable, economically and emotionally. Women also exerted a degree of pressure when deciding to migrate: "Maybe my husband decided to take me because he loved me very much," commented Doña Tita while chuckling, "because the majority of the men did not [take their wives]. Well, it was because one day I told him, 'Why don't you get me a tourist visa, come on, let's go to

Guadalajara, to the consulate.' . . . They told us to get the permanent residency instead so that I could come and go as I pleased. Then my children told their father that it would be better for me to go north so that we could all be together."[46]

At the same time, many San Ignacian men believed that the United States provided a licentious atmosphere that would be detrimental to Mexican children's and women's socialization and thus adherence to patriarchal hierarchies: "I didn't want to go with so many children and my mother sick. And my husband used to say that over there [Detroit] was too promiscuous and he didn't want my children to be raised there."[47] Notwithstanding the many hurdles that both Mexican men and women considered and overcame, the flow of migration from San Ignacio to Detroit had begun.

Once women began to migrate to Detroit in the 1970s, a new set of social networks emerged that enlarged and to some extent replaced the older networks established by Latinas and consequently San Ignacian men of the bracero generation. Through these networks townspeople arriving from San Ignacio continuously renewed and replenished the social and cultural life of the growing San Ignacian community in Detroit.

Recent scholarship has only begun to explore the gendered ambiguities of these networks. For example, Denise A. Segura and Patricia Zavella employ an approach from the fields of Chicana/o Studies, arguing that "[immigrant] women are constructing their identities in spaces 'located in the interstices between the dominant national and cultural systems of the United States and Mexico' as they live, work, and play in communities on both sides of the border. Women in the U.S.-Mexico borderlands construct a new diasporic subjectivity that may be oppositional and transformative as they reflect on their experiences of migration, settlement, work, or social reproduction that are affected by globalization and structural violence."[48] Inherent contradictions embedded in the immigrant experience also contribute to the construction of this diasporic subjectivity, however; while many women disliked Detroit's isolating weather and impersonal texture, they enjoyed the company of their family and the cultural familiarity created by the influx of more and more San Ignacian co-nationals.

Doña Minerva complained that Detroit was ugly and she did not like the snow. But she added, "Well now, I don't like to come to San Ignacio, because of my children [who are all in Detroit now]."[49] Doña Chavelita also illustrates these contradictions and difficulties concerning mobility:

I didn't know how to survive anymore [while her husband, Jesús Hernández, was going back and forth between Mexico and Detroit] and support so many [thirteen children] there [in Detroit]. Besides, I was worried about how we were going to fit in that house, because my husband's brothers were there and also some of my children and my nephews. We didn't have money to buy another house [in Detroit]. It was very hard for me because we couldn't go out and the winter was very hard. Then my husband would get some time off and we would go back to San Ignacio for a short period and we would bring some of the other kids.[50]

Working-class San Ignacian women began to negotiate within their dislocating transnational experience in order to carve a familiar space in their new geographical site. Making a home in Detroit required, first of all, owning a home. Their Mexican predecessors of the first three decades in the Motor City "did not purchase homes. The main reasons were their short time in the city; an unstable job market, which made a steady income impossible; and the prohibitive cost of real estate."[51] San Ignacians, however, aggressively pursued the purchase of a new home in the neighborhood that welcomed new arrivals. Settling in Detroit and the availability for jobs in the 1970s facilitated the creation of new social networks among San Ignacians as well as the formation of a transnational community.

By the end of the 1960s and early 1970s Detroit had suffered one of the most savage racial battles in the history of its urbanization (after the racial riots in 1943): the July 1967 race riots that left the city's racial, social, and architectural infrastructure severely injured. "After five days of violence, forty-three people were dead, thirty of them killed by law enforcement personnel. . . . The property damage, still visible in vacant lots and abandoned buildings in Detroit, was extensive. Rioters looted and burned 2,509 buildings."[52] Due to the aftermath of the race riots, property values in southwest Detroit became much more accessible to new arrivals from San Ignacio. Burned homes remain a fixed neighborhood landscape in Mexican Town. Don Chuy's son Jaime and his wife, Irma, settled in Detroit in 1992. In 1994, Jaime said, "We bought the house, right? Two years after we arrived. But it was very expensive [laughing and joking]. I only paid $5,000, right there in Mexican Town where all of us San Ignacians live. At that time they were almost giving away houses. The barrio was . . . well, there were a lot of Cubans because of the *Mariel* . . . but we arrived and now it's mostly Mexican and on the other side of the street it's mostly African American."[53] Segregation practices led to the devaluation of southwest Detroit properties; by the time San Ignacians began to settle in Detroit in the 1970s, white flight had diversified the area, marginalizing Latinas/os and African Americans into the poorest urban enclaves of the city.[54]

Once working-class San Ignacians began to settle in Mexican Town, they began to purchase their own homes. First the Mercado brothers bought their home, and then the Hernández brothers one by one purchased their own homes. These financial transactions were facilitated by the existing Latina/o networks, such as the Cuban woman who welcomed Don Chuy and the woman from Santiaguito (a small town near San Ignacio) who rented to the Hernández brothers. As Doña Tita recollects, "[My husband] ended up buying a house for all of us and we were all right. . . . When they [the brothers] arrived [in Detroit] they lived in a *casa de asistencia* of someone from Santiaguito, from a town that is very close to Arandas."[55] After San Ignacian men had accessed Latina social networks they were able to purchase their own homes. Doña Tita exercised pressure for her husband to buy a house in order to accommodate so many co-nationals and of course for her to have her own private space and at the same time reduce the amount of domestic labor she had to endure while having too many visitors at once.

San Ignacian immigrants began to purchase homes in the part of southwest Detroit that is now called Mexican Town, where houses were affordable for them. Doña Tita is believed to be the first woman from San Ignacio to settle in Detroit, in 1969. Her husband, Delfino Hernández, had worked out the petitions to bring his family; and after she had her last child they all moved to Detroit to join him. Doña Tita did not know any other women in Detroit, but as soon as she arrived she remembered meeting a woman from Chihuahua, Mexico, who immediately befriended her and began to inform her about the different schools for the children, the health centers available to them, and the nearest food market.

> I met a woman named Lupita; she was from Chihuahua. She immediately became my friend and gave me protection, and helped me so that my children that were of age could go to the school—Héctor, Martín, Gustavo, Graciela, and Lorena. And also Father Francisco helped me get them to the Holy Redeemer School, because I had to pay and when I got there it was already time for them to start school. For me to pay the tuition, I needed help from someone because I had to come up with the money. I had another friend from around here [San Ignacio]

in Atotonilco, her name was Raquel Fonseca, and Lupita Anaya from Chihuahua. . . . [If my children got sick] they would inform me. Raquel moved here after her marriage. They were both older than me.[56]

Following the Mercados' migratory pattern and then settlement, Doña Tita tapped into existing networks of working-class Latinas, which facilitated their mobility and entrance into a process of socioeconomic and political transnational socialization. Working-class Mexican, Chicana, and Latina women had been making a home in Detroit many years before San Ignacians arrived. Moreover, these existing networks facilitated the mobility and the creation of the San Ignacian transnational community. Intra- and intergroup relations within transnational communities help explain the spatial versatility that the immigration experience provided for new settlers in Detroit's last three decades of the twentieth century. Mexican working-class women occupied public spaces throughout the twentieth century: "The border journeys of Mexican women were fraught with unforeseen difficulties, but held out the promises of a better life. . . . Women built communities of resiliency, drawing strength from their *comadres*, their families, and their faith. Confronting 'America' often meant confronting the labor contractor, the boss, the landlord, or *la migra*. It would also involve negotiating the settlement house, the grammar school, and the health clinic."[57]

Unlike her predecessors, Doña Tita socialized or "acculturated" through these networks rather than through the earlier Americanization programs launched in the first three decades of the twentieth century in order to Americanize Mexicans and other minorities. Her first experiences with Euro-American institutions, such as enrolling her children in school, were facilitated not only by Lupita's previous experience in making a home in Detroit but also by Lupita's capital accumulation, since she loaned the money for Doña Tita to enroll her children in a private Catholic school. In many ways, for women arriving in the 1970s networks previously established by Latinas/os served as substitutes for "state and church-sponsored Americanization projects [that] could portend cultural hegemony, individual empowerment, vocational tracking, community service, or all four simultaneously."[58]

Although there were not yet any other San Ignacian women in Detroit, Doña Tita established cross-Mexican and cross-Latina affiliations that helped her lay the groundwork for the social networks that she and other San Ignacian women would build via their socioeconomic relations and their collective reproductive and paid labor. A second major socializing facilitator for newly arrived San Ignacian women was the presence of the Catholic Church. Lupita from Chihuahua informed Doña Tita about the churches that surrounded the neighborhood; and Doña Tita made the decision to take her family to Holy Redeemer, which was close to her home.

The two main Catholic churches in Mexican Town were Most Holy Redeemer and St. Anne, known as Santa Ana. These centers for religious rituals became (just like San Ignacio's local church) social centers for newly arrived immigrants. As a bastion of spirituality and comfort, the Catholic Church and its multiple religious iconography provided something that San Ignacians could identify with in Detroit, despite the social and cultural challenges they faced—including, for many, lack of language proficiency and the racist sentiments of native white Detroiters and other ethnic groups.

Continuing a tradition of strong religious fervor, most San Ignacian families arriving in the early 1970s chose to go either to Holy Redeemer or to Santa Ana. San Ignacians participated in the Cristero Revolt of 1926. This was a war against the religious persecution plaguing Mexico in the end of the 1920s, when Mexican president Plutarco Elías Calles and thus the Mexican state "had begun to close Catholic schools and convents, place restrictions on the numbers and activities of parish priests, and prohibit public worship. . . . They [San Juan peasants from the neighboring state of Michoacán] did know of the rebellions under way in the neighboring states of Jalisco, Colima, and Guanajuato."[59] This national rhetoric carried a strong anticlerical message that affected several states in Mexico and caused an insurrection that lasted more than three years. The state of Jalisco strongly championed the Cristeros, whose war cry was "¡Viva Cristo Rey!" (Long live Christ our King!). Images of Cristero heroes beautifully adorned in golden rococo-style frames parade on the main avenue in San Ignacio along with the Virgin of Guadalupe and the national immigrant heroes and heroines in the yearly festivities. Membership in a church was a sociocultural ritual that signified markers that were known to San Ignacian women as they began to construct their own transnational spaces. San Ignacians chose their place of worship according to location, recommendations from other parishioners, and familial preferences.

Once settled in Detroit, Doña Minerva and her husband, Luis Mercado, initially preferred Santa Ana because it was the first church to celebrate mass in Spanish, but they changed to Holy Redeemer because it was

TABLE 1.3. MEXICAN POPULATION RESIDING IN THE UNITED STATES
AND PERCENTAGES OF MEN AND WOMEN

Year	Mexican Population in U.S.	Women (%)	Men (%)
1970	760,000	51.1	48.9
1990	4,766,000	44.9	55.1
2000	8,527,000	46.1	53.9

Source: Mexican Ministry of Foreign Affairs–U.S. Commission on Immigration Reform, Washington, D.C., *Mexico–United States Binational Migration Study: Migration between Mexico and the United States* (Austin, Tex.: U.S. Commission on Immigration Reform/www.utexas.edu/lbj/uscir/binational.html, 1998); U.S. Department of Commerce, Bureau of the Census, *Census 2000* (Washington, D.C.: U.S. Government Printing Office, 2000).

close to their Detroit home. Later Holy Redeemer also acknowledged the growth of the Mexican population in the neighborhood and began to offer a Spanish-language mass in the church basement. Doña Minerva remembers when the mass was in English: "To begin with I did not understand anything but I still went there. Once they began to say mass in Spanish, it was nicer."[60] Eventually the Spanish-speaking population outgrew the church basement: now Santa Ana and Holy Redeemer both celebrate three masses on Sundays in Spanish, attended mostly by the San Ignacians who live in Mexican Town.

From the 1970s onward it was women who did the most to construct, support, shape, and contest the social networks that facilitated the flow of San Ignacians to Detroit (Table 1.3). Taking over the social networks that the Mercado brothers had initiated by tapping into existing Latina social networks, Mexicanas from San Ignacio began to create community and help each other make a home in a geographical area that was new to them. Within these new social networks, San Ignacian women built a strong and substantial base for their transnational community, facilitating the dissemination of imperative information pertaining to the acquisition of jobs, access to health and education, English-language proficiency, and important issues concerning their new lives in Detroit. This taking over of the management and sustainability of social networking by San Ignacian women from their male counterparts metaphorically illuminates

Father Ignacio's story at the beginning of this chapter; it was as if Mexicanas told their male family members what the Virgin of Guadalupe told San Ignacio de Loyola: "Get out of the way because here I come."[61]

As soon as San Ignacian women joined the migratory flow to Detroit only a few years after Don Chuy arrived, their deployment of economic and social capital became obvious. Church attendance became a part of their new transnational social and cultural routine in their new home. Mexicanas and their male counterparts joined a circular migration that placed in stark contrast their lives in Detroit and their yearly visits home to celebrate not only their religious affiliation but also their regional transnational loyalties.

Unlike the small intimate receptions that their bracero husbands received when returning home, San Ignacian women joining the migratory flow in the 1970s experienced the radical changes that this seemingly simple celebration underwent. It was transformed from a familial affectionate reunion to a magnificent procession, perfectly orchestrated and displayed as a regional major event. Mexicanas residing in Detroit are now an integral element of the yearly week-long celebrations held during the last week of January. Women and their families stand in line, participating in the long religious procession that shows off their success as San Ignacian immigrants—transnational subjects. This procession is the centerpiece of many processions that are part of the weeklong celebrations. Every year *los hijos ausentes* (and of course now *las hijas ausentes*), like heroes and heroines, wait impatiently for the procession to move forward, with their families and friends by their side, proud to show off their regional and religious affiliation as well as their membership in a transnational network. Their heroic deeds are displayed in full force all around town, starting with the beautifully paved main avenue (subsidized by remittances), which these long lines of transnational workers will cross on their way to their final destination: the church. The local priest and his entourage of ecclesiastical authorities lead the procession, which will eventually end inside the church, where they have prepared a special mass for the *hijos ausentes*.

A CHANGING CELEBRATION

Mexican rural women have been praying for the *hijos ausentes* for centuries, offering *exvotos* and *retablos* (votive offerings and altarpieces) for the loss of a son, husband, boyfriend, or brother to forced conscription. A colonial legacy, *exvotos* and *retablos* have been a socioreligious reality for many poor rural peasants, imprinted with their anxieties. For many women, religious faith and hope were a way of asserting control of the safety of their loved ones through their prayers. These *exvotos* were very popular in the nineteenth century, when women and men (mostly from rural areas) would ask a particular Virgin or saint for a miracle in return for a promise. The payment-promise and the timeline involved in repaying the miracle varied, depending on the parishioner and the locality. Some included yearly visits to the Virgin's or saint's shrine or yearly pilgrimages to a church from a particular point of departure; others included offering an important symbol of personal sacrifice, such as leaving a long braid of hair next to the *exvoto*. The believers would commission local painters to represent (to the best of their ability) the actual moment of suffering and thus the reason for the miracle. Patricia Arias and Jorge Durand describe the *exvoto* as "giving thanks for a favor granted like a miracle, in return which they must offer a public and lasting expression of gratitude."[62] Regions in Mexico with strong *exvoto* historical production include Guanajuato, Jalisco, Querétaro, Michoacán, San Luis Potosí, and Zacatecas—the center-west Cristero region.

According to rural historical experiences, "absent men" were associated with conscription during periods in the nineteenth and twentieth century in Mexican history that caused rural mayhem: mainly the Mexican-American War, 1846–1848; the Reforma in the 1850s; the dictatorship of Porfirio Díaz, 1876–1910 (known as the Porfiriato); and the Mexican Revolution of 1910–1921, later compounded by the Cristero Revolt. These rural/urban armed conflicts resulted in separations and uncertainties, particularly in the last two centuries: "This reason for anguish [the absence of loved ones] has been dated or assumed to have become popular in the mid-nineteenth century, when political turmoil brought about social violence. During this time, it became an everyday experience to implement the forced enrollment of young men from small towns and villages into the federal troops and then take them to different and distant locations."[63] In 1858 Luz García's mother prayed: "In the month of October of 1858 when Luz García went to take care of some business in Tepatitlán [Jalisco], he joined the federal army. Coming from Silao, his mother, along with his brother, looking for García . . . is asking El Señor de la Misericordia [Lord of Mercy] to care for him, who has been separated from his mother for a year and seven months, for a miracle."[64] Rural women from Jalisco and other regions represented their social and emotional dislocations visually through *exvotos*.

In the nineteenth and twentieth centuries workers traveling north in search for better opportunities became another embodiment of the *ausentes* and thus a major concern for the economy of the rural household. Many women expressed the emotional and economic anxieties and fears that plagued the journey and consequently the absence of a loved one during a long peregrination with dangerous as well as rewarding consequences. In 1955 Candelaria Arreola wrote: "I thank the Virgin of Tlalpa for returning my son from the United States. He was there for a long time and I started to pray my novena [prayer lasting nine days] and before I could finish it he was back. Thanks, my mother!"[65] Yearly religious celebrations in this area (the center-west, also know as the Cristero Region) have formed part of the constellation of religious rituals followed by thousands of fervent Catholic believers. Long pilgrimages are part of traditional affiliation and proof of religious devotion. Many of the promises imprinted in the *exvotos* left behind by rural women included long peregrinations on their knees to the sanctuary of the Virgin of Guadalupe.

While living in San Ignacio, I was awakened one morning by loud bells ringing from the church, announcing another of the many celebrations I had already experienced. I managed to put on whatever I could (it was five in the morning), grabbed my camera, and headed toward the church. As soon as I reached the corner, from which I had a clear view of the main entrance of the church, I saw an endless line of small bodies swaying rhythmically from side to side and attempting to climb the stairs leading to the main hallway. Stunned by the sight, I began to take pictures of mostly older women (in their fifties through eighties) and a few younger ones on their knees. These women had been walking on their knees for long distances before reaching their destination at San Ignacio's main church. Peregrinations and processions have been a cultural trait in rural Mexico for centuries. Moreover, the transformations that these local festivities underwent in the last three decades of the twentieth century in San Ignacio signify the way in which religious rituals and economic systems influence and are intertwined in the lives of these transnational subjects.

San Ignacio was a small town in the 1950s. Doña Ana, the wife of Rubén Hernández and a nurse assigned to work in San Ignacio in 1959, remembered it undergoing renovations to expand and having about a hundred very small houses.[66] The town was isolated and lacked access to communications media, aside from a few radios.[67] People in general were absorbed with strategies for survival, and social life revolved around the family and church-organized activities. The church was a place of worship but also a place to gather and talk to friends and relatives after mass. The priest, as the principal supervisor of knowledge, was a central figure in the social, cultural, and religious lives of San Ignacians. As a Cristero state, Jalisco—with a strong tradition of religious political intervention by the church—represents the importance of the effect that the presence of the Catholic Church and its priest has on townspeople and vice versa. The Cristero Revolt took place when the Mexican government wanted to enact the anticlerical measures stipulated in the 1917 Constitution, in particular the implementation of the Calles Law of 1926, which supported agrarian reform (private property) and advocated anticlerical sentiments.

Postrevolutionary Mexico's nationalist agenda pushed forward two major agendas: the agrarian reform, which meant the dismantling of *ejidos* (communal land) and the division of communal land for private ownership, and dismantling the political and economic power of the church by advocating an anticlerical view that adamantly supported the separation of church and state. "Education, whether public or private, was to be completely secular in content; monasteries and convents were abolished; the clergy were prohibited from making any statements in opposition to existing laws and institutions; religious publications could include no political commentary; no political organization could bear a name including any religious references; political meetings could not be held in church buildings; all religious worship was to take place in churches under supervision of local authorities; religious clothing could not be worn in public; and the Church was prohibited from owning all forms of real estate."[68] It was clear that the Mexican state feared the political and economic power of the church, including its proselytizing through private education.

Most working-class San Ignacians (both in Detroit and in San Ignacio) expressed not only their loving relationship with and eternal respect for the priests assigned to their locality but also their expectations of the priest's local obligations:

> When I got married, the priest was Raúl Cortés. . . . But the one we have now [Ignacio Ramos Puga] is the one that has changed the town most. He planned the religious ceremonies and all the celebrations. But now we are very sad because they just relocated him. The day before yesterday my sister [who is in San Ignacio] told me. It's very sad because he was there for fifteen years. And the religious ceremonies, he planned them so beautifully. We don't know what the new priest will do for our town.[69]

Alina's religious affiliation is expressed through her interest in spiritual guidance, but she also expects the priest to "do something for our town," despite the fact that she lives in Detroit. In this statement she also expresses the sociopolitical commitment that is expected from the priest, aside from all the social engagements through which a priest validates his spiritual authority over civil leadership. Births, baptisms, first communions, marriages, and burial rituals are not recognized or ratified by the state unless registered through civil services—such as obtaining a marriage license or a birth certificate issued by the state.

Women's prayers and promises to God and the saints offer testimonies that underline the major circumstances surrounding the life of rural women in the Mexican provincial landscape. Most recently, they have turned to *exvotos* "as a way to confront the sadness and constant anxiety about the absence of a loved one; with her promise, the petitioner also expects to cover the *ausente*'s safe return home. Moreover, from the petitioner's point of view, this religious commitment also works as a kind of talisman that accompanies the *ausente* in all of her/his travels and activities while away."[70] Recently Guadalupe Dorante Franco asked: "Señor de Chalma, protect my sister who is in the United States. It's been days since she left and I don't know when she'll return. Please protect her and have her return soon."[71] Women are now part of the pantheon of the *ausentes*, not only present in prayers and during the festivities in the last week of January in San Ignacio but also exerting presence and authority through their paid labor in the United States and their economic participation in the town's social, economic, and cultural infrastructure through their remittances.

When braceros from San Ignacio returned home in the 1950s and 1960s, their arrivals were private family affairs. They returned primarily to see their families and make sure that they were well taken care of but also to celebrate their religious affiliation. During the bracero years the annual religious celebrations for the Virgin of Guadalupe were local, usually celebrated by different *colonias* (communities) in the towns. Small traveling carnivals and food vendors gathered around the plaza in front of the church, with bands playing. The celebrations lasted only a few days. The festivities also served as commercial hubs, where townspeople came to buy and sell their products. Although immigrants on home visits enjoyed these celebrations with their families, they were not publicly recognized during them. But their heroic deeds were recognized through personal prayers. This changed dramatically, however, as more women joined the migratory flow and the transnational community became more significant economically and culturally.

Unlike their male counterparts during the bracero era, San Ignacian men and women who moved to Detroit in the late 1960s and early 1970s were welcomed by an incipient Latina/o community. Labor demands along with tougher immigration policies began to disrupt the circular migratory patterns established by the bracero generation, thus limiting the mobility of these transnational subjects. Most of the early immigrant workers tried to visit Mexico every year or two, but it was not always easy, because they had to petition for time off from the factories where they were working. As the postwar industrial boom began to deteriorate in the 1970s, however, Mexican immigrants largely shifted into construction work and landscaping. These jobs enabled them to leave Detroit at the beginning of winter, in October or November, and return in March or April. They were usually laid off during this period, and some even collected unemployment benefits. The months that they were not working coincided with the traditional religious festivities in San Ignacio.

Today the elaborate celebrations honor the town's heroes and heroines—first and foremost their eternal protector, the Virgin of Guadalupe—and the current heroes and heroines—the returning immigrants. It is a time when immigrants and residents come together in San Ignacio to share their common experiences as a dynamic transnational community. In San Ignacio immigrants stand proudly alongside hundreds of their conationals, lined up behind a banner of the Virgin of Guadalupe and a big sign that reads "DETROIT." They wait patiently for the procession to begin, dressed in their best clothes and accompanied by their families. They carry gifts that the priest has instructed them to bring: candles of a particular size that will fit the candle holders in the church, wine of a specific brand name that is used for mass, flowers of all colors, and of course the one gift that is less visible yet supremely important: dollars.

In 2003 the immigrants from Detroit donated $14,000 to purchase an enormous image of Christ that is now housed in the church. These religious *ofrendas* (offerings), much like their personal *ofrendas* through *exvotos*, continue to exemplify the historical participation and leadership of women in religious rituals. These *exvotos* are proof of the maintenance of an economic religious infrastructure that enables the church to exert its influence while collecting monetary *ofrendas* as well. At the same time, women play a more central role in making personal decisions on how to participate in these yearly magnificent celebrations. Fittingly, these religious celebrations are no longer called only *la fiesta de la virgen*; they are now also *la fiesta de los hijos ausentes*: the celebration of the town's current absent children—the immigrants.

One obvious change is that women now take advantage of the occasion to challenge notions of appropriate female behavior. They do so by per-

forming their transnational identity (starting with their choices of clothing), including how to express their sexuality in courting rituals that take
place during the months when most immigrants return to San Ignacio.
In 2003, when I witnessed the fiesta for the first time, a few women were
lined up in the procession that ended at the church for mass. Some of
the Detroit women were dressed very provocatively, according to older
women of the town. They were wearing tight dresses that were considered
too short and revealing, challenging religious and social mores concerning appropriate feminine behavior. Although the priest, Father Ignacio,
did not address this issue, many older and even some younger women were
heard to gossip and criticize the visitors' attire. The regional bishop, who
was hosting the mass that day, did not intercede either, focusing his ser-
mon on thanking the immigrants for their big financial contribution to
the church.[72]

*The Mexican men here [Chicago] say that the Mexican girls of the
United States have too much liberty. They want to marry the girls
newly from Mexico. Mexican girls here [Chicago] want Mexicans
who have been in the United States.*

—MEXICAN HIGH SCHOOL BOY, CHICAGO, ILLINOIS, 1937[1]

*In my opinion it doesn't matter if they come from there [the
United States] or from here [San Ignacio]. . . . But the problem is
that young men here are very jealous. . . . I guarantee you that the
majority of young women here [in San Ignacio] have boyfriends in
the United States.*[2]

—ALMA (EIGHTEEN), INTERVIEW IN SAN IGNACIO,
JANUARY 2003

I could hardly maintain a steady shot while walking and filming video
during the *fiestas patronales* in 2003: hundreds of youths were dancing,
pairing up, listening to music, kissing, and renting local *bandas* (bands) to
follow them around. Many young men took the opportunity to market
themselves as potential romantic partners and hard workers by flaunting
their impeccably decked out cars, among other things. Today capitalist
consumer culture is fully displayed in San Ignacio during the fiestas; local
requirements for courting rituals are integrated with modern commercialized leisure in a way that that resembles early twentieth century urban
amusement parks like Coney Island, where "carefully marketed sexual
titillation and romance in attractions threw patrons into each other,
sent skirts flying, and evoked instant intimacy among strangers."[3] These
amusement park–like carnivals also satisfied transnational needs of Mexicanness by offering spaces where regional and traditional leisure activities
such as cockfights, *lotería* games (similar to bingo in the United States),
and rodeo competitions took place. Vendors seduce their patrons with

portable national/religious symbols like bumper stickers with the image of the Virgin of Guadalupe with a Mexican flag in the background or colorful velvet quilts with enormous images of the Virgin of Guadalupe elegantly posing with La Malinche—her historical rival.

Love and attraction are very subjective, as are personal experiences linked to social relations and ideologies about romance and sexuality. Alma and the young man in Chicago expressed their visions of desirability in a partner. For the high school boy in 1937, Mexican women who had not migrated or were "newly from Mexico" were definitely more attractive than those who had been in the United States for some time. He categorized Chicanas and Mexican immigrant women living in the United States as "undesirable." His justification for this transnational preference was primarily that Mexican women living in the United States were too independent and consequently were a threat to male dominance.

Two generations later, Alma, residing in San Ignacio in 2003, described immigrant men living in the United States and Mexican American males born in the United States as more desirable candidates for romantic relationships and possibly marriage. These two subjects, speaking from particular geographical locations at different historical times, offered biased transnational viewpoints about the desirable/acceptable "womanhood" of the Mexicana who had just arrived and "manhood" of the Mexicano who had been more assimilated. They offer a glimpse into the kaleidoscope of gender nuances intersecting with race, class, sexuality, and nation within transnational fields. And they reveal, in turn, how transnational fields produce and reproduce gender ideologies about sexual, racial, and class attitudes.

Social constructions of appropriate "womanhood" and "femininity" are directly linked to confrontational and transformative sexual categories that transnational subjects balance when experiencing mobility from one nation to another: Edna A. Viruell-Fuentes states that "while transnationalism can sometimes function as a tool for belonging, it can also highlight difference, particularly for women whose life trajectories might be perceived as 'too liberal' and not conforming to prescribed gendered expectations. A certain degree of assimilation is an integral component of transnationalism but not necessarily expressed or interpreted as a final product."[4] Assimilation thus becomes a process embedded in transnational circuits.

This chapter maps out how social constructions and expectations about working-class sexual identities both in the United States and in Mexico shape and are shaped by the Mexican immigrants' experience.

Building on academic work on immigration studies, gender, and sexuality, my investigation supports the argument that "women are constructing their identities in spaces 'located in the interstices between the dominant national and cultural systems of both the U.S. and Mexico' as they live, work, and play in communities on both sides of the border. Women in the U.S.-Mexico borderland construct a new diasporic subjectivity that may be oppositional and transformative as they reflect on their experiences of migration, settlement, work, or social reproduction that are affected by globalization and structural violence."[5] The chapter also introduces what I call transnational sexualities: the oppositional and confrontational experiences that Mexican transnational subjects accumulate while constructing sexual identities through their participation in transnational circuits. These transnational sexualities are multifaceted and include interpretations and constructions of "womanhood" in Mexico and in the United States as San Ignacian women transitioned from rural working-class experiences to urban environments.

Not only is this network gendered, but younger generations of Mexicanas experience courtship, sexuality, and decisions about contraception, childbearing, and family size in radically different ways than their mothers and grandmothers did. The immigrant experience has affected their attitudes about dress, dating, premarital sex, use of contraceptives, and family size, all of which are dynamic and historical; San Ignacians who have emigrated and those who have remained at home have dialectically constructed transnational sexualities specific to their gender and their generation.

In her work on Mexicans in interwar Chicago, Gabriela Arredondo coined the term *mujeridades* to reframe the way we understand these complex and multiple transnational constructions. For Arredondo, *mujeridades* means "the competing visions and beliefs about what Mexican women could and should do. This concept of *mujeridades* provides a way to capture the multiple, often conflictive meanings of Mexican 'womanhood' that affected various aspects of their lives from migrations to marriages, families, to workplaces."[6] Transnational subjects undergo complex socio-economic and political processes while migrating and establishing transnational networks. Many of these processes are not only conflictive and confrontational but also dislocating and extremely daring when trespassing the gendered lines imposed by two distinct patriarchal nations—the Mexico-U.S militarized border. Transnational sexualities represent such challenges and provide an in-depth analysis of how Mexicanas and Mexicanos make sense of socially constructed ideologies about sex and sexual

TABLE 2.1. INFORMATION ON MEXICAN WORKING-CLASS IMMIGRANT WOMEN FROM SAN IGNACIO CERRO GORDO RESIDING IN SAN IGNACIO AND DETROIT

Pseudonym	Age	Marital Status	Birth	Work Experience	Family Background	Migration Experience
Bianca	Teens	Single	SI	None	Large family in SI	Resided in SI; had a brother in D and three uncles in Michigan; Mónica's sister
Lily	Teens	Single	SI	None	Large family in SI	Resided in D with her family; Don Chuy's granddaughter
Elena	Teens	Single	SI	None	Small family in SI	Resided in SI; had four brothers and two sisters in D
Mónica	Teens	Single	SI	None	Large family in SI	Resided in SI; had a brother in D and three uncles in Michigan; Bianca's sister
Reyna	Teens	Single	SI	None	Large family in SI	Resided in SI; had a sister and two brothers in D
Alma	Late teens	Engaged	SI	None	Large family in SI	Resided in SI; moved to Fresno, California, after marriage
Gaby	Early 20s	Married	SI	Homemaker; nail stylist	Small family in SI	Resided in D; went back to SI for two years

Gela	Mid-20s	Married	SI	Homemaker; waitress	Large family in SI	Resided in D with her husband and two sons; Gaby's sister-in-law
Nena	Late 20s	Married	SI	Homemaker; waitress	Large family in SI	Resided in D with her husband; Gabriel's sister-in-law
Vivi	Late 20s	Single in a relationship	SI	Homemaker; waitress	Small family in SI	Resided in D; Gaby's older sister
Angeles	Late 20s	Single	SI	Homemaker; waitress	Large family in SI	Resided in D; Nena's older sister
Rosi	Early 30s	Married	SI	Homemaker; retail salesperson	Large family in SI	Moved to D with husband but was deported and resided in SI
Mari	Late 30s	Married	SI	Homemaker; retail salesperson	Large family in SI	Worked in California but returned to SI to reside; two daughters resided in D
Sonia	Early 40s	Married	SI	Homemaker	Large family in SI	Resided in D with her family; married to Doña Toña's son
Irma	Late 40s	Married	SI	Homemaker	Large family in SI	Resided in D; Don Chuy's daughter-in-law
Tina	Late 40s	Married	SI	Homemaker; auto industry worker	Large family in SI	Resided in D with all of her family

TABLE 2.1. CONTINUED

Pseudonym	Age	Marital Status	Birth	Work Experience	Family Background	Migration Experience
Mercedes	Late 40s	Widow	SI	Homemaker	Small family in SI	Resided in SI; Gaby's mother; most of her children (except two) resided in D
María	Early 50s	Divorced	SI	Homemaker; factory worker	Large family in SI	Resided in D after leaving abusive husband in SI; all of her children resided in D
Lidia	Early 50s	Married	D	Homemaker	Small family in SI	Moved to D with husband and all of her family; Gaby's mother-in-law
Magda	Early 50s	Married	D	Homemaker	Large family in SI	Chicana from D, met her husband in D then followed him back to SI
Karla	Early 50s	Married	SI	Homemaker; brickmaker	Small family in SI	Resided in SI; had three sons in D
Alina	Early 50s	Married	SI	Homemaker; auto factory worker	Small family in SI	Doña Tita's daughter-in-law; her family resided in D; mother resided in SI

Doña Toña	Early 60s	Married	SI	Homemaker; nursery worker	Large family in SI	Resided in SI; traveled back and forth with husband to D, where most of her family resided
Doña Ana	Early 60s	Widowed	SI	Homemaker; nurse	Large family in SI	Resided in SI; Rubén Hernandez's wife; traveled to D to visit her son, who resided in D
Doña Minerva	Late 60s	Widowed	SI	Homemaker; nursery worker	Small family in SI	Resided in D but went back to SI with her husband during the winter months
Doña Chavelita	Late 60s	Widowed	SI	Homemaker; retail salesperson	Small family in SI	Moved to D with her husband; moved back to SI in old age; most of her family resided in D
Doña Luna	Early 70s	Widowed	SI	Homemaker; nursery worker	Small family in SI	Traveled back and forth with husband from D to SI; when her husband died she moved permanently to D, where most of her family resided
Doña Tita	Early 70s	Widowed	SI	Homemaker; domestic worker	Small family in SI	Moved to D with husband, Delfino; moved back to SI; believed to be the first San Ignacian woman to move to D

Note: SI = San Ignacio; D = Detroit.

practices through courting rituals and their choices of clothing, among others.

Historically the construction and dissemination of a concept of appropriate national "womanhood" has served as patriarchal propagandistic nationalist rhetoric. Mexican Porfirian elites (1876–1910) expressed moral indignation "over adultery, over the loss of virginity before matrimony, over sex without reproductive ends, over the exhibition of women's unclothed legs, and over the knowledge of anatomy."[7] In other words, the state formulated and disseminated an exclusive appropriate national notion of "womanhood" that included the control, management, and possession of women's bodies through their public and private (sexual) behavior, through their demeanor, and through rigid dress codes that symbolized those very privileged and sanitized ideals of national integrity.

Victorianism in the United States promoted the very same values of female morality and sexual management and their correlations with nationhood. Furthermore, studying immigrant women in New York, Kathy Peiss found that "reformers, social workers, and journalists viewed working-class women's sexuality through middle-class lenses, invoking sexual standards that set 'respectability' against 'promiscuity.' When applied to unmarried women, these categories were constructed foremost around the biological fact of premarital virginity, and secondarily by such cultural indicators as manners, language, dress, and public interaction."[8] Transnational subjects express their experiences through their representations of social categorizations such as ideologies about "womanhood." In turn these ideologies affect the way in which working-class San Ignacians negotiate gender while courting and selecting what they consider to be "appropriate" dress codes reinscribed in the transnational experience.

COURTING AND DRESS CODES

The significance of transnational sexualities is on full display in San Ignacio in the last week in January during the religious festivities that both honor the return of townspeople living abroad and celebrate their patroness, the Virgin of Guadalupe. The scene in town during fiesta week gives a panoramic view of how these religious/leisure activities reflect the changes in courtship practices and in attitudes toward women's dress codes, which are closely linked to attitudes about women's sexuality in general. In her study on Latina immigrants, Olivia M. Espín found that "immigrant women's identity conflicts and identity transformations continue to be expressed in our time through clothing and sexuality."[9] Cloth-

The main Catholic church in San Ignacio Cerro Gordo, built on one side of the plaza. San Ignacians celebrated the first corn harvest in October 2002. Farmers selected their best corn and cooked corn on the cob for the townspeople in the middle of the plaza. The celebration began with mass, followed by a community brunch.

Some San Ignacian women took the opportunity to transgress patriarchal mores regarding dress while asserting their ideologies about sexuality and "acceptable" behavior within their transnational social fields.

ing thus becomes a tool of resistance that many San Ignacian women appropriate to challenge patriarchal socioreligious boundaries during the *fiestas patronales.*

During these festivities, as was customary, many San Ignacians took the opportunity to flirt and look for potential partners while the town was vibrant with people returning home from different places (but predominantly from Detroit). Every night for a week in 2004 there were paid *banda* groups everywhere following reunited relatives, who were dancing and overwhelmed with excitement. The air was filled with the smell of all sorts of local foods like *tortas ahogadas* (dipped sandwiches) and *buñuelos* (fritters). There were hundreds of vendors in endless corridors of consumer products, some promising romance from imported perfumes and others auctioning velvet blankets (with jaguar prints or an image of the Virgin of Guadalupe).

I met him a day before my birthday, in the plaza. Thanks to a friend of mine, Ramón, that's where he started talking to me. . . . His name is Alonso, and we met here during the fiesta. He used to live here, but he just left for Detroit. His parents are there, so he went to work.[10]

For rural working-class Mexicans in San Ignacio, religious rituals such as Sunday mass and the *fiestas patronales* offered social public spaces where members of the community came together not only to pay their religious respects and conduct commerce but also to form family alliances through possible marriages. Historically, the *fiestas patronales* have had a great impact on rural inhabitants' sexual practices and ideologies about sexual behavior. In the nineteenth century, "the local fiesta made it easier to bring the two genders together; it was in the plaza and in front of the church where there was more tolerance for young single women to talk and flirt with local ranchers."[11] Like the *fiestas patronales*, these courting rituals have historically undergone several changes. One major influence on these changes has been the exodus/influx of political, economic, and very importantly sociocultural capital and the experiences of San Ignacians as transnational subjects.

These multiplicities of transnational experiences, in turn, affect and are affected by understandings about sexuality and "appropriate" sexual behavior while migrating to and from the United States and Mexico. Courting processes in San Ignacio are socioreligious rituals where gender is negotiated; these rituals also provide the social space for youths to explore and express their sexuality during fiesta week (under the watchful eye of the church and the community).

Socioreligious processes are the organic intertwining of San Ignacians' religious, social, and ecopolitical attitudes. For example: "These entertainments [*fiestas patronales* and *serenatas*] were intimately linked to the church. This way the respectability of the young women involved was not put in doubt with this strange symbiosis. Before going to the plaza and participating in the *serenatas*, young women had to go to mass, say the rosary, and be involved in the procession."[12] The importance and the complexity of this set of socioreligious and political relationships add to the nuance of transnational sexualities within transnational circuits. The priest and the church in San Ignacio and the central-west region of Mexico have historically played a major role in the control and management of sexual desires and sexual practices by orchestrating these rural working-class courting rituals.

The women that I interviewed, regardless of age, attended or had attended the traditional courting ritual (*la serenata*) most Sundays after mass and every night for a week during the yearly *fiestas patronales*, in the main plaza in front of the church. In this ritual men line up around the *kiosco* (a kiosk at the center of the plaza) in two large circles facing each other. Women, usually in pairs or small groups, walk around the inside of the circle, making the circuit several times as the men throw confetti and chat with them. Men are not supposed to touch the women, but one woman commented: "I don't like *la serenata*, because now they not only touch your hair but also your buttocks You know all that comes from years past, and I don't know why."[13] Once a man or a woman chooses a partner, the man offers the woman a rose and they break away from the circle to stroll in the park and the plaza.

Women from different generations chose to describe their courting in various ways, giving us insight into how they made meanings of contradictory and confrontational socioreligious ideas about purity, virtue, and family honor and also helping us to understand their experiences when meeting a young man and exploring their sexuality. Tina's experience sheds light on these complex socioreligious rituals: "We used to live on nearby ranches. He [her husband] used to come by my house selling milk. That's how we met. I was fifteen when we started to talk. We used to talk through a hole in the wall."[14] Many other older women in San Ignacio began their courtships by sneaking conversations with their boyfriends (through holes or cracks in walls or wooden doors). Sometimes they would manage to exchange a few words at a fiesta or while attending the Sunday *serenatas*.

According to many San Ignacian women, their parents, regardless of class, were very strict about their daughters' dating. María, a Mexicana living in Detroit, recalls her youth in San Ignacio: "I couldn't go out with him. No, I had to chat while standing by the door of my house. Every so often maybe I saw him in a *serenata* in the plaza. There in the plaza was where we would see each other."[15] Thus the public space and *la serenata* became the sites through which rural youths explored their sexualities. These historical working-class courting rituals also served to match young single women with fellow San Ignacians. For working-class San Ignacians, the availability of potential partners changed gradually with the influence of immigration.

In interviews older women who recalled the courting ways of their youth emphasized the secrecy of the encounters and the physical separation between their suitors and themselves. Several couples and widows from different generations said that they had communicated with suitors through a small gap in a door or wall. Others were allowed to leave the door partially open while one parent kept a watchful eye on the couple. Doña Chavelita remembered her first "dates" with her husband, Jesús, when they were boyfriend and girlfriend in 1949:

> We had to talk with the door closed. Through a hole in the wooden door we would look at each other like this [makes a sign with her fingers surrounding one eye] with one eye and the other and that's how we saw each other.[16]

During the same interview, however, Doña Chavelita playfully stroked her gray hair, and her blue eyes lit up when she commented:

> He looked very handsome, wearing his chauffeur's hat. Not the new driver's hats; the ones worn in older times, those that displayed the chauffeur's shield. Sometimes his sisters and I, two or three of us, would ride with him in the bus. . . . We would talk for a while on the way.[17]

San Ignacian rural working-class youths found ways, given their socio-economic realities, to escape parental supervision to explore their sexual identities.

When I asked older women if the *serenata* had been practiced when they were young, they all agreed that it had. Younger women also recalled their mothers talking about it as an experience prior to marriage.[18] It is understood that all the participants in the *serenata*, both male and female, are unmarried and available for a possible match. Older women in particular emphasized the ban on close contacts with men while courting individually as well as the physical proximity of men and women in these collective, working-class rural courting rituals. Because of patriarchal domination, however, rural working-class women had few chances to express and explore their sexual identities. San Ignacian women found ways to balance discourses and expectations about *mujeridades* while enjoying opportunities to meet mates.

Like their ancestors a century ago, young women in San Ignacio today are more likely to meet a transnational boyfriend or future husband during the yearly *fiestas patronales*, when hundreds of immigrants return from Detroit on their yearly visits home. But now San Ignacian rural working-class women (both those living in San Ignacio and those residing in Detroit) have a much greater menu of choices when selecting a mate than their predecessors did. These choices, however, also include taking greater risks than older generations of San Ignacian women did when crossing the border.

For San Ignacian workers, current immigration experiences include life-threatening risks while crossing the U.S.-Mexico border as well as familial separations that are often final.[19] Transnationalism has increased economic opportunities for many, but at the same time the labor risks for immigrants have become exponentially more dangerous. Nonetheless, rural working-class Mexicanas have long tested and transgressed cultural and social boundaries with respect to courtship. Courting rituals are not fixed and immutable but fluid and constantly changing over time.[20] In other words, transnational sexualities have transformed the way San Ignacians negotiate and experience gender within courting rituals.

Courting rituals are now centered on the time when the immigrants return to their communities of origin each year. Typically they begin to arrive in October and November, stay to celebrate Christmas and the religious festivities in January, and return to the United States in February. These dates accommodate the many male immigrants who work in construction or landscaping and are unemployed in the winter months (unlike their predecessors in the 1950s and 1960s, who worked mostly in industrial jobs). Women usually work in factories yet may still get time off for the Christmas holidays to return to Mexico.

One crisp, cold, and beautiful night during my stay in San Ignacio in 2003, I made my way through the crowd in the plaza, past the *kiosco*, to get to the end of the street where the grandiose San Ignacian amusement park began. Among the multitude of images I encountered while walking in the tight narrow streets of San Ignacio, the Virgin of Guadalupe stood out everywhere. I could see her on different functional articles: on lampshades in different shapes, in images with plastic frames in gold that gave out psychedelic neon colors when plugged in, in candles, and on mouse pads. Interestingly, the image of the Virgin of Guadalupe has been transformed, not just transplanted, from images depicted by hegemonic religious institutions such as the Catholic Church. Nowadays many enjoy her portability and mobility in T-shirts and key chains. The Virgin of Guadalupe has also become a representation of Mexicanas' and Chicanas' struggles for gender equity and social justice.

The Virgin of Guadalupe can be seen and experienced "on the northern side of the border. She is painted on neighborhood walls and on storefronts, emblazoned on sweatshirts and baseball caps; her portrait hangs in living rooms and in every barrio church from East L. A. to El Paso."[21] Most important, however, has been the portrayal of this national/religious icon both as an active agent of historical processes and as an advocate for gender and social justice, as depicted in Yolanda López's painting

Portrait of the Artist as the Virgin of Guadalupe. These changes in gendered symbolic representations reflect, among other things, how Mexicanas and Chicanas have embraced a new mobility and self-assertion of the Virgin of Guadalupe as a symbol of feminine power. This imagery has made available a selection of ideologies about *mujeridades* and "womanhood" that supersede the hegemonic naturalized madonna/whore dichotomy usually represented in nationalistic discourses. Social dress codes represent some of these transformations in ideologies about representation of women's bodies.

Immigrant women's choices in the way they represented themselves via their clothing usually have been linked to their morality or lack thereof. As Espín noted, their identities are still expressed through clothing and sexuality.[22] Women who have migrated to the United States from San Ignacio and some who have remained in the community of origin have chosen to transgress certain parameters usually associated with "decent" (*decente*) women. These daring San Ignacian women were challenging not only religious dress codes of "appropriate morality," however, but also transnational collective social ideologies of what constitutes "appropriate" attire for a feminine and decent woman within a transnational field. Chicanas and Mexicanas have challenged such images by deconstructing and reappropriating these very rigid sociocultural images of acceptable "womanhood" influenced less by geography than by the transnational experience.

The provocative attire worn by some visiting young women plays into the nuances represented in transnational sexualities. Many Mexicanas living in Detroit seized the opportunity, on their return to San Ignacio, and overtly challenged traditional expectations of acceptable behavior, demeanor, and dress for women as well as deep-seated notions of femininity and sexuality. During the 2003 festivities in San Ignacio a few women taking part in the procession of *los hijos ausentes* wore dresses that other San Ignacians found inappropriate because they were seen as "too revealing"—especially since the procession ended at the church, where several priests and the bishop celebrated the yearly awaited mass.

In interviews older women tended to blame this dress code transgression on the social evils of immigration, but younger women contested this notion by asserting that some women from the town had always dressed in such fashion, whether they were immigrants or not. But younger women agreed that attitudes toward dress differ in San Ignacio and Detroit. Fourteen-year-old Elena commented:

I think that people there [in Detroit] are more open. They don't care what you wear, not like here. For example, a tattoo, here people would talk and criticize whereas in Detroit you get one and that's it. Also, in Detroit you can wear shorts and it's seen as normal, but when you wear them here people almost die. You can distinguish between the people because they [Detroiters] are more daring, cooler, it's people with means—yuppies.[23]

Wearing the more revealing shorts immediately is associated with upward social mobility, confirming the collective idea that migration does allow women a certain degree of social mobility and in turn a greater flexibility to develop and explore their transnational sexualities. These young women also associated dressing in a more revealing or comfortable style with class: wearing Detroit styles distinguishes a person as *gente más popis* (someone of a higher social status). While immigrant dress styles may violate certain religious and social protocols, older San Ignacians acknowledge that being an immigrant, especially a successful immigrant, does afford a person some freedom from local cultural constraints.

Women who have transgressed the boundaries of certain sites associated with men, particularly public spaces, have always been associated with inappropriate "womanhood" and lack of morality. Young working-class San Ignacian women have carved out new ways to represent their transnational sexual identities within transnational circuits, including wearing more seductive attire that reflects their transnational mobility in public—showing off the latest Detroit fashion—but also their rural-urban realities experienced in both nations. Working-class women have had to deal with ideologies about sexualities that categorize *una loca* (a crazy woman) "as any woman who crosses the threshold of the home and steps beyond the traditional bounds of proper, womanly behavior."[24] Women's choice of dress while challenging socioreligious courting rituals defines their transnational attitudes toward sexual desires.

Provocative attire also represents upward class mobility, a status attributed to all members of a transnational circuit, thus challenging patriarchal religious stigmas about proper feminine attire and demeanor. These so-called *locas* are now active economic participants in the town's economic and social infrastructure and particularly in providing for religious *ofrendas*. One example of this transnational generosity was the enormous $14,000 statue of the crucifixion adorning the church during the 2003 celebrations.

As part of these yearly celebrations, visiting working-class men make a self-conscious display of affluence, parading in expensive cars and trucks. Elena said with a laugh: "Most of them [immigrants] think, 'I'm going to go there [Detroit] and buy a car and then bring it back here to show it off.'"[25] But Reyna replied, "It is good too, because he saved his money and bought his car."[26] Elena added, "[That shows that] he didn't leave to be a bum, that he made an effort and that's what he could afford."[27] Young women in San Ignacio agreed that they were aware of the young men's working-class status and realities despite the display of automotive and other consumer luxuries. They knew that most of these young men in Detroit owed money for their cars and that they worked hard to attain these capitalist luxuries; this made them ideal working-class mates.

Since most young women in San Ignacio had relatives in the United States and were constantly exposed to the immigrant experience, they knew that they most likely would have to join the labor force to contribute to their households if they migrated. For example, Alma commented: "At first, yes, I will work in the restaurant, but it is not my aspiration to be a waitress. No, I want something more after a while. I know that I have to learn English and everything and later I can get a good job."[28] San Ignacian women's understanding of the realities of migration enabled them to choose among prospective mates and strategize on how to achieve a successful immigrant experience. Nonetheless, this process of selection, while mostly based on the young men's economic prospects, was also influenced by several other factors: the women's relationships with their families, their sense of adventure or desire for security, and their own financial situations.

Eager to demonstrate their successful immigrant experience and perhaps attract a mate, the visitors flaunt their U.S.-acquired goods around town, from clothing and jewelry to expensive trucks and decked-out cars. Powerful sound systems in these vehicles flood the town with *banda*, hip-hop, and reggaeton rhythms, a raucous mating call that has all but replaced the secretly passed notes and sweet whispers of bygone days. Their transnational experience has posed new possibilities and choices and has given rise to new constructions and understandings about sexuality, both for women who live in San Ignacio and for those visiting from Detroit. These public expressions of alternative forms of sexual behavior—in opposition and at the same time sanctioned with socioreligious ideologies—expand young people's choices about how to experience, explore, and practice their transnational sexualities.

SEXUALITY AND MARRIAGE

On a frosty morning in January 2003 Father Ignacio Ramos Puga married Lily (seventeen) and Camilo (twenty-three), an immigrant who had been going back and forth between the United State and Mexico for a decade. The ceremony resembled many Catholic weddings, with its eucharistic rituals, incense burning, and bells ringing from the majestic cathedral on the town plaza. What made this wedding extraordinary was the time of day (7:00 A.M.) and the fact that the whole town knew that the bride, clad in a long, ornate white dress, was seven months pregnant. The church, magnificently ornamented for the January festivities, was empty except for the wedding *padrinos* (godparents) and a few family members and friends. From afar I could hear the echo of every word and breathe the coldness of every movement that Father Ignacio, in his role as moral disciplinarian, executed in the chancel as he joined the couple in sacred matrimony.

Lily looked beautiful; although we had all had to wake up early, the ceremony was lovely and the bride and groom seemed happy. The white dress, however, became a contentious symbol. In religious and cultural codes, white bridal attire represents purity, which in turn symbolizes female virginity; for many townspeople, a pregnant bride in a white dress challenged their moral values and their loyalties to religious mandates:

> Oh my god, they just feel really bad. It makes me sad that discrimination occurs because only our Lord should be able to punish us. I don't want our priest to do it. That's my opinion. [But] one should be pure and wear white when one marries. White signifies purity and virtue. So all I would say is that they shouldn't marry in white, but they should marry at whatever time of day they would prefer. Women should say, "Well, I will choose a dress in a different color, like pink or an off-white ivory tone. If everyone already knows that I have been living with him or whatever, I won't wear white. I am not pure in entering into this sacred institution." But they should marry whenever they want. I think it's not nice to marry them on a Saturday at seven o'clock in the morning.[29]

Lily's pregnancy and wedding, complete with white dress, illustrate how transnational sexualities have challenged and influenced socio-religious norms and values. The priest agreed to marry the couple and granted absolution for their premarital sexual transgression, even though they were advised to delay the wedding in order to attend the premarital talks mandated by the church. Father Ignacio complained:

Since they [San Ignacians in Detroit] have their girlfriends here [San Ignacio] they want to come and get married *en caliente* [very fast], even though they know that the "talks" [premarital counseling] are supposed to take place for a whole year, once or twice a month. They have to attend their retreats with catechists.[30]

Lily and Camilo timed their wedding to coincide with the *fiestas patronales*, which meant the wedding had to be quick because the groom's godparents (Camilo's oldest brother and his Chicana wife) were immigrants from California who had to leave San Ignacio within a particular timeframe and Camilo was preparing to leave for Detroit, where he currently resided.

In her examination of immigration from Degollado, Jalisco, Jennifer S. Hirsch found a similar phenomenon: "Even couples who themselves do not go north often wait until November and December [when they celebrate their *fiestas patronales*] to marry or baptize, counting on the help of returning relatives as *padrinos* and thus cosponsors of the party."[31] Moreover, many San Ignacians living in Detroit wait to marry and baptize their children in San Ignacio rather than in Detroit, thus forcing local religious authorities to adapt and accept the immigrants' transnational timetable for these celebrations.

This wedding planned around a transnational time-frame/reality gave Lily the opportunity not only to wear white while showing off her protruding belly but also to challenge and feminize the very male-dominated space of the church through her transnational experience. In her investigation on the Pachuca culture of resistance, Rosa Linda Fregoso argues that "refusing to stay in the place assigned to them by Chicano society, pachucas are trespassers in public spaces, violating the boundaries of femininity."[32] Like a Pachuca, Lily challenged a contested public/religious site, and the symbolism of the white dress representing virginity and purity was completely offset by Lily's rounded belly. Hanging to the left of the Virgin of Guadalupe's portrait, adding a touch of aesthetic and visual drama to the ceremony, was the "blessing" that Camilo and Lily received from the colossal image of Jesus that the immigrants from Detroit donated that year. Marriage to Camilo, an experienced migrant, opened up Lily's future options when exercising her rights as an immigrant's wife in San Ignacio. This meant, among other things, the possibilities of future migration for herself or even citizenship for her offspring. For now, this union also allowed her access to the social networks available to her new husband.

Nonetheless, an obviously pregnant bride dressed in a beautiful white dress marching down the church's aisle was not the perfect symbol of *mujeridad*. The Mexican rural landscape changed dramatically from 1940 to 1970, when Mexican society became more urban than it had been in the agrarian past;[33] and "45% of the [Mexican] population lived in localities of more than 15,000" by 1970.[34] This meant that Mexico was changing, and national ideologies about *mujeridades* were also changing through the modernization of public services as well as media accessibility.

Despite religious and societal stigmatization, several young women I interviewed became pregnant before they married. This is partly because of cultural changes in Mexican sexual ideologies and partly because of the influence of the mass media in both Mexico and the United States.[35]

When I asked a group of teenaged girls in San Ignacio what they thought about premarital sex, they all agreed: "We want to be virgins when we get married!" But their reasoning did not emphasize religious mores or even parental prohibitions. Rather, they were preoccupied with the respect that a man would or would not accord them based on whether they were virgins or not. Elena expressed her views on the topic: "I wouldn't like it if after I was married if we had any problems my husband would say something like, 'Well, you're not a virgin, so who knows how many men you were with.'"[36] For these young women, virginity was a valuable bargaining tool that left their husbands no way to question their integrity. The oppressive religious commoditization of sexual practices, enshrining unequal heterosexual marital relations, triggered a degree of anxiety in Mexicanas.

Most of their practical concerns with premarital sexual practices, however, were directly linked to their fears of personal disgrace within a patriarchal and sexist system. Gloria González-López, who interviewed women from Jalisco, asserted that "in theory, the Catholic Church formulated moral values that are sexually controlling to heterosexual Mexicanas. But in practice, family and male-defined codes of sexual conduct establish and enforce gender politics linked to a Mexicana's need to preserve her premarital virginity."[37] In other words, the prospect of social marginalization and resentment from their husbands if they were found to have engaged in premarital sex seemed to influence young Mexicanas' sexual ideologies more than the religious definition of premarital sex as a sinful transgression did.

Despite continued efforts by the church to mandate silence on issues related to sexual practices, younger Mexicanas are becoming more open in talking about their experiences:

[I knew about sex] because I had friends and some had already had sex and they would say, "You're missing out, silly." And I think that I really had an idea of what it was but I was embarrassed to talk about it. But I had sex with my husband [before they were married] and it was about five years ago. I was only twenty, so for me it was something new. It was great![38]

Mexicanas and Mexicanos are continuously constructing sexual identities and ideologies about sex influenced by the many variables—cultural, social, religious, political, and economic—that affect their lives. Generational differences emerge, but as we dissect Mexicanas' narratives about sexuality and sexual practices, the differences emerge mainly in how women of any age or generation choose to narrate them.

Vivi, who lives in Detroit, commented:

I think that now that I have my partner it's a stable relationship. It's important that you get to know each other completely, and sex is very important to a couple. I think that understanding each other in that way is very important. I don't think it's vital to be a virgin when you marry, although many men are still very sexist—not just San Ignacian men, but all men in general.[39]

Confrontational underlying discourses are always lurking in these narratives: on the one hand a liberated sense of communication with your sexual partner, but on the other the socioreligious transgression and its consequences.

Younger women talked more freely about sex and about how they perceived their sexuality. Although older women disclosed significant amounts of information about their intimate courting rituals and their notions of sexuality, especially around the issue of motherhood and reproduction, they tended to repeat during the interviews that they did not know much about sex and were not supposed to talk about it. According to the Mexicanas I interviewed, information about sex was very restricted, especially in San Ignacio, since it was such a Catholic community and its residents followed an old tradition of "not talking about sex." Both younger and older women agreed that information about their reproductive systems was hard to come by. As one young woman noted:

Sometimes my sister asks my mother, "Ay, how come you never told us that we were going to suffer so much having children and everything else?" And my mother just says, "Well, who told you to go and do it [have sex]?" But she never told us anything and neither did my father. We had to figure it out by ourselves.[40]

This statement delineated the parameters of silences about reproduction by constructing these silences as natural. In his study on Jaliscans in Guadalajara, Héctor Carrillo noted:

> Besides maintaining silence about sex in the family, parents also used proscriptive messages to exert control and ensure that their children grew up to fit within the social core of "normality." In the process, the children also learned how to participate in the reproduction of "sexual silence"—a widespread method used to keep transgressive sexual behavior under wraps in order to maintain the appearance of normality.[41]

It is clear that Jaliscans had a widespread culture of constructing specific silences around sexuality.

When I asked older women how much they had learned from their mothers about their sexuality, they all agreed that it was close to nothing. And when I asked them if they had talked to their daughters about it, most of them said no. The discourse on sex was therefore "unarticulated" by San Ignacians, yet it was ever-present in the lives of Mexicanas both in San Ignacio and in Detroit when bargaining about gender relations.

These obvious contradictions are inherent in the politics of any identity, whether sexual, personal, or national. Identities are not fixed; they are fluid and mutable, and sexual identity is no exception.

Although younger Mexicanas are more explicit about their sexuality, older and younger women reported similar circumstances that affected their knowledge (or lack thereof) about sex and reproduction. These included their experiences as immigrants and the changing cultural and social mores in Mexico and in the United States. In this complex and shifting set of circumstances, simplistic dichotomies such as categorizing the United States as more "modern" versus Mexico—a developing country—as "traditional" fail to explore the nuances of transnationalism. Most of the young women I interviewed both in San Ignacio and in Detroit acknowledged having had premarital sex.

Moreover, when young women became pregnant out of wedlock in San Ignacio, this sometimes—although not always—led to migration. As Gela commented, laughing:

> I was pregnant with Galan, my oldest son, and Polo [her husband, who was her boyfriend at that time] was going to migrate. So I told him,

fine, leave, but I'm pregnant. So he said, "No, we will go together then." And that's why we decided to come here together, because I was pregnant and I could not stay in my house and he wanted to leave.[42]

For Gela, pregnancy became the vehicle by which she convinced Polo to take her to Detroit. Sexual bargaining among working-class women is not a new phenomenon. Kathy Peiss found that a certain degree of sexual bargaining was accepted and normalized among urban working-class youths: "In their workplaces and leisure activities, many working women discovered a milieu that tolerated, and at times encouraged, physical and verbal familiarity between men and women, and stressed the exchange of sexual favors for social and economic advantages."[43] San Ignacian women like Lily, living in a small town, had to use the available resources to adapt to their transnational realities.

Even though both older and younger Mexicanas consistently denied knowledge of sexual practices in interviews, in actuality they were and are engaging in sexual activities. Many San Ignacian women in my study had engaged in premarital sex; and some, like Lily, had gotten pregnant. In accordance with my findings, sociologist Gloria González-López found that among the forty Mexican immigrant women in her study (many from Jalisco) 70 percent were not virgins prior to marriage.[44] Moreover, many, whether young or old, enjoyed their sexual experiences. This was true of Mexicanas who lived in Mexico and of those who lived in the United States. The immigrant experience thus is a subjective conceptualization of collective experiences that include agency and resistance within contested terrains—in particular ideologies about sex—in Mexico and in the United States. Transnational sexualities serve as places of negotiation between conflicting beliefs systems about how sex is articulated, practiced, and experienced.

CONTRACEPTION, CHILDBEARING, AND FAMILY SIZE

After the Mexican Revolution, the Mexican state launched a campaign of health promotion by making clinics available throughout the countryside to combat diseases that were affecting the rural population. "I was a nurse and was assigned here [San Ignacio] in 1959 . . . it was a campaign against diarrhea."[45] With lower mortality rates and better health resources, the Mexican state promoted population growth: for example, by reducing the age for marriage to fourteen for women and sixteen for men in 1947. The state even "granted prizes to large families."[46] These messages promoting demographic increases were compounded by popular culture, which also promoted reproduction for the benefit of the state; motherhood then was perceived as a national as well as a social obligation. ¡A parir, madres latinas, a parir más guerrilleros! (Give birth, Latin American mothers, give birth to more warriors!) demanded Mexican protest songwriter and musician José Molina in one of his songs.[47] The development of film production in Mexico facilitated the dissemination, normalization, and nationalization of this socioreligious glorification/demonization of "motherhood"/"whorehood" as inherent in understandings of mujeridades. According to Doña Ana: "Here [San Ignacio] women would die giving birth and others would say that they morir en la raya [die in the trenches]" (although raya may also mean line or border, in this context it means a trench).[48] Dying in the trenches the way Doña Ana contextualized it meant dying in battle.

Mexican women's situation differed from that of their Euro-American counterparts, for whom "being a woman after World War II often meant being in reproductive conflict, knowledgeable about contraception, in a position to get it, and determined to use it. On the other hand, for good reason many women still felt the heavy hand of the cultural mandate that pressed them to reproduce."[49] It was not until 1960 that the first clinic for family planning opened in Mexico (in Mexico City).[50]

When Luis Echeverría was campaigning for president of Mexico in 1969 his stand on population growth was clear: Gobernar es poblar (To govern is to populate). In the early 1970s, after attending a conference on population growth and poverty, Echeverría introduced population control for the first time in the history of Mexico as part of the national rhetoric, much to Catholic society's chagrin. His campaign slogan La familia pequeña vive mejor; vámonos haciendo menos (Smaller households live better; let's diminish our population numbers) shocked Mexican society. There were twenty-nine family planning clinics in the cities and sixtynine in the states by 1974.[51] Needless to say, this message of "responsible paternity," as the state called it, and its information on and distribution of contraceptives were an outright blow to religious codes on reproduction and sexual practices. Clearly the state had a new agenda that included the monitoring of population numbers (in particular indigenous populations and the poor) as an inherent component of nation building.

The United States and the Mexican state disseminate ideologies about heteronormative "appropriate" sexual practices, such as encouraging women to have more children (or fewer depending on the socioeconomic circumstances), through multiple nodes of information sharing.

In the first three decades of the twentieth century in the United States modernity—associated with urbanization, industrialization, and capitalist consumer culture—formulated packaged characteristics of the "modern woman" that affected working-class transnational subjects. These urban categorizations of "womanhood" in the United States worked in opposition to and in tandem with rural socioreligious traditional beliefs about appropriate *mujeridades* for women migrating to and from San Ignacio and Detroit. This collectivity of experiences, compounded by the processes of migration, informed the way in which Mexican women construct their subjective notions on transnational sexualities.

Information about the use of contraceptives was and continues to be very contested terrain for working-class Mexicanas, both in San Ignacio and in Detroit. In many towns such as San Ignacio, religious and civic institutions compete with government health clinics for influence over women's reproductive systems. Civil authorities have exerted their power over marriage, which used to be strictly the domain of the church. By requiring a civil ceremony to make marriage official, civil authorities have continued to displace religious power over civil society's main nucleus, the contractual union of the family. But the influence of the Catholic Church is still strongly felt. Doña Ana expressed her confrontations with these two dialectically opposing institutions:

> When he [her husband, Delfino Hernández] started to process his documentation [to become a legal resident] we were not married by the civil authorities. In the past what was important, especially in this town of Cristeros, was the church wedding. So my husband said, "Tomorrow we'll go to the presidency and get married," and I replied, No, not me. Where I come from [a nearby town] a woman who goes to the *presidencia* is eloping with her boyfriend. I'm not going, they're going to say that I married wrong [*mal*]. So we never had a civil union.[52]

Doña Ana was the only wife of one of the Hernández brothers who did not migrate to Detroit.

While Mexico was modernizing, president Manuel Avila Camacho (1940–1946) pushed his national agenda through film: "In picking national unity, industrialization, international respectability, capitalism, and 'modernity,' they [his administration] were launching Mexico into a brave new world that required a modified approach to nationalism."[53] By 1945 Mexico was producing eighty-two films under the state's auspices. In these films representations of women adhered fervently to the madonna/

whore dichotomy, where sexual silences were the norm. Popular ranchero films glorified motherhood while demonizing "modern" women who expressed their sexualities outside the norm.[54]

Working-class women from San Ignacio born in the 1930s, 1940s, and even 1950s generally felt that having children was an important manifestation of womanhood. They took pride in their stories of childbirth, boasting that they had endured labor pains stoically. Despite this pride there was also a sense of obligation. Notwithstanding cultural demands, many of these women feared the consequences of repeated births. Doña Ana started to use contraceptives out of fear for her well-being after having had six children:

> I don't want to die [from multiple births]. So I went to see a male gynecologist in Guadalajara and he said, "You are going to take this and have no more children." And I still had two more! My mother-in-law used to say that she didn't even complain while giving birth. I did! I yelled and kicked while it was coming out.[55]

Women of this generation had to consider several factors before they even thought about ending their childbearing. The church and its strict rules about contraception as well as women's own social and cultural understandings of *mujeridades* weighed heavily in their decision making. Most apparently had internalized the notion that pregnancy and childbearing were a woman's essential duty. The politics of contraception thus were very difficult for women of the second half of the twentieth century in San Ignacio, even though some, at least, understood that having many children could be detrimental to their health.

Minimal access to education and information clearly played a role in how women dealt with their reproductive choices. Older women who had their children in San Ignacio often attributed their multiple pregnancies to the lack of information on reproduction available in the 1950s and 1960s. Doña Toña commented: "In those times we didn't know anything, so we would have one after another. We didn't even know how we were going to educate them or support them. We didn't think about that at all, we just relied on God to help us keep going."[56] Older women often recalled that they never received any information from their mothers about sexuality and that lack of information caused them many tribulations, including repeated births. Many agreed that access to information in Detroit and in Mexico provided options for the younger generation that they themselves did not have.

People had very little access to health education in the 1950s and 1960s in San Ignacio. Doña Ana, a nurse educated in Guadalajara, arrived in the town in 1959 to work at the clinic:

The clinic here in San Ignacio was improvised back then. It was just a large room like a holding cell that we separated to make small examining rooms and a waiting room, and that was all. . . . It was very hard because I had to educate people. There were a lot of flies back then, and conditions were unhygienic. There were no bathrooms; we had to teach people how to build latrines. We would visit houses to tell them how to boil water and how to treat stomach parasites because everyone had parasites. We were engaged in a campaign against diarrhea, giving people medication and conducting tests.[57]

Despite her own education and access to information, Doña Ana did not take contraceptives until after her sixth child and had to go to Guadalajara to get a prescription from a gynecologist (as noted above). Moreover, she had two more children after she had been prescribed the contraceptives.

Doña Toña and Don Jacinto, another working-class couple dealing with these issues in the 1950s, had eighteen children: "When I had ten children I started to hear, 'Look, you can take care of yourself if you use this or the other.' But it didn't work for me. I couldn't take the pill because it gave me headaches, and it also made me very nervous. But there was nothing else."[58] Many women from San Ignacio, both young and older, complained about the physical and emotional side effects of the pill. Mexican women were not alone. The chemical composition of the pill has changed several times since its inception, and its side effects and detrimental symptoms affected many women, though "symptoms such as nausea, breast changes, fluid retention, headaches, depression, abdominal cramp, weight increase and glucose intolerance were initially dismissed on the grounds that they also occurred during the menstrual cycle and pregnancy."[59] Many women in San Ignacio warned younger females about their experiences with the pill through personal anecdotes. Doña Chavelita commented:

If they [younger women] want to take care of themselves, they should not do it in a way that goes against the church or that damages their health. When I was going to a psychiatrist for a nervous condition, I saw many women locked up in there, and they told me that all of them were ill because they had taken contraceptive pills that harmed them and made them crazy. So I tell my daughters that the pill is detrimental to their health and they have followed the natural way, the Billings [rhythm] method, and it has worked for them.[60]

Doña Chavelita's statement illustrates the conflicting and sometimes harmful options that San Ignacian women had to balance between their socioreligious and economic realities, between church mandates and national attitudes toward women's reproductive systems. It also delineates how religious and civic "experts," both priests and doctors, located themselves vis-à-vis these rural working-class women and the management and control of their reproductive systems. For different ideological and religious reasons, both stood against the use of the pill when it became available to San Ignacian women.

The Catholic Church in San Ignacio has been instrumental in regulating and responding to women's sexuality through its discourse on morality and definitions of normativity. As this investigation has pointed out, the priest and the church are the main producers and arbiters of culture and overseers of moral values. Moreover, the plaza, with the church as the centerpiece, has been the nexus for social activities in San Ignacio. Capitalizing on its influence, the church as an organization has attempted to regulate and dictate women's reproductive "obligations" through confession and through the many church activities that target the control of women's sexuality, such as church-sponsored premarital counseling.

There are enormous differences in the ways in which both the state and the church in Mexico and in the United States approached women's reproductive capabilities. While the Mexican church promoted adherence to what it considered "traditional" behavior, Americanization programs in the United States, often run by religious institutions, promoted assimilation into Euro-American culture. These programs often countered the norms dictated by the immigrants' communities of origin. In an interview, Father Ignacio expressed his fears of cultural loss:

> We can say that the mass [prepared every year for the immigrants' parade in the last week of January] emphasizes for the immigrants the importance of adhering to our traditions so they don't lose their Christian moral values, their traditions, their customs. It's up to us—the families that remain here, the priest, and the townspeople—to remind them of that.[61]

According to the priest, the *fiestas patronales* and the immigrants' yearly return served, among other things, to revitalize and reenergize the immigrants' socioreligious "traditional" capital.

Father Ignacio's fears were not unfounded. Americanization programs targeting Latinos began in the United States in the early twentieth century and intensified after World War II in tandem with a nationalist discourse as the United States asserted its global hegemony and Cold War stance. This national effort to assimilate Latinos, especially Mexicans, was intended to acculturate and integrate them into the "social" working-class fabric. In the Midwest these Americanization programs were instituted by several social and religious organizations, including settlement houses and the Catholic Church.[62]

While the Mexican state along with socioreligious discourses glorified motherhood and naturalized large families (until the 1970s), its counterpart in the United States was forcefully discouraging women of color from procreating. Led strongly by advocates of eugenics, who promoted white supremacy, many states began forced sterilizations of women of color, justifying the surgeries as "benefiting" the racial integrity of the United States. Michigan was at the forefront of these campaigns: "soon this state mandated process (forced sterilizations of the feeble minded) became a way for the government to eliminate potential offspring of those it deemed a problem, including people who were poor, sexually deviant and racial minorities."[63] In Michigan forced sterilization became law in 1913, after a campaign led by Victor Vaughan, who is still honored in the Medical School's Hall of Honor.[64]

Both church-sponsored and state-sponsored programs involved racist and pernicious stereotypes about Mexicans. Unlike the church in San Ignacio, which encouraged immigrants to hold onto their "traditional ways," the Catholic Church in Detroit joined the Americanization frenzy and began a series of programs to promote the un-Mexicanization of immigrants.[65] Rickie Solinger found that "in many states, public officials defined poor mothers of color as reproductively expensive and as producers of worthless children. Their race, their poverty, and their gender, and all the vulnerability inherent in those statuses, cast the reproductive capacity of these women as the source of social problems and the site of solutions to a number of postwar social ills."[66] In this manner, the nation turned motherhood into a race/class privilege that working-class women of color were not entitled to.

One of the "traditions" that the Mexican church is most concerned with preserving among Americanized immigrants is that of producing large families through the grace of God (*los que Dios me mande*). The changes in sexual and reproductive behavior in recent years, compounded

TABLE 2.2. NATIONAL FERTILITY RATES IN MEXICO (1976–2000)
AND WOMEN'S KNOWLEDGE OF CONTRACEPTIVES

Year	Fertility Rates	Married Women with Knowledge of Contraceptives (%)	Women of Fertile Age with Knowledge of Contraceptives (%)
1976	5.7	30.2	89.0
1981	4.4	N/A[a]	N/A
1987	3.8	52.7	92.9
1992	3.2	63.1	94.9
1996	2.8	68.4	96.6
2000	2.4	N/A	N/A

Sources: for 1976: Secretaría de Programación y Presupuesto and Instituto de Investigaciones Sociales de la UNAM (SPP-IISUNAM) (Mexico City, SPP-IISUNAM, 1979), *Encuesta mexicana de fecundidad, 1976* (Mexico City: Instituto Nacional de Estadística y Geografía [INEGI], 1979); for 1981: *Encuesta nacional demográfica, 1982* (Mexico City: Consejo Nacional de Población [CONAPO], 1985); for 1987: Secretaría de Salud (SSA) *Encuesta nacional sobre fecundidad y salud, 1987* (Mexico City: SSA, 1989); for 1992: INEGI, *Encuesta nacional de la dinámica demográfica, 1992* (Aguascalientes: INEGI, 1994); for 1997: INEGI, *Encuesta nacional de la dinámica demográfica, 1997* (Aguascalientes: INEGI, 1999); for 2000–2004: CONAPO, *Proyecciones de la población de México, 2000–2030* (Mexico City: CONAPO, 2002).
[a]Information not available.

by decreasing fertility rates in Mexico, have given rise to new worries on the part of the church in San Ignacio about fertility and childbearing.

When I attended mass one Sunday morning during the 2001 religious festivities in San Ignacio, Father Ignacio was literally scolding the immigrants in the pews for not having enough children. He lamented that young couples who married in San Ignacio would leave for Detroit and would only have two children when they came back after some years. In an earlier interview Father Ignacio had raised similar concerns:

[The immigrants] also have been influenced by that [Detroit] custom [of having fewer children]. It's easier, more comfortable. And they morally promote it: "Don't be silly, just have two children," whereas

TABLE 2.3. FERTILITY RATES IN JALISCO AND MEXICO

Year	Fertility Rates: Jalisco	Year	Fertility Rates: Mexico
1960	7.3	1976	5.7
1970	6.8	1981	4.4
1980	4.9	1992	3.2
1990	3.91	1996	2.8
2000	2.47	2000	2.4

Sources: for 1976: SPP-IISUNAM, *Encuesta mexicana de fecundidad, 1976* (Mexico City: SPP-IISUNAM, 1979); for 1987: SSA, *Encuesta nacional sobre fecundidad y salud, 1987* (Mexico City: SSA, 1989); for 1992: INEGI, *Encuesta nacional de la dinámica demográfica, 1992* (Aguascalientes: INEGI, 1994); for 1997: INEGI, *Encuesta nacional de la dinámica demográfica, 1997* (Aguascalientes: INEGI, 1999); for 2000: CONAPO, *Proyecciones de la población de México, 2000–2030* (Mexico City: CONAPO, 2002).
[a]Information not available.

their traditions and customs here in their town have been large families of ten or twelve. And in Detroit the young woman who comes from a large family of twelve will lose those values. I am not saying that she has to have eight, nine, or ten children, but it has to be what we call responsible parenthood. That means that there are two parents and that the couple has to be mindful of God's teachings in light of the times and circumstances that we are living in today. They should organize and plan their family, but adhering to the norms of the Catholic Church. And the immigrants in Detroit are no longer guided by the Catholic Church.[67]

Aside from the heteronormative assumption (a couple is defined as a man and a woman), Father Ignacio believed that immigrants in the United States displayed "irresponsible parenthood" through their use of contraceptives, which allowed sexual relations for pleasure and not purely for reproduction.

Interestingly, women of the older generation, whose reproductive lives had been heavily influenced by the church's strictures, did not necessarily agree that contraceptive use was a bad thing. Among the older women I interviewed who had started families in the 1950s, the average number of births was thirteen. For example, Doña Luna was born in 1929 and married Don Andrés when she was fifteen. He had worked as a bracero since 1945 in Texas and California and moved to Detroit in 1978. Don Andrés returned to Mexico once or twice a year to see his family during those years in the United States, so Doña Luna continued to get pregnant, eventually giving birth seventeen times. When I asked her if she agreed with the priest's attitude toward responsible parenthood, she responded:

> Nowadays there are ways to avoid getting pregnant. In my time those ways weren't used. That's why I had seventeen children. I learned about that [contraception] in Detroit with my friends and my daughters. I also ask my daughters and my daughters-in-law: "Why would you want to have so many children?" Today it's very difficult, especially to support them financially and to educate them. I tell them to take care of themselves.[68]

After she answered my question, Doña Luna laughed. Covering her face with both hands, she added: "Oh my, if the priest [*el señor cura*] could see me he would get angry."[69] Only eight of her seventeen children survived. She began talking to her daughters about using contraceptives when they were very young. Despite her Catholic beliefs, she felt that having as many children as she had would be even more challenging in Detroit, particularly because of the cost of rearing children in the United States. She noted that very little information on reproductive issues had been available to her when she was younger; however, her transnational experience had granted her not only access to more information but also the opportunity to share this experience with her friends and daughters. She also complained that the "Billings method" (the rhythm method of fertility control prescribed by the church through premarital counseling sessions for couples) was potentially dangerous, since she herself had lost nine: "In the past there was only so much we could do, and we didn't say anything. Nobody said, 'Here there's this or that' to avoid pregnancy. And one expected to have as many as God granted. It didn't matter how badly or hard we [women] suffered: we saw ourselves struggling."[70] For this reason she thought it prudent to have a more open conversation with her daughters and with her only son as well.

For years Doña Luna and Don Andrés traveled back and forth between Detroit and San Ignacio. All their surviving children, now adults, live in Detroit. When I asked whether she thought that her ideas about reproduction had changed with her immigrant experience, she said that they had. She underlined the importance of taking care of one's body and one's sexuality as a woman and at the same time emphasized the difficulty of economic survival in Detroit and the expenses that came with raising children. Doña Luna not only noted the easy availability of information on contraceptives in Detroit but also remarked: "Well, I'm going to tell you a thing or two. I support the use of contraceptives even though in my experience I had all my family and most women had large families."[71] These changing ideologies about sexual practices are inherent in transnational sexualities.

Despite the availability of information on contraception in Detroit, many San Ignacians continue to balance their options and express their concerns about contraception. In 2004 I attended a birthday party in Detroit that included a large group of San Ignacians, both young and old. At one point nine women were talking about contraceptives. They all started to complain about different detrimental symptoms from contraceptive methods and their availability at the local clinic. Gela commented:

> [I started to use] the Depro injection every three months, but since I have a nervous condition it was bad for me. My neck was tense, and it made me very nervous. So the doctor here [in Detroit] told me that I could not use any contraceptives because I had a problem with my nerves and everything would affect me, with bad headaches.[72]

Many San Ignacian women I interviewed (both in San Ignacio and in Detroit) who were of reproductive age have continued to allow their partners to take the lead in spacing births by performing coitus interruptus (the withdrawal method), which they referred to by saying *mi viejo me cuida* (my old man takes care of me). They still rely on this method despite its ineffectiveness and despite the health risks involved with unprotected sex in the age of AIDS. Nena got pregnant in San Ignacio then immigrated to Detroit and married her partner. She commented: "I didn't want to have another child, but now I'm two months pregnant. My husband was taking care of me, according to him, but apparently not. I used pills before but they were bad for me and I didn't feel well. I used them for a year, but I stopped last October, and now after seven months I'm pregnant."[73] Even though younger women in Detroit have more access to information about contraception than they claim they had in San Ignacio, some unwanted pregnancies continue. Most apparently result from reliance on the withdrawal method, suggesting that the ideological baggage about contraceptives weighs heavily even in Detroit.

CHANGING IDEOLOGIES IN SAN IGNACIO AND DETROIT

What made a Mexican woman living in Mexico or "freshly" arrived from Mexico a much more desirable partner for a young Mexican man residing in Chicago in 1932? And what makes a Mexican resident or native of the United States a better candidate for marriage according to some young Mexican women in the twenty-first century? Transnational sexualities include new patterns of courtship and ideologies about premarital sex that reflect ideological changes in both Mexico and the United States. Most importantly, these ideologies reflect the circumstances surrounding the immigrant experience in both geographical sites. These transnational circumstances informed Mexicanas' and Mexicanos' concepts of masculinity and femininity. My research shows that women in San Ignacio have responded to immigration trends by creating and reshaping courting rituals to enable themselves to choose suitable mates and enhance their bargaining power before and during marriage.

Transnational sexualities cannot be broken down according to useless dichotomies grounded in Western ideologies about how the "Other" may construct sexualities. Developed in the course of people's everyday lives in San Ignacio and Detroit, transnational sexualities cannot be separated into two distinct and opposing sets of experiences in these two places. Mexicanas' ideologies about sex and reproduction are shaped by their experiences both in their communities of origin and in the United States. These ideologies permeate the consciousness of Mexican women, I argue, whether they decide to migrate to the United States or stay in San Ignacio. It is precisely the connection between these two sets of gendered experiences that defines transnational sexualities.

The two communities have become so closely knit that San Ignacians experience the cultural changes associated with immigration even if they themselves do not make the journey north. At the same time, San Ignacians in Detroit experience immigration not only through their own physical relocation but also through the experiences of their family members, fictive kin (*comadres* and *compadres* [godparents]), and friends still living in San Ignacio. Transnational sexualities have become a common denominator as San Ignacian immigrants and townspeople constantly redefine their understandings of gender-appropriate behavior in the light of economic, cultural, and social changes in the United States and Mexico and in response to their everyday experiences in both places.

In the process, Mexicanas and Mexicanos have increasingly challenged the gender-specific notions of femininity and masculinity that are rep-

licated and disseminated through heteronormative patriarchal institutions—religious and civil—in both the United States and Mexico. In part
as a result of migration, they continuously resist and reinscribe the rigid
societal and religious mandates informed by patriarchal systems of oppression. In particular, women from different generations are constructing new notions of "womanhood" in the United States versus *mujeridades*
in Mexico as they examine and question old precepts about abstinence,
the church-sanctioned rhythm method of fertility control and the use of
contraceptives, and family size, weighing their own experiences and aspirations against their religious beliefs and the entrenched social stigma
attached to female sexuality. In the process they construct what I have
called transnational sexualities.[74]

Over the next decades, working-class Mexican women not only altered
their sexualities but also confronted new labor demands and challenges
in creating a community that stemmed from their migrations to *el norte*.
Social networks nurtured by immigrant women were key to the continuing flow of San Ignacians to Detroit and other parts of the United States.
These elaborate systems of reciprocity and obligation offer a glimpse of
the ways in which gender divisions are essential in understanding the process of immigration and the creation of a dynamic transnational community in Detroit.

No, I will not go back [to Mexico] by crossing through the desert.
No, because I was so afraid when we crossed even though we made
it all right. I will not do it again; it's better if I stay put here.[1]

—VIVI (TWENTY-EIGHT), INTERVIEW IN DETROIT,
JUNE 2004

Demographic changes altered the ethnic landscape of Detroit throughout
the twentieth century. But Mexican immigrants arriving in the 1920s and
1930s suffered severe dislocations that affected transnational community
formation in different ways. The Great Depression in the early 1930s hit
the Mexican community living in Detroit like a tsunami, diminishing its
vitality until the early 1970s. National nativist sentiment against Mexican immigrants and Chicanos triggered the implementation of inhumane
campaigns for massive repatriation of Mexican co-nationals.[2] Mexican
communities all over the United States were suffering the ripple effects of
an economic downturn that would claim many victims—primarily Mexi-
canas/os and Chicanas/os. In Detroit the campaigns were carried out by
welfare officials, who set up "the first tent colony in the city . . ., located
in Clark Park in the heart of the Mexican district."[3] It was clear that city
officials were targeting Mexican immigrants. The economic crisis sev-
ered the Mexican community, however, leading to massive deportations
of Mexicans and Chicanos (many of whom were children born in the
United States whose parents were immigrants).

In 1932 some visible celebrities such as Mexican artists Diego Rivera
and Frida Kahlo got involved in the repatriation project. Rivera was com-
mandeered to paint a mural about the struggle of the proletariat at the
Detroit Institute of Arts; and Kahlo was expressing her inner feelings
about capitalist inequalities in the United States and in Mexico when she
produced the painting *My Dress Hangs There* during her stay in Detroit.
While Rivera and Kahlo supported voluntary repatriations and worked
alongside the Mexican consulate in Detroit at the very beginning, it did

not take them long to realize that most repatriations were coercive and not voluntary and that the Mexican government was not prepared to aid repatriates—both artists retracted their support. While these two radical Mexican artists were in Detroit to support workers, a large portion of the working class was pushed to leave the city for former homes, and in many cases new homes in Mexico.

While many Mexicans were coercively sent to Mexico, the Department of Public Welfare absorbed a cost of $21 per Mexican being sent back home. As many as 1,246 Mexicans were repatriated from Detroit. "By the middle of December 1932, only 3,000 Mexicans remained in Detroit. By 1936, the population dwindled to 1,200, a nearly 90 percent reduction of the population residing in the city in 1928."[4] Other cities were certainly affected, like Los Angeles, which lost "one third of its Mexican residents."[5] Due to restrictive politics of movement—forced repatriations—and a plummeting economy, Mexican migration from Mexico slowed down while Chicana/o migration from Texas accelerated.

During World War II women and minorities were called upon to join the labor force. Many Tejanas/os also responded to the call for workers and took agricultural and factory jobs in Detroit. Sugar beet agricultural industrialists and foundries started "recruiting workers directly from Texas during World War II."[6] Migratory flows from Texas into the Midwest continued to settle in Detroit. Chicanas/os and Mexican immigrants had to struggle against several obstacles while creating "a home" in Detroit; among the most detrimental were postwar urban developments that disregarded the integrity of Mexican and other neighborhoods that housed mostly minorities.

In his study of Mexican immigrants in the Midwest, Dionicio Nodín Valdés notes that "new construction [in Detroit] destroyed hundreds of homes, caused a sharp increase in noise and air pollution, displaced thousands of residents, and shifted the heart of the barrio toward the Southwest, from Bagley and Porter to the Clark Street District."[7] Ironically, in the 1960s a Cuban immigrant woman would welcome newcomer San Ignacian Don Chuy while he was sitting on a bench at Clark Park in the Clark Street District. By then a community of Latinas/os and recent immigrant arrivals had settled in southwest Detroit.

Following Chicanas/os and other Latinas/os, in the 1960s Mexican immigrants began to establish themselves in Detroit, initially attracted through the gendered Bracero Program and later enticed by the dwindling auto economy to move on to construction and service jobs. Although the Mexican immigrant community was relatively small and spread out after

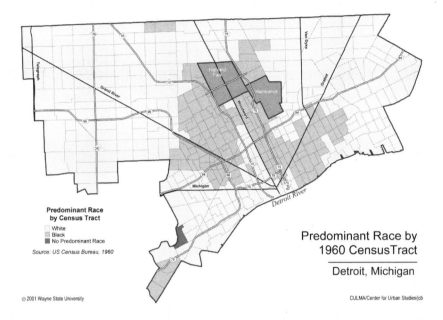

MAP 3.1.   *Predominant race by 1960 census tract, Detroit, Michigan. From Wayne State University, College of Urban, Labor and Metropolitan Affairs/Center for Urban Studies, 2001. Source: U.S. Census Bureau, 1960.*

the Depression, World War II initiated an aggressive campaign to re-cruit Mexican labor through the Bracero Program (1942–1964). In the late 1960s the Mexican immigrant community slowly began to gain momentum, aided by the implementation of the Bracero Program, increasing migration of Mexican workers in Texas to the Midwest, and most importantly existing Latina/o social networks. It is estimated that approximately 5 million working-class Mexicans entered the United States under the auspices of the Bracero Program. Many of them processed their documentation in order to remain—temporarily or permanently—in the United States.

By the 1970s a small number of male immigrants from San Ignacio had settled in Detroit, mostly former braceros who had followed Jesús Mercado and his brother Luis, the pioneers who arrived in the early 1960s. Moreover, Valdés points to the slow increase of the Mexican population residing in Detroit from 1900 to 1980 and emphasizes the radical increase of the Mexican population in the 1980s:

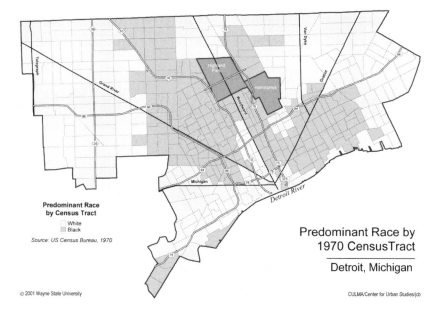

MAP 3.2. *Predominant race by 1970 census tract, Detroit, Michigan. From Wayne State University, College of Urban, Labor and Metropolitan Affairs/Center for Urban Studies, 2001. Source: U.S. Census Bureau, 1970.*

During the generalized recession of the 1970s, detractors characterized the region as "The Rust Belt," and with the exception of Illinois, even the rate of Mexican population growth was slow. As economic restructuring accelerated during the 1980s, the number of Mexicans grew by more than 40%, representing more than half the total increase in the region. During the boom of the 1990s, the regional Mexican population grew at record levels, and by the end of the decade it approached two million inhabitants.[8]

The employment of Mexican immigrants gradually changed from industrial jobs to service and public work such as construction and landscaping.

The community would change radically once women began to arrive and settle in southwest Detroit in what today is known as Mexican Town. Capitalizing on Latina/o networks in Detroit, San Ignacian men began to delineate the contours of their transnational community. Having set

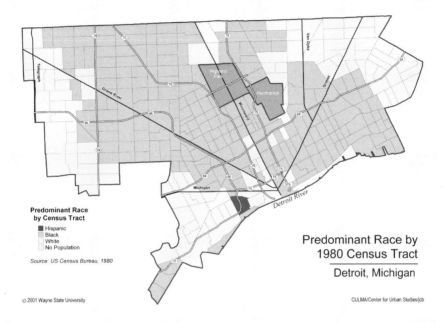

Predominant Race
by Census Tract

■ Hispanic
▨ Black
□ White
□ No Population

Source: US Census Bureau, 1980

Predominant Race by
1980 Census Tract

Detroit, Michigan

© 2001 Wayne State University

CULMA/Center for Urban Studies/jcb

MAP 3.3.   *Predominant race by 1980 census tract, Detroit, Michigan. From Wayne State University, College of Urban, Labor and Metropolitan Affairs/Center for Urban Studies, 2001. Source: U.S. Census Bureau, 1980.*

down the blueprint for the migratory networks, men gradually stepped back as women became the primary nurturers of the social networks that helped bring a steady flow of migrants from San Ignacio to Detroit.

More than a quarter-century later the city's population of Mexican immigrants had grown exponentially, and many of them were from San Ignacio. By 2000 an estimated 15,000 San Ignacians lived in the Detroit metropolitan area, mainly in southwest Detroit.[9] As the transnational community swelled with new arrivals, women's social networks, sustained by their productive and reproductive labor, remained the bedrock of the community.

This chapter deconstructs San Ignacians' social networks and analyzes more deeply how women weave the social fabric that sustains the migratory flow to and from San Ignacio and Detroit through their participation in the migratory fields. Moreover, I contend that it is San Ignacian women who have played the most important role in this transnational movement. This means that gender roles and relations, in particular the gendered

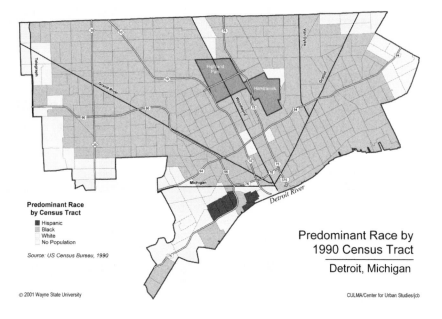

MAP 3.4. *Predominant race by 1990 census tract, Detroit, Michigan. From Wayne State University, College of Urban, Labor and Metropolitan Affairs/Center for Urban Studies, 2001. Source: U.S. Census Bureau, 1990.*

division of labor within transnational circuits, have been central to the development of these networks. This chapter also assumes that the intersection of class, gender, and nationality is embedded in the construction and maintenance of transnational social networks, which in and of themselves are gender specific.

Scholars have often debated whether the experience of migration for Mexican women changes traditional sexist gender roles and especially whether immigrant women's entry into the paid labor force gives them more decision-making power within the family. I suggest that this mode of inquiry is ineffective when studying transnational communities because gender relations are constantly changing and readapting to the particular social, economic, and cultural circumstances of people's lives.

Many San Ignacian women have figuratively crossed national borders, even before leaving Mexico themselves, by experiencing the migration of family members (usually their husbands in the 1940s and 1950s and their husbands, daughters, and sons in the 1960s). Such women often have

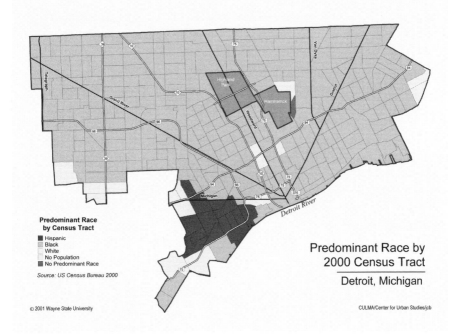

MAP 3.5. *Predominant race by 2000 census tract, Detroit, Michigan. From Wayne State University, College of Urban, Labor and Metropolitan Affairs/Center for Urban Studies, 2001. Source: U.S. Census Bureau, 2000.*

adopted traditional male roles in the sending community, even becoming heads of households, providing a sense of autonomy and freedom even in the midst of their economic uncertainty.

As scholars of gender and women's studies, we often find ourselves searching for women's outright resistance to patriarchy, and in the process we sometimes miss the nuances of the ways in which women negotiate and contest histories and adapt to oppressive and patriarchal systems. This study deconstructs and unpacks social networks to include not only the connection and construction of a transnational community but also the vicissitudes, contradictions, and dislocations surrounding this very complex transnational phenomenon.

To understand how San Ignacian women made meaning of their lives, I began by listening to women's narratives of their experiences over the past four decades; these narratives then became the foundation for an analysis of gendered processes that both affect and are affected by immigration. My point of departure is not how much more "liberated" Mexicanas have become through immigration, but how women both in San Ignacio and in Detroit met challenges and at times contested spaces despite omnipresent patriarchal systems. Their narratives are essential to understanding how these transnational subjects slowly work their way into the weaving of these very complex sets of transnational social relations.

These social interactions have forced San Ignacians to reformulate their relationships with their blood relatives and to accommodate newly formed ties to other San Ignacians in Detroit. The immigrant experience has had an impact on kinship systems in San Ignacio and in Detroit, creating new relationships that have sometimes challenged long-standing ethics, morals, and familial obligations. The conflicts, tensions, and dislocations associated with the immigration experience in turn shape and reshape the contours of the social networks that link San Ignacio and Detroit.

BUILDING A TRANSNATIONAL COMMUNITY

Doña Tita is recognized by her co-nationals as the first woman from San Ignacio to settle permanently in Detroit. Unlike some San Ignacian men who were reluctant to have their families migrate, Doña Tita's husband, Delfino Hernández, applied for residency for her and for all of their children shortly after he came to Detroit in 1969. Although Mexican immigrants had migrated to Detroit for decades, it still represented a harsh northern frontier. Doña Tita remembered her first impressions of Detroit when she arrived in 1970: "I didn't like it too much, nor did I like the small house. But I was happy because I had all my family and my husband there."[10] For Doña Tita, familial unification took precedence over her geographical dislocation.

Once in Detroit, San Ignacians replicated their socioreligious adherence to community building by turning to the Catholic churches located near their neighborhood.

> When I arrived I started to go to Santa Ana church because they [her husband and his brothers] were already going there. The church is more welcoming [than Holy Redeemer]. It's a place where people meet: there's a coffee shop with someone making coffee and pastry, some donating money for the church, and people sit around in little groups and talk with their family or friends. There were people from everywhere, not from San Ignacio at first, but from Santiaguito [a town close to San Ignacio]. There were Puerto Ricans and Cubans. I made a

lot of friends, partly because I had several older sons, and they're not bad-looking at all—I'm boasting [she laughs]. So I made a lot of friends because some people wanted my sons for their daughters, so they became my friends.[11]

Doña Tita's fond recollections of the church reveal its significance for the construction of this transnational community.

On one of my visits to Mexican Town in the summer of 2004, my friend Gaby gave me a tour of the neighborhood. We started at one of the two Catholic churches that many San Ignacians attend in Detroit, Most Holy Redeemer, and from there we moved on to St. Anne, known as Santa Ana. Beyond their beauty, these churches are important as the primary spaces where San Ignacians gather informally to socialize. Families and friends get together after mass to catch up on local news and family gossip. During our visit I recognized almost everyone, including many people I had seen just a year before at the *fiestas patronales* in San Ignacio.

Doña Chavelita (who was interviewed while she was visiting San Ignacio) praised the warmth of the growing San Ignacian community in Detroit: "I like being there [in Detroit] because there are so many people from here [San Ignacio]. We enjoy seeing each other when we meet in the stores, at church, everywhere, and we help each other a lot."[12]

Doña Tita's and Doña Chavelita's recollections vividly illustrate how their transnational community has grown over the years and how San Ignacians began to "San Ignacize" Detroit by transplanting familiar regional and local cultural rituals such as socializing at church. Their comments also underscore the importance of women's social networks for the survival and growth of this transnational community. While navigating racialized institutions and enduring often-hostile attitudes in Detroit, Mexican immigrants have turned inward to the strength of their own community and have transformed Detroit into a second home.

The stories of individual Mexicanas make it clear that the development of these networks through women's labor is a complex and contradictory story. On the one hand, women emphasize their satisfaction in sharing their lives with their families and friends arriving from San Ignacio, to whom they feel a strong sense of obligation. On the other hand, the gendered division of labor means that the burden of helping new arrivals falls heavily on women, who feel the strain of accommodating them and helping them adjust to a new home. In particular, the crowding of relatives and acquaintances into small dwellings can lead to tensions and conflicts. While women recall fun celebrations such as birthday parties, they also

A transnational family posed in San Ignacio with some of their relatives from Detroit. Of the nineteen offspring, only four resided in San Ignacio; the rest had settled permanently in the United States. These transnational grandparents had grand-children born in both San Ignacio and Detroit, some of whom spoke only English. In sharp contrast to their parents' minimal educational experience, many were enrolled in college.

note that accommodating so many people in their households compro-mised space and privacy. Mexican immigrant women built communities of resiliency, drawing strength from their *comadres*, their families, and their faith.

Women were more likely to engage directly with U.S. social struc-tures, often crossing gendered and racial borders across language and cultural barriers. In her analysis of Mexican women in the United States, Adelaida R. Del Castillo comments that "in the United States, Mexican immigrant women make possible access to institutions and agencies that serve the family such as schools, clinics and religious groups."[13] While Mexican men worked long hours at their jobs, many women managed to take new arrivals around to schools and health clinics to obtain needed services while juggling domestic chores and wage labor.

The generational divide regarding work and "obligations" illustrates a whole new set of contradictions plaguing Mexican immigrant women.

TABLE 3.1. OCCUPATION OF EMPLOYED SPANISH-ORIGIN PERSONS
IN DETROIT

Year	Total Employed	Spanish-Origin Women	Mexican Women
1970[a]	8,703	2,871	
1980	8,302	3,379	
1990[b]	6,957		2,777
2000	13,565		4,286

Source: U.S. Department of Commerce, Bureau of the Census, *United States Census of Population, 1970–2000* (Washington, D.C.: U.S. Government Printing Office, 2000).
[a]For the 1970 and 1980 census information, Mexicans were not classified separately; the census lists them as part of "General Characteristics of Persons of Spanish Language for Areas and Places."
[b]In 1990 the census began to classify Mexicans separately.

In interviews, older women (many of whom had joined the labor market while in Detroit as factory workers, nursery workers, waitresses, and cashiers at one time or another) tended to take pride in their wage-earning roles. Younger women, while not wanting to be seen as complaining, were more open in talking about the conflicts associated with these responsibilities regarding wage work and about how they had to negotiate them.

The politics of movement (the crossing of the Mexico-U.S. militarized border) must be seen as gender-specific. Mexicanas in Detroit both performed gendered labor to support migration flows and, in some cases, contested the patriarchal ideologies embedded in this division of labor. These processes have restructured the meanings of kinship and friendship in both San Ignacio and Detroit. But the politics of movement meant that men had to make difficult journeys and decisions before deciding to settle (semi)permanently in Detroit.

DECISIONS AND DILEMMAS FOR MIGRANT MEN

Once the bracero generation of male migrants was established in Detroit, they were faced with the question of whether to bring their families to live with them. This decision-making process was influenced by several

TABLE 3.2. LABOR FORCE CHARACTERISTICS FOR SELECTED
HISPANIC-ORIGIN GROUPS IN DETROIT, 1970–2000

	1970[a]	1980	1990[b] Mexican	2000 Mexican
Professionals, Managers, and Administrators	486	993	741	1,112
Sales Worker and Clerical Worker	1,175	1,054	1,220	1,506
Construction Extraction and Maintenance	515	537	2,894	3,587
Farming, Fishing and Forestry	14	13	78	195
Service Worker	556	626	942	2,661

Source: U.S. Department of Commerce, Bureau of the Census, *United State Census of Population, 1970–2000* (Washington, D.C.: U.S. Government Office, 2000).
[a]For the 1970 and 1980 census information, Mexicans were not classified separately; the census lists them as part of "General Characteristics of Persons of Spanish Language for Areas and Places."
[b]In 1990 the census began to classify Mexicans separately.

factors, beginning with men's uncertainty as to whether they would stay permanently in Detroit or go back to San Ignacio once they had saved enough money. Moreover, some Mexicanos worried that their family's journey north would erode their patriarchal power and challenge their identities as men and heads of household.

A year after the Hernández brothers arrived in Detroit in 1969, Delfino brought his wife, Doña Tita, and his children. Like most men who migrated to the United States during the Bracero Program, the Hernández brothers processed their residency status and became eligible to petition for their families. Although he had the same opportunity to petition for his own family, Rubén Hernández decided not to. Unlike his brothers, Rubén believed that bringing his family to Detroit would diminish familial "traditional" values and erode his authority over the family, in particular his children. He saw the inability to control his family as a loss of patriarchal power and a form of emasculation. His decision was allegedly influenced in part by his brother Delfino's difficult experience after his family arrived in the United States. Rubén's wife, Doña Ana, remembered:

Yes, Delfino brought his whole family there to live, but we learned from that experience, because his sons rebelled against him. Delfino arranged the papers for his oldest sons and then for his wife and the rest of the children. It was a family of thirteen. But when Delfino's sons began to rebel against him, Rubén said, "No, that's not for me, that's why I won't bring my children."[14]

Rubén, like some other Mexicanos, demonized the United States for familial rebellion and patriarchal erosion. This fear influenced his decision not to bring his family to Detroit. Rubén's household structure placed him at the top of the hierarchy, and the thought of losing his authority deterred the possibility of reunifying the family sometime in Detroit, at the same time granting his mobility and curtailing his family's. The United States, while seen as an economic haven, was also perceived as a more liberal society that would allow women and children to gain more power within the family structure and ultimately to challenge male parental authority. Vicky Ruiz has notably underlined the processes by which gendered structures of control and management of young females within Mexican families in the United States are tied to ideologies of family honor and morality and how migration seriously challenged cultural constructions of sexual identities. She breaks down the transitioning of rural working-class sexuality and urban working-class sexuality after migrating to big cities.[15]

Some of these transitions had serious repercussions for females who had recently migrated from San Ignacio and were exploring their working-class transnational sexualities while courting in Detroit. Parental authority was exercised over female control of sexuality, and women's control of sexuality translated into more control over the family and its honor.

Like Rubén, Don Chuy feared that his patriarchal hegemony over the family would be eroded if he brought his family to Detroit. Don Chuy, however, explained his decision not to bring his family to Detroit by referring to the serious repercussions caused by some women's transgressions of what he considered "gender-appropriate" behavior. He recalled the experience of his Detroit neighbor Santiago, who had two daughters. In the early 1970s, when the daughters were approximately sixteen and eighteen years old, they went out with their boyfriends one night and allegedly came home very late. According to Don Chuy, they had been drinking so much that they could hardly stand up. He remembered that Santiago was extremely angry and gave the young women *una mula* (a beating) so severe that his wife called the police. Santiago was jailed, and Don Chuy posted bail for him. Santiago burned some of his family's documents in the park and shortly afterward took his family back to Mexico and never returned to Detroit.[16] Transnational sexualities and the more libertine sexual environment in the United States challenged rural working-class courting rituals as well as patriarchal social/regional spaces.

What Santiago and Don Chuy found so offensive, Vicky Ruiz found to be endemic to Mexicans' experiences in the United States: "In contrast, parents in the barrios of major cities fought a losing battle against urban anonymity and commercialized leisure."[17] In turn the anonymity of the city of Detroit provided a new alternative space within a transnational field whereby Mexicans explored their sexualities, albeit sometimes with violent consequences.

Like Rubén and Don Chuy, many Mexicanos perceived risks in bringing their families to the United States. At stake, they believed, was their families' honor, their manhood, and their power as authority figures. Although the rebellions of young sons challenged fathers' authority within the family structure, the transgressions of daughters were regarded as even more serious; gendered expectations of sons and daughters and expressions of female transnational sexualities were considered a direct threat to masculinity, patriarchy, fatherhood, and most importantly family integrity and honor. By the 1970s the United States (with its women's movement) and Detroit (with its urban dangers) were perceived as places where female family members might well become unmanageable—an expectation borne out by some families' experiences with transnational dislocations.

Men's concerns were not only about moving from one country to another but also about the movement from the countryside to the city—rural life versus urban life. Many of these concerns were shaped by collective ideas of how life in a small town, with its country values (respect for family, religion, and authority), might contrast with life in a big city.[18] These ideas were not nostalgic or romanticized but were based on Mexicans' actual experiences in San Ignacio and in Detroit. San Ignacians knew that in their small town the church, family members, and townspeople in general functioned as informal social supervisors and disciplinarians. In Detroit most San Ignacians live in proximity to each other, and community gossip circulates much as it does in San Ignacio. Yet this reality was overshadowed by the fear of anonymity and lack of social control in a big city. Perceived dissimilarities between life in Detroit and life in San Ignacio were not always considered threatening, but they permeated the beliefs and feelings of San Ignacians in Detroit and in San Ignacio and influenced men's decisions about whether to bring their families.

THE GROWTH OF MEXICAN TOWN

Over time, some San Ignacian women were reunited with their husbands and families; meanwhile, more women also began to migrate on their own. It was the women who made possible the further growth of Mexican Town by housing thousands of newcomers from San Ignacio as they arrived. Shortly after Doña Tita moved to Detroit in 1970, she and her husband welcomed some of their thirteen grown children and their families. From there Doña Tita and other immigrant women branched out to support the arrival of more distant kin and townspeople. She recalled cooking for large numbers of San Ignacians, many of whom were not related to her but were friends of either her husband or her sons and daughters.

> I cooked soup and salad and roasted meat for them, and by the time they came home from work everything was ready because I had made it in advance. I used to get up very early and pack lunches for everyone. Can you imagine, I had up to seventeen people in my house! My sons would bring their friends from San Ignacio, and they all slept crowded together in the basement until I had to say, "I can't have so many people in the house anymore." But my husband and my sons didn't say anything to them.[19]

Despite the hard work of housing and feeding so many, Doña Tita recalled the camaraderie and sense of obligation associated with helping her co-nationals:

> We had fun because we would have parties and sing. We celebrated everyone's birthdays in my house because it was big and I was not very strict [about cleanliness]. Also, I would think to myself, if I do not welcome my own people and make them comfortable then they will not feel at home here.[20]

Doña Tita recognized that her reproductive labor was indispensable for the survival of her community in Detroit, and it reflected the maternal obligation she felt toward her family and their guests. This sense of obligation toward *mi gente* (my people) was the foundation for the social networks that allowed the movement of thousands of San Ignacians to Detroit over three decades. Her resiliency and demand that she would not have so many people in the house motivated her husband to buy another home where she would have much more space to accommodate others. This female need to execute reproductive labor in better conditions also expanded the barrio as more and more San Ignacians purchased new homes in Mexican Town. New moral and emotional bonds formed among San Ignacians in Detroit as the immigrants stretched the meaning of familial obligation to include people from their hometown in addition to blood relatives. Doña Tita positioned herself as a kind of surrogate mother to all the *muchachos* (young men), thus redefining the parameters of kinship systems in response to the unique imperatives of the immigrant experience. In practice, this meant having people arrive on her doorstep without much notice, allowing numerous guests to stay for an undetermined number of months, carrying the financial burden of supporting all the parties involved, and, most importantly, doing the intensive domestic labor necessary to maintain a household of seventeen. Many San Ignacian women in Detroit shouldered similar burdens of reproductive labor while also joining the labor market and working in paid jobs outside the house.

Thanks to this female support, the flow of San Ignacians to Detroit grew rapidly from the 1970s through the 1990s. Because of de facto housing segregation in Detroit and Latino families' desire to live close to each other, San Ignacians along with other Latinos began to rebuild what is now called Mexican Town. It had been severely affected first by the Great Depression and then by the 1970s deindustrialization of Detroit. A reporter for the *Detroit News* wrote in 2005: "Some 60,000 people live in the area commonly called Mexican Town, roughly bordered by the old Tiger Stadium, East Dearborn and the Detroit River. More than 4,000 people have moved there since 1990."[21] The area was surrounded by small businesses that catered to the growth of the Latino population.

By the 1970s deindustrialization was already underway in Detroit. The dismantling of the auto industry and the closures of steel factories and meat-packing plants led to thousands of job losses, devastating the city.[22] Much of the literature on deindustrialization, however, overlooks the brighter picture in certain areas of the city such as southwest Detroit, where "marginal" groups such as Mexican immigrants were creating a new, albeit informal and less grandiose, economy.[23] San Ignacians in Mexican Town bolstered their community of origin by sending dollars home to Mexico, but they also did their part to sustain the flagging economy of Detroit.

TABLE 3.3. LABOR FORCE CHARACTERISTICS FOR SAN IGNACIANS IN
THE UNITED STATES, JULY 2000

Job	Percentage	Job	Percentage
Service Worker	40.18	Sales Worker	4.46
Construction	18.75	Professional	1.34
Manufacture	12.05	Other	4.91
Housewife	11.16	Unemployed	2.23
Agricultural Activities	4.91		

Source: Departamento de Estudios Regionales, Instituto de Estudios Económicos y Regionales (INESER), Programa de Estudios para la Decentralización, Universidad de Guadalajara, "Encuesta sobre migración: impacto de las remesas y potencialidades de desarrollo local en San Ignacio Cerro Gordo, julio de 2000," *De Vinci* (Universidad de Guadalajara) 3, no. 6 (April 2001): 40–55.

San Ignacio depends on Detroit, but at least one part of Detroit depends on San Ignacio. Many of the estimated 15,000 San Ignacio immigrants in Metro Detroit live in southwest Detroit, the state's oldest and largest Latino neighborhood, and have helped make it one of the few city neighborhoods gaining population and businesses. . . . San Ignacio natives joined dozens of Mexican immigrants who opened restaurants, grocery stores, record shops and other businesses in the past decade.[24]

After the first wave of bracero families in the 1960s and early 1970s, the influx of Mexican immigrants into Detroit was largely undocumented. This new migrant stream made its way to Detroit with the help of a well-organized, clandestine, and exploitative network of professional smugglers known as coyotes. Although coyotes have been well established since the beginning of the twentieth century, their roles have changed over the years.[25] In the past three decades smuggling undocumented people and forging *papeles chuecos* (fake Social Security cards and "green cards" attesting to legal residence) have been their main focus. They have established a sophisticated network that extends to most of the United States. Most men and women who migrated after the 1970s and had no family relationships with the bracero generation had to depend on their co-nationals' social networks and on these coyotes for their journey to *el norte*.

Growing nativist rhetoric in the United States and tightening restrictions on immigration laws meant that entering the country would only become more difficult. A significant change came in 1976, when Congress passed Public Law 94-571, which not only limited the number of visas available for the entire Western Hemisphere to 20,000 but also raised the age limit from eighteen to twenty-one for U.S. citizens to petition on behalf of their parents. This unfair distribution of visas heavily affected and hindered legal Mexican immigration and indirectly sparked undocumented migration.[26] Many San Ignacians migrated with the idea of settling permanently in Detroit to avoid the hardships of crossing the border undocumented. This meant ever-larger numbers of San Ignacians arriving in Detroit and needing help from their co-nationals. The social invisibility of Mexican immigrants within a society grown increasingly hostile to immigration added to the sense of obligation to help "one's own people," even as it intensified the strains and burdens involved in doing so.

WOMEN'S REPRODUCTIVE AND PRODUCTIVE LABOR

Women who had relatives and friends staying in their homes bore the brunt of these tensions. These situations led to gendered family dislocations that were difficult and unstable for many San Ignacians. Young women I interviewed were not having as many children as their elders, and this was not necessarily due to what Father Ignacio called "betrayal of traditional religion" (using contraceptives to enjoy sex for pleasure rather than for reproduction).[27] Greater acceptance of contraceptives, economic constraints, and the acculturation to contemporary U.S. and Mexican ideologies about family size all contributed to the downsizing of large families (see Tables 2.2 and 2.3). But I contend that another reason for a lackluster birth rate was that most women in Detroit became surrogate mothers, sisters, and daughters to large numbers of San Ignacians, whether they were blood relatives, *compadres* or *comadres* and their children, or friends; hence this new transnational commitment influenced (decreased) the number of children that Mexican immigrant women had.

Mexicanas' contribution to the creation of their transnational community was dependent on both their reproductive and their productive labor. Historically, scholars of women's studies have struggled to foreground the importance of women's reproductive labor within patriarchal and economic systems. Feminist approaches to the topic of migration have tended to emphasize women's challenges to traditional gender roles when they join the paid labor force. But the experiences of San Ignacian women prove that this process is more complicated than it may seem. Women who feel empowered by their participation in the paid workforce may still adhere to gendered divisions of labor at home. And while they may stagger under the burden of domestic tasks, some women feel that their authority over the domestic space gives them some power to make decisions concerning all the residents of the household. In gendered immigration studies we have to connect reproductive labor with the subsistence of transnational communities.[28] It is through the gendered division of labor that we can begin to understand how gender relations are interlinked and embedded within the immigrant experience and the maintenance of transnational social networks.

Most San Ignacian men I interviewed did not regard reproductive labor as "work" or acknowledge its value. Don Antonio brought his family to Detroit in 1972. He and his wife, Imelda, had nine children. When asked whether his wife worked, he replied: "No, she just took care of the house. I supported her." But he later added that his wife worked with a neighbor who prepared meals for retired older people and also got a job in a factory.[29]

Don Gabriel and his son Sergio offered a similar argument. Don Gabriel and his wife, Lupe, had ten children. She had to care for them before and after she migrated to Detroit. When asked whether his wife had worked in Detroit, however, Don Gabriel adamantly replied, "No, [over there] she never worked, not one minute!" When I asked Don Gabriel and Sergio one more time if Lupe had worked in the house, Sergio responded: "Oh, yes, she did do housework, she was a very active woman. But the houses there aren't as large, and she didn't have to mop every day because the house in Detroit had carpeting. So I think her workload was lighter." Sergio also mentioned casually that at one point more than eighteen people lived in their house, including his wife and the wives and husbands of his ten siblings.[30] Downplaying domestic chores within transnational fields points to the patriarchal unequal gendered division of labor as well as the transnational domestication of domestic labor by Mexican immigrant women. For male San Ignacians, domestic labor in the United States seemed easier, given the modern domestic appliances like vacuum cleaners and the like, but also normalized as an extension of personal obligations.

The case of Don Raúl and his wife, Eli, illustrates how some women struggled to negotiate the terms of their reproductive labor. Don Raúl arrived in Detroit in 1970 and, like other San Ignacian pioneers, lived with the Mercado brothers until he was able to rent his own apartment. In 1972 he processed his family's residencies, and they joined him in Detroit. According to her son Benjamín, Eli loved Detroit: "Over there she had all of us, her family, and she did not have to work as hard as here [San Ignacio]. She only had to pick up the house because we helped her vacuum the rug. She was happy to have all of us with her." Don Raúl, however, added: "We had to buy a house because the apartment was very small. My wife started to become very *delicada* [touchy] because a lot of people arrived in the apartment and I let them stay there to help them. So I thought, let's buy a house, because I liked it there and I wanted to stay for a long time. So I got the idea to buy the house and then I bought another one four years later that I turned into small apartments to rent."[31] Eli not only rebelled against having so many tenants in the apartment but, like Doña Tita, also used this as leverage to get her husband to buy a house.

Eli was not the only one who complained about having so many people around. Doña Chavelita also persuaded her husband to buy a house when she complained about the crowded conditions they were living in and the extra work she had to do. "All his [her husband's] brothers came, and he arranged for several of his sons to come too. We all lived tightly crowded together. Anyone who arrived could stay with us until he found work, and my husband didn't charge for food or anything. . . . They all helped with the house, my children all living in the same place. It was bad, and I was not used to it. Finally we bought a house."[32] Under the stress of overcrowding, some women were able to negotiate with their husbands for better living and domestic labor conditions. These negotiations sometimes led to the purchase of homes and thus to more permanent settlement in Detroit, helping solidify the transnational community.

Women's entry into paid work opened up additional spaces for Mexicanas to expand the development of transnational communities. Most of the women I interviewed had worked and are currently working in paid employment in Detroit. Due to their immigration status, many held low-paying jobs such as working in auto parts industries and other service and food sectors. The shop floor became one more contested arena where women revisited their cultural constructions of gender roles and further expanded their social networks, often recruiting other women to join them at their place of employment.[33]

Doña Tita's daughter-in-law Alina arrived in Detroit in 1972, about a year after she was married in San Ignacio to Javier Hernández, Doña Tita's oldest son. While most of the men in the Hernández family worked in steel factories, the women found jobs in auto parts factories. Alina worked in a factory sewing covers for cars. She remembered how kinship networks on the shop floor facilitated transitions into a new job market and created spaces for Mexicanas to socialize.

I didn't like the job at the beginning, it was very difficult, so when I got pregnant with Fabiola [her first daughter], I quit. But after I had Araceli [her second daughter], I started to work there again. We sewed car covers with industrial sewing machines. I started working there because my *comadre* [Doña Lola, her aunt] recommended me. Right after I started, my friend Aurora, may she rest in peace, joined the factory and she worked there for about twenty-seven years. So at first we were a small group from San Ignacio, only Lola and Aurora, but Elia joined after I did and then more people arrived. We would get together after work and visit each other all the time because we were the only ones [from San Ignacio]. I would run to my Aunt Lola's house in the evenings so that I wouldn't be alone.[34]

While Alina's productive labor at the factory gave her an opportunity to meet other women, her reproductive labor at home allowed more San Ignacians to move to Detroit. After Alina arrived in the city, Doña Tita went back to San Ignacio to bring her youngest children to Detroit. Doña Tita stayed in San Ignacio for a year before returning to the United States. During that year Alina cooked and cared for fourteen family members and friends and also worked in the auto plant. Her husband, Javier, had been the first of Doña Tita's children to marry, placing the responsibility on Alina, as his wife, to take care of younger family members and San Ignacian guests as well. She recalled learning how to cook in Detroit thanks to her *comadre* Lola from San Ignacio. Although the workload was heavy, she commented: "I felt good here with all of them because I was not alone. Thirty-one years ago there was almost no one here from San Ignacio, not like now."[35] Alina recalled with nostalgia the times when she appreciated having so many members of the family there, while she downplayed the story of having to perform intensive domestic work in order to sustain the household.

The complexity of gender relations in immigrant households makes it difficult to determine whether the effects of women's entry into the paid labor force have been "liberating" in terms of challenging traditional gender roles. The case of Gela illustrates the plurality of experiences among Mexicanas and their ambivalence regarding their position as wage earners. Gela commented: "We could definitely support ourselves on what he [her husband] makes. So whatever I earn I can use for things that are not . . . [necessities], like for new clothes or going out, or to save. I can do what I want with whatever I make."[36] Gela described her contribution to the household's finances as supplemental income, even though she had been working consistently since she arrived in Detroit nine years earlier, doing factory work and waitressing in several restaurants. Although she underestimated the importance of her wages, it was clear that her financial contribution did cover some essentials, like clothing for the family. Her comment portraying her income as minor and supplemental suggested a desire to defend her husband's sense of manhood as the breadwinner, showing how women must constantly navigate patriarchal assumptions pertaining to women's paid work and its importance in the household economy.

Some women who had previously taken care of agricultural duties in San Ignacio used their transnational experience and entry into the labor force in Detroit to reprimand their partners for not being able to support them and their families, as traditional gender roles prescribed in their community of origin. Tina commented: "If men take care of their obligations better [i.e., make enough money to support the family], then I don't think women should work, they should care for their families. But if the men do not, then it is better there [in Detroit], because here [in San Ignacio] there aren't many jobs for women."[37] Tina was in San Ignacio for the January festivities when I conducted the interview, but she and her family live in Detroit. Her comment appeared to reflect what Emma Pérez calls the "third space," where San Ignacian women claim their transnational experience to negotiate and maintain some kind of power over the family dynamics.[38]

Yet despite their assertion of some resistance due to their transnational experiences, the comments of San Ignacian women—contesting men's economic adequacy and their own competency—include an ironic acceptance of traditional gender roles, in which they assume that women do not work outside the home (even when they do so while also performing domestic labor). They reveal the contradictions inherent in social norms and their lived transnational realities. But when I asked Tina if she enjoyed working, she replied: "Yes, at first it was hard but now I like it, it's fine. You don't have to worry about anything."[39] Tina was laid off from the company she worked for in Detroit. The company offered two years of English lessons as part of a severance package, and she expressed enthusiasm about the prospect of looking for another job as soon as the lessons were finished. Tina's resentment toward her husband for not fulfilling his obligations as breadwinner stemmed from her guilty feelings about not spending much time with her children rather than from any dislike of paid work. Indeed, she recalled having fun with her friends at work. "I have many women friends. The factory has been closed almost a year, but we still keep in touch and we see each other when we go to English lessons."[40]

Her ambivalence about her participation in productive labor reflects the multiplicity of experiences available to transnational Mexicanas as they weigh adherence to socially assigned gender roles against their feelings of empowerment and, in some cases, enjoyment as members of the transnational/global workforce.

CONTRADICTIONS IN WOMEN'S LIVES

As women take on different surrogate roles, they must contend with conflicting moral imperatives about how much they should tolerate when taking care of extended family members and other long-term houseguests. Moreover, San Ignacian women had to pay the physical and emotional costs involved in the development of transnational social networks. While doing my research in San Ignacio and Detroit I spent time with Gaby (twenty-two), Gabriel (twenty-eight), and their son Luis (six). Luis was born with a muscular disease that impeded his ability to walk. Gaby was advised by a friend to seek accountability from Henry Ford Hospital in Detroit, where her son was born, and to file a lawsuit. Gaby did not speak English and the lawyer that someone recommended did not speak Spanish, so they used a friend as an interpreter. Gaby asked me if I could help her fill out the thick questionnaire that the lawyer had sent her in order to begin the lawsuit. While we were working on the many pages of forms, Gaby received a phone call from her oldest brother. In an instant I saw her attitude and tone of voice change. She began to complain about her younger brother Camilo, who had recently arrived in Detroit from San Ignacio and was living with her family. She said that Camilo was not paying for his long-distance phone calls to Mexico or contributing for the food he ate. He scattered his clothes everywhere, and she had to pick them up and put them away.

In appealing to Beto, her oldest brother, Gaby made use of family hierarchies based on patriarchal social structures in order to discipline her younger brother. While she honored one tradition, acting as "mother" to her brother by picking up after Camilo and paying his expenses, she also asserted her sense of equality by appealing to the family patriarch to impose fairer family roles. When I asked Gaby why she did not just tell Camilo to straighten up, she replied, "No, I can't, he's my brother."[41] Here was a woman who was undertaking a lawsuit against a hospital, a daunting task (especially in light of her limited English skills), yet she was not able to tell her own brother to act responsibly.

The sense of obligation toward extended family and friends and the burdens on women that this entailed frequently provoked gender conflicts within families. Vivi, Gaby's sister, was married and had two little girls. While I was interviewing Vivi in her living room in Detroit, another woman came down the stairs with two other little girls. It turned out that Vivi's husband's brother, the brother's wife, and their two daughters had arrived two months earlier from San Ignacio and were living in the house. While Vivi was telling me this, she and Gaby began to whisper so that the other woman, who had gone into the kitchen with her daughters, could not hear us. Vivi was on the verge of desperation. Her sister-in-law never cleaned the top floor, which was completely taken over by the woman's family, and never helped with the cooking or dishes. Her husband was only working three times a week, which meant that it would most likely take them forever to move out and make it on their own. The list of complaints went on and on until the sister-in-law returned to the living room.

On another occasion, when Gaby and I were on our way to visit Vivi again, we stopped at McDonald's to get a kid's meal for Gaby's son Luis. While we were waiting in the takeout line she remarked: "Oh, we should get one for my niece." She continued: "Well, should I get two more for the woman's little girls?" But she immediately concluded: "No, hell no, I'm not responsible for the other two girls, right?"[42] Her comments reveal resentment about the extension of family obligations to distant kin and the tensions that women experience as they try to guard some privacy and boundaries in this situation. They also show a changing sense of familial obligation in the new transnational setting of Mexican Town.

A week later Gaby received a distressed call. Vivi was crying uncontrollably and asked Gaby to pick her up. Vivi had repeatedly asked her husband, Genaro, to give his brother a time-frame to leave and rent an apartment for his family. Her husband had criticized her for making a big deal out of nothing and insisted that he could not tell his brother to leave before he was ready to move out on his own; this, he said, would be an insult. Vivi would just have to put up with it. But Genaro was hardly ever home. He and his brother would leave early in the morning, ostensibly to go to work, and would not return until late in the evening, leaving Vivi to deal with the everyday conflicts and tensions that arose between the families. Ultimately Vivi was able to negotiate with her husband a time-frame for his brother to move out. This was possible because she continued to stand her ground but also because Genaro had more siblings in Detroit with whom his brother's family could stay. Nevertheless, for four months Vivi and Genaro argued continuously, causing turmoil within the household.

Despite this very contested and unfair situation, Vivi commented:

> Many people helped us. It's very important when you come here that you have someone to extend their hand to you. I know a lot of people who didn't have anywhere to stay when they came, who didn't know anybody, who didn't even have a place to sleep or anything to eat until they found a job. Thank God I was lucky because I had my sister here. It's so nice and it encourages you to come when you have a place to stay, because life here is not easy, and if you're not working it's even harder, but it's easier when you have family here, thank God. [Once you get settled] you want to help other people because you know what they're going through. We've all gone through the same thing, all of us.[43]

Vivi's comment pointed to the contradictions and ambivalences that the construction of transnational social networks has created in women's lives. Even though she was having problems with her husband because of his relatives' extended stay, she also felt obligated to do for her in-laws what Gaby had done for her and understood the reasons for having them remain in her house. Gender relations are shaped and reshaped by the immigrant experience, and this makes it hard to determine when and how Mexicanas challenge traditional gender relations. I contend that they do, albeit in increments, as they construct their lives in their transnational community. Women see themselves as the creators of their community even though they must continuously stake their claim to contested spaces in which the division of power is unequal and unfair.

Compared to the bracero generation of Mexicanas who moved north in the 1970s, younger women who have settled in Detroit more recently have had certain advantages. Because there were so few San Ignacians in Detroit in the early years, women faced a difficult moral choice between housing their newly arrived relatives and friends or letting them fend for themselves while they got on their feet. Today the large transnational community in Detroit offers arriving San Ignacians more options in terms of places to stay, somewhat lessening the burden on the families already there. As the transnational community has grown, it has opened up spaces for younger Mexicanas to negotiate and challenge patriarchal dominance by appealing to members of their families and to other San Ignacians already residing in Detroit. Gender relations and patriarchal systems are not monolithic or stable, and women are constantly changing the ways in which they negotiate and challenge these systems. Younger Mexicanas are also influenced by cultural expressions of feminism and individualism and are more open-minded about relationships than their elders are. This has allowed young women like Vivi to express discontent and to act on it, often by negotiating with their male partners issues that affect the family's well-being.

These examples provide a glimpse of the hardships and struggles that Mexican women have experienced as they work to support the social networks that sustain immigration. Painful tensions and conflicts within families have required immigrants to renegotiate gender roles and kinship relations. Even so, the main burden still falls on Mexicanas, who are the primary caretakers of their immediate families and any guests staying with the family and who also frequently work full-time outside the home. The Mexicanas I interviewed have found various ways to negotiate and contest gender oppression, even though these efforts often fall short of overt resistance to patriarchal norms.

TRANSNATIONAL DISLOCATIONS AND REUNIONS

Attitudes about permanence and transience were gender specific; thus San Ignacian men and women had different reactions to residing in Detroit permanently or going back to San Ignacio. Contradictions also attach to women's feelings about where to live and for how long, and especially about being separated from their children. Older women, in particular, struggle with the choice between living out their lives in Mexico or in Detroit, where most of their families reside permanently. Although they expressed various views in interviews, most Mexicanas who moved to Detroit in the early 1970s concluded that they preferred their lives in Detroit to their former lives in San Ignacio. Older women who lived in San Ignacio repeatedly commented that they would rather be living in Detroit, especially if they had children there. While they had several reasons for staying in San Ignacio, often it was the deterioration of their health that was the primary cause. They had grown old, and some were physically unable to travel back and forth. Others humored their husbands, who liked to stay in San Ignacio for the winter and return to Detroit when the weather was less harsh. Doña Chavelita commented:

> My children are there [Detroit] and I enjoy doing things for them. I know they love me and I love them too and they like it when I'm there,

but there are so many of them! Now I'm older and my heart is weak, and I can't handle bad news or work too much because I have already had minor heart attacks.[44]

Doña Minerva and her husband, Luis Mercado, divided their time between the two places and expressed mixed feelings based on gendered transnational experiences. Luis commented: "We're happy here [in San Ignacio]. When we go back I do odd jobs here and there, but I don't work anymore." Although they went back and forth, Doña Minerva said that she felt sorrow when she was in San Ignacio because she missed her children, who were in Detroit.[45] Doña Luna was an older woman who made the choice to live permanently in Detroit. While her husband, Don Andrés, was alive, he and Doña Luna went back and forth between Detroit and San Ignacio; but after Don Andrés passed away, Doña Luna moved to Detroit to be taken care of by her sons and daughters.

Familial separation is one of the most difficult dislocations for San Ignacians, who may go months or even years without seeing immediate family members. In 1976 Saúl de la Torre left San Ignacio to find work in Detroit while his wife, Tina, stayed behind to care for their four children. He traveled back and forth for two years; in 1978, after the birth of a fifth child, they decided that being together would be best for the family. In addition, Tina could join the labor force in Detroit and help the family's economic situation. Tina and Saúl hired a coyote to smuggle them into the United States. But the whole family could not migrate together. Tina remembered: "I went with him. I took my youngest—he was seven months old—and left my other four children with my relatives."[46] Tina and Saúl paid $1,100 each and crossed the border through Tijuana to Chula Vista, California, near San Diego. Although the crossing was difficult, especially carrying the baby, they arrived safely. Saúl borrowed the money to pay the coyote from family members who were waiting for them in Detroit.

Tina remembered the anguish that she and Saúl experienced while they were saving money to pay for their other children to cross the border:

> After three months I started to work in a hotel doing housekeeping and saving every penny to bring my other four children. Once we had the money, we couldn't find anyone who would take them from San Ignacio to Tijuana. We didn't see them for six months. I was going mad, oh my God! I kept telling Saúl, if we don't bring them here soon I'm leaving. At night I couldn't sleep, I would go outside and weep for hours until finally we came up with the idea of who could bring them to us. My rela-

tives who are retired and live in San Ignacio agreed to take the children and we paid for their travel. They crossed safely with a coyote. As soon as the children got to Detroit I enrolled them in school and we began our new life.[47]

For many San Ignacian immigrants, crossing the border was a horrendous experience, but the descriptions were gendered.[48] In interviews older Mexican women tended to downplay the dangers, however, except when talking about the border crossings of their children. They emphasized instead the anguish caused by family separation and the importance of reuniting their families. In contrast, men rarely described separations with such emotion.

Family separation has contributed to the constant shaping and reshaping of migrant families in Detroit and in San Ignacio. One morning in San Ignacio in 1988 Gustavo and Mari decided that Gustavo needed to go back to Detroit to improve the household finances. He had gone there a few times but had never stayed longer than a year. The day after Gustavo got to Detroit he called Mari to let her know that he had arrived safely and was now with his sister. Mari turned to her young daughter, who was sixteen, and said: "Your father just called to let us know that he's okay. So with the money [he will earn] I'm going to have the doctor run some tests to see why you're not getting your period."[49] Mari was already suspicious, so she was not surprised when Lily opened up and confirmed that she was in fact five months pregnant. Lily had been going to a clinic in Arandas (a town near San Ignacio) and knew that she was carrying a girl. Though Mari had suspected the pregnancy, she was distressed when she found out the truth.

> I asked her, "Why did you have to wait until your father left? Why didn't you say something while he was still here?" I prayed to God that nobody would tell him until I talked to him. Eight days later he [Gustavo] called and I said to him, "You know the van broke down." He was very angry because I was unable to pick up the van from where it broke down, and he said, "How can you not make arrangements to pick up the van, kids are going to break the windows and who knows what else!" So I said, "I wish our only problem was with the van. Our daughter is pregnant." He started to cry and to hit the wall.[50]

Gustavo did not speak to his daughter for more than eight months. His first reaction was to blame the father of the child and ostracize his daughter. Months after the baby was born, Lily and her older sister announced that they wanted to go to Detroit. Gustavo objected but Mari intervened, challenging patriarchal authority, and supported the emigration of both her daughters. Mari advised Lily not to take the baby until she found a job and felt more stable. Both daughters moved into their aunt's house in Detroit, where they have lived for four years.

This situation shows how women navigate difficult situations, drawing on networks of female relatives and other women in order to support the well-being of their transnational families. Mari's family members in Detroit welcomed the young women, alleviating the parents' anxiety about having their young daughters so far away. The story also shows how women constantly reposition family roles in order to cope with the circumstances surrounding immigration. In this case, Mari allowed her teenaged daughter to escape her maternal obligations by leaving her infant behind. The grandparents became the parents of the baby, the older siblings became authority figures in relation to the child, and the aunts in Detroit took over some of the responsibility for parenting the young mother herself.

For many of the transnational families I met, separations were eventually followed by reunions—often, though not always, involving the regrouping of the extended family in Detroit. When I was conducting research in Detroit in 2004, I was invited to a birthday party for Alex, eight years old. Alex's father, Antonio, had left San Ignacio for Detroit in 1994 with the four oldest children in the family, leaving Sandra, her mother, with the younger five. The mother moved to Detroit with the remaining siblings in 1995, and Alex was born a year later. Both parents and all ten siblings now live in Detroit.

I drove to Gaby's house and from there she, Gabriel, Luis, and I walked to Gabriel's sister's house for the party. Gaby's sister-in-law, Mayra, had decorated her backyard with colored ribbons and a sign that read: "Feliz Cumpleaños [Happy birthday], Alex." There must have been about thirty people, including immediate family, extended family, and friends. Mayra's husband and Gabriel had thrown a long rope from one side of the backyard and hung a piñata in the shape of a pink heart with Minnie Mouse carrying a present. We all sang as the children took turns hitting the piñata. When it burst, candies went flying in the air, and the children rushed to scoop up as many as they could carry.

This transnational family, like many others, includes some family members who are legal permanent residents (green card holders); others who are U.S. citizens (like Alex, who unlike her siblings was born in Detroit); and still others who are undocumented immigrants, like Gaby.

She is married to Gabriel, a legal permanent resident, and her son Luis is a U.S. citizen. The parents and the four oldest children in Alex's family do not speak much English, and their formal education is limited. The two oldest siblings were only able to attend school for a few years in San Ignacio since they had to help their father with his work. The situation is different for the younger siblings, who grew up mostly in Detroit. Three of them (Teresita, eighteen, Armando, nineteen, and Juan Pablo, twenty) are enrolled at Michigan State University, Wayne State University, and the University of Michigan, respectively. Alex, the only one born in Detroit, wants to become a doctor when she grows up. Thus Mexican immigrants have to construct and reconstruct new meanings of what it means to be a San Ignacian and a Detroiter at the same time. Immigrants of the younger generation have made Detroit their home, despite their desire to return every year to San Ignacio for the *fiestas patronales*. This construction of the Mexican transnational family at a more intimate level also points to the fluidity of roles within the family as well as hierarchies based on levels of education and migratory status.

The former braceros who moved to Detroit in the 1960s would have had little impact had it not been for the women who ventured north and became involved in community formation. As women create and sustain transnational social networks, they develop strategies to navigate contested patriarchal spaces in order to maintain a sense of identity and dignity for themselves and their families. They experience ambivalence, contradictions, and conflicts as they gradually conquer public and private spaces. The creation of transnational communities reshapes gender roles and family structures and calls into question the whole notion of geopolitical borders, acknowledging their transparency and fluidity. As they meld two different, albeit intertwined, experiences in San Ignacio and Detroit, immigrant families develop new narratives of transnational identity and citizenship.

*It [Detroit] was very ugly and it had snow. . . . Now we go back
and forth and spend time here and there. But I came here [San
Ignacio] with sorrow because of my children [who are in Detroit].*[1]

—DOÑA MINERVA (SIXTY-SEVEN), INTERVIEW IN
SAN IGNACIO, DECEMBER 2001

One sunny afternoon in the summer of 2004 I found myself unexpectedly
humming Jorge Negrete's nationalistic anthem *México lindo y querido* as I
strolled down the street in Detroit's Mexican Town.[2] On one side of the
street was a typical multipurpose immigrant business selling everything
from music CDs to frilly *quinceañera* (fifteenth-birthday celebration)
dresses, groceries, and cowboy boots. Across the street was my favorite *taquería* (taco stand), La Lupita, and next to it a bakery selling *pan
dulce* (sweet bread); its aroma brought back a rush of childhood memories.
There was no doubt about it: just being in Mexican Town made me feel
more Mexican.

A sense of Mexicanness, based on collective recognition of national
and local identity and reflected in familiar cultural products and social
rituals, pervaded this public space in the city of Detroit. Mexican Town
is not the only U.S. neighborhood to have become Mexicanized by the
presence of large numbers of Mexican immigrants, Mexican Americans,
and Chicanas/os, but it is a prime example of this process. This particular
day I was touring Mexican Town with my friend Gaby, a twenty-two-
year-old San Ignacian residing in Detroit. We were bombarded by the
cultural images and sounds of Mexico: a painted mural of the great Aztec
pyramid next to a muscular Aztec man and a voluptuous woman in a sheer
costume; altars carefully constructed at the entrances of many homes; the
Mexican flag fluttering as a curtain in a small room on the second floor of
a house; young children chattering in Spanish. Pieces of Mexico had been
transported to Detroit and tantalized all my senses.

Advertisements in Spanish offered us a multitude of services—lawyers, money transfers, bail bonds, psychic readings—and touted consumer goods ranging from the necessities of food and clothing to charm bracelets to bring me happiness and stop my husband from drinking. Clearly, Mexican immigrants were recognized for their purchasing power, though they might be ignored in many other ways. Just like the Mexican anthem I was humming, the images of the mural and the Mexican flag by the window were exalting my sense of Mexicanness. At the same time, they were strong national signifiers of Mexico's gendered male nationalist pantheon of symbols.

Mexican women—in Mexico and in the United States—are seen through an implicitly gendered male nationalist lens. The voluptuous and sensual Aztec princess represented in the mural rested motionless (passive and oversexualized) on the lap of her heroic savior—the Aztec warrior. Nationalist agendas both in the United States and in Mexico have been anchored in gendered male ideologies of civic representation and national citizenship. As Rosa Linda Fregoso puts it, "Modern societies privilege the public (masculine) citizen-subject in the formation of the nation-state."[3] The granting of suffrage rights illustrates this historical devaluing of women's civic participation as members of a nation and at the same time reveals the historical erasure of women as "official" sociopolitical citizens. It was not until the first half of the twentieth century that women in the United States (1920) and Mexico (1950) were able to achieve suffrage. For working-class Mexican female immigrants, transnational identification includes the integration of two separate albeit both patriarchal systems of nation building. Situated within the sociopolitical misogynist constructions of the nation, Mexican women who are undocumented also find themselves having to work out alternative ways of experiencing themselves in relation to the state.

Driving through Detroit's Mexican Town, Gaby and I reflected on the sudden death of our mutual friend Tori's fifteen-year-old son Manuel. Tori had been living in Detroit for over thirty years, and his son was born in Detroit. Nonetheless, the boy's body was going to be sent to San Ignacio after the funeral. His entire family planned to fly back for the burial at the local cemetery. I realized that at least three deaths had occurred during the period of my research on Mexican immigrants there, and all of the bodies had been sent back to San Ignacio for interment in the cemetery there. I asked Gaby if she wanted her body to be sent back when she died. She replied: "Hell yes, I don't want my body to be buried here in Detroit, are you kidding? *Ni modo que me desparramen acá* [I would not like to be scattered here]. No, Luz María, I would never want to be *desparramada* here in Detroit." *Desparramada* literally means broken into little pieces and scattered everywhere. Yet Gaby had been in Detroit for more than five years; although she had been obliged to return temporarily to San Ignacio because of a family illness, she appeared to like living in Detroit. She was not alone in her perceptions of fragmentation.

Working-class San Ignacians in Detroit vacillated between feelings of permanence and transiency. Their everyday experiences shaped and reshaped the way they saw their residence in the United States. While they had enduring emotional ties to Mexico, they had invested substantial emotional and economic capital in both San Ignacio and Detroit, becoming active participants in the construction of a transnational community. This dual allegiance was gendered and constantly challenged San Ignacians' sense of belonging to a particular place. That is why most made arrangements, or maintained an unspoken understanding with family members, to ensure that when they died their bodies would be returned to San Ignacio so that they would not be *desparramados* in Detroit. Family members were also more likely to visit this eternal resting place in San Ignacio, thus forging a more permanent historical memory.

This chapter addresses the complex role of women in this transnational community by mapping out the ideological context in which Mexicans constructed new lives within their transnational community and created new understandings of transnational identity and citizenship. Immigrants from San Ignacio have defined themselves both as San Ignacians and as Mexican Detroiters, whether they reside at any given moment in San Ignacio or in Detroit. They have invested time, skills, and capital in both places. Despite this dual loyalty, contradictions arise on an emotional level as immigrants grapple with issues of residence and permanency and with their marginalization in a country that depends on their labor but relegates them to social invisibility.

MEXICAN IMMIGRATION

Early literature on Mexican immigration once centered on the idea that Mexicans migrated to the United States solely in an effort to increase their financial opportunities.[4] Contemporary immigration scholars recognize that the drivers of migration are more complex than the simple desire to improve livelihoods. The literature now highlights structural differences between the two countries as well as international labor agreements that involve the aggressive importation and exportation of large numbers of workers—the Bracero Program being an obvious example.[5] It also emphasizes the social networks that tie immigrants to both their sending and their adopted communities.

Deciding whether to reside permanently in the United States is a complex and contested process that taps into Mexican immigrants' feelings of being transnational subjects. These include complex connections to two different and at times contradictory cultural, social, and geopolitical sites embedded in the transnational process. One of these processes involves the politics of movement through the rigid management and policing of the U.S.-Mexico border. Over the last three decades immigration reform and the acute militarization of the border have forced many undocumented immigrants to stay in the United States rather than travel back and forth as they had previously done. I have argued elsewhere that prior to the severe immigration restrictions imposed in the 1990s (such as Operation Gatekeeper) the United States engaged in a cat-and-mouse game between U.S. agencies like the Border Patrol and several groups who have historically had vested interests in Mexican labor that alternately aggressively recruited and curtailed immigration.[6] After severe militarization of the border and restrictive immigration legislation during the 1990s, however, this semi-innocent labor turnover became a mortal cycle that claimed the lives of more and more Mexican immigrants.[7] These immigration reforms along with severe demonization of Mexican immigrants as "illegal aliens" defined the Mexican immigrant as the quintessential un-American and thus noncitizen. Furthermore, this taxonomy of un-American prospects extends far beyond those who are marked as "illegal aliens." Chicanos and Chicanas have borne the brunt of these racist attitudes and political and economic erasure. Being a citizen of the United States does not guarantee that all members of civil society will be integrated into the national white hegemonic polity.

What is citizenship? This study recognizes Maxine Molyneux's definition of citizenship: "the legal and cultural foundation of the relationship between the state and society, citizenship specifies the basis of social membership and of the social contract that it implies."[8] In her study of state formations in Latin America (which I extend to the United States) Molyneux adds that "the social organization of power, not only in the state but in much of civil society, retained a predominantly masculine character": none of these state formations had gender equality as an integral variable in the political sphere.[9] Undocumented Mexican women thus face an intricate web of gender marginalization within nationalist political discourses while at the same time engaging in civil/social daily activities that include their participation in productive and reproductive labor. This study focuses on ideological discourses produced by Mexican immigrant women (many of whom are undocumented) while they preserved "home" and memory in San Ignacio via their remittances—economic, cultural, and emotional—and their active participation in a transnational network.

The United States persecutes immigrant workers, even though they are considered highly desirable as a source of low-wage labor. Experiencing this situation affects Mexican immigrants' sentiments when considering the United States as their new "home." Regardless of their immigration status, Mexicanas and Mexicanos define themselves and their lives in relation to the anti-immigrant and hostile environment in the United States and their transnational experience. These sentiments are gendered and constitutive of the way in which Mexicanas construct their lives as transnational subjects/citizens both in Detroit and in San Ignacio.

TRANSNATIONAL ECONOMIC TIES: IMMIGRANT DOLLARS FOR SAN IGNACIO

In 1982 Tori, a longtime San Ignacian resident of Detroit, drove from Detroit to San Ignacio with a bulldozer in the back of his *troka*, ready to upgrade the town's main plaza and its kiosk. According to townspeople, the *municipio* of Arandas, to which San Ignacio belongs, had ignored its obligation to provide resources for public services such as maintenance of the plaza. Tori became involved with the committee that organizes the *fiestas patronales* and collected more than $6,000 from San Ignacians in Detroit to renovate the plaza and refurbish the *kiosco*.

Towns and cities throughout Mexico feature a central plaza facing a Catholic church. Surrounding the plaza are small businesses and restaurants along with civic buildings such as the police station and municipal offices. Political, social, and religious events and gatherings of all kinds are held on the plaza. A central feature is an elevated kiosk facing the church, which provides a venue for entertainment and speeches. This pseudocolonial architectural landscape was the place where San Ignacians celebrated the *serenatas* (the courting rituals through which they expressed their transnational sexualities and experimented with their ideologies about sexual identities) during the *fiestas patronales*. The plaza thus not only represented regional adherence and local membership but was the main stage for socioreligious and political rituals.

With the permission of the municipal authorities in Arandas, Tori and other San Ignacians tore up the old plaza and began building a new one.

But the money ran out midway through the project, and the municipal authorities in Arandas took it upon themselves to finish the construction. Much to residents' dismay, the town was left with a disappointing plaza, "like over there, very European-looking, that did not look good in front of our church. People were not happy."[10] Three years later Gustavo and other San Ignacians appealed to the authorities and collected money so that they could tear down the "European-looking" plaza and build something new in its place. Contributions were raised from a benefactor in San Ignacio and from San Ignacians in Detroit.[11]

> We complained to the authorities, saying that we wanted to tear it down and rebuild it, until finally they accepted. Before we tore it down I went to Don Alfonso Patiño and asked him if he could help us rebuild the plaza. When he saw the photographs he agreed, saying, "That plaza is not for my town." . . . The next day we started to tear down the *kiosco* and the plaza. We went to Irapuato with Don Alfonso and he gave us the first check, for 11,700,000 pesos, so that we could get started, and then he gave us 50,000,000 pesos for the *kiosco*. . . . The *kiosco* that we have is a replica of the *kiosco* in Chapala. We looked for ways to embellish the plaza, and I think we succeeded in getting what we wanted.[12]

San Ignacians, including those living in Detroit, wanted a beautiful plaza and *kiosco* as symbols of their love for and commitment to their hometown. It had to be a plaza that was aesthetically in harmony with their transnational tastes. San Ignacians in Detroit were as much involved in the planning as were those in San Ignacio, illustrating the immigrants' continuing economic participation in their hometown and the deepening of the economic ties between San Ignacio and Detroit.

The plaza was not the only project that the immigrants became involved in. Another was the construction of two ceremonial arches at the town's entrance as a symbol of local identity and pride. Father Ignacio recalled:

> The arches are not there thanks to the authorities. None of them can say, "During our administration those arches were built." The town is witness that those arches at the entrance to the town were built with money and labor donated by the people of San Ignacio, both here and in Detroit. People would give a brick, or a sack of cement, or a week of labor; that's how the arches were built. And the same goes for the landscaped lines of trees that separate the main streets. Before, a dirty

stream ran along what is now our main avenue. We thought that it would be worth it to have a main avenue. . . . The same thing happened with many other streets that are now paved.[13]

The annual processions during the *fiestas patronales* proceeded down this main avenue. Beginning at the arches, the processions moved along the avenue to the plaza and from there to the church.

Since the 1940s immigrants have gradually become social and economic protagonists in San Ignacio by making generous contributions toward the betterment of the town. In addition to aiding in civic projects, their assistance enabled numerous renovations of the town's church over the years. At the same time, immigrants used their earnings to benefit themselves and their families, building luxurious houses in San Ignacio, starting or expanding small businesses, and sending remittances home. Women in particular have gotten involved in the planning and construction process of the *casas solas* (empty homes), as they are called in San Ignacio, as well as assigning female immediate family relatives to care for them during their "absence." This form of "presence" through public and personal economic ties to their community of origin (owning property there while residing in a different nation-state) highlights immigrants' sentiments about their "imagined community" or "imagined transnational community." David G. Gutiérrez and Pierrette Hondagneu-Sotelo introduce a conceptualization of what transnational spaces are: "Defined by proponents as the interstitial social spaces traversed and occupied by migrants in their sojourns between places of origin and places of destination, transnational spaces are envisioned as multisided 'imagined communities' whose boundaries stretch across the borders of two or more nation-states."[14] Thus immigrants invest a dual emotional and sociopolitical capital that pays off differently depending on the specific trans-location in which they find themselves—San Ignacio or Detroit.

The transnational experience and historical protagonist role of immigration in Jalisco is highlighted by Paul S. Taylor's research on Mexican immigrants to the United States. Most specifically, when he documented immigration from Arandas (the municipality that San Ignacio belonged to until 2003), Jalisco, in 1933, he found that many immigrants from Arandas—primarily men—went to Texas, following the citrus belt, but others leapfrogged to the Midwest, satisfying labor needs throughout the United States.[15] Thus the immigrant experience of San Ignacians has unfolded in several stages. Influenced by the state's long historical experience with immigration, the integration of San Ignacians into the Bracero Program facilitated the transition of a small town into a transnational community. San Ignacians from the bracero generation, with men who migrated north to satisfy immediate survival needs, initiated a pattern of migration that was to last for many generations. As transnational networks expanded with the arrival of women and more San Ignacians moved to Detroit to take up job opportunities, families slowly began to accumulate capital. Often their first investment in Detroit was the purchase of a house to make sure their families were taken care of. Once they achieved a measure of economic stability, many became avid consumers of various goods, including trucks, cars, and domestic appliances (such as washing machines), both in their sending community and in Detroit.

They also sent money home. In 1999–2000 townspeople in San Ignacio received more than $1.6 million in remittances from family members residing in the United States according to some estimates.[16] Tori, however, who owns a very profitable money transfer business in Detroit that sends remittances to San Ignacio, estimated that San Ignacio received much more than that annually from his store and that of his only business rival. Tori asserted that in 1996, without having any business competition, he sent $5 million annually. He calculated that the total for remittances from his store and his business rival's store and the money that immigrants carried with them when returning for the fiestas would come to $10 million annually. It is difficult to cite the exact amount of remittances received since the sources vary, but nonetheless it is clear that money sent back to San Ignacio from the United States was more than significant. According to official estimates, remittances to San Ignacio average $1,053 per family. This money sent by San Ignacians living in Detroit has rippled through the economy of San Ignacio.[17] More recently, an economic bulletin from the Banco de México reported that Mexico received a total of $23.54 billion in remittances from the United States in 2006. Jalisco alone received $991.8 million, second only to Michoacán in Mexico in the amount of dollars from the United States in the form of remittances.[18]

In contrast to the economic boom of San Ignacio through immigrants' experiences and remittances, Taylor found that immigrants from Arandas that had been employed "in 20 of these, on track: California, Nevada, New Mexico, Texas, Oklahoma, Kansas, Missouri, Oregon, Nevada, Utah, Wyoming, Colorado, Nebraska, North and South Dakota, Iowa, Illinois, Ohio, Michigan, Pennsylvania" sent a total of $580,719 from 1922 to 1931, with an annual average of $58,071.90.[19] Taylor added that the majority of Arandans who had experienced immigration "spent their money as fast as it was earned, in the United States, in Mexico or in both countries, for food and clothing for themselves and families or for pleasures of various kinds." Moreover, he stated: "For the most part, the material gains were ephemeral." San Ignacians' economic development thus stands in stark contrast to their regional predecessors who had initiated their migratory patterns in the early decades of the twentieth century.

The economy of San Ignacio was stimulated by the rapid expansion of small businesses such as construction companies, which boomed due to the demand for construction of houses, financed mainly by immigrants. Bars, restaurants, and small retail businesses sprang up. A study showed that 12 percent of the businesses in San Ignacio in 2001 were subsidized by dollars coming from the immigrants.[20] In 2002, after living in Detroit for five years, Gaby and her husband, Gabriel, returned to San Ignacio because of their son's illness. While in Detroit, Gaby worked in a nail salon, where she learned how to make acrylic nails and offer pedicures and manicures. On her return to San Ignacio she and her husband invested in a small retail store, where Gaby offered her services as a pedicurist and manicurist. Like Gaby, many San Ignacians invested in small retail stores with skills acquired in Detroit. By the end of the twentieth century Detroit and San Ignacio had obviously become interdependent parts of a complex transnational economic network, and the immigrants became active contributors to the economies of both their sending and adopted communities.

TRANSNATIONAL POLITICAL TIES: BECOMING A *MUNICIPIO*

The rising economic participation of immigrants in San Ignacio has contributed to their social status as influential (though mostly absent) members of the community. It has also given many of them a measure of political clout. One illustration of this is the immigrants' role in San Ignacio's successful effort to become a *municipio* (municipality). This politically and economically motivated attempt to become independent from Arandas exemplifies the transnational identities that evolve as unique phenomena of the immigrant experience. In this particular case, both San Ignacians and San Ignacian Detroiters joined forces to accomplish a goal that would benefit them regardless of their geographical residence and/or permanence.

The states of Mexico are divided into *municipios*, which in turn are divided into *delegaciones*. Local authorities called *cabezas municipales* con-

The kiosk adorned San Ignacio's main plaza and was also the main stage for socio-religious and political events. During the political meetings for San Ignacio to become a municipio, *the kiosk served as a political platform where representatives of the Comité para un Nuevo Municipio held their meetings.*

trol and allocate state and federal funding intended for the localities and decide where and how local budgets will be spent. Until 2007, when San Ignacio Cerro Gordo held its first municipal elections, it belonged to the *delegación* of Cerro Gordo, which belongs to the *municipio* of Arandas in the state of Jalisco. Many San Ignacians had grown discontented with Arandas's lack of consideration for their particular needs and expressed suspicion about the integrity of representatives such as the *presidente municipal* (municipal president), who allegedly favored his interests over those of San Ignacio. San Ignacians claimed that Arandas misspent the money by favoring structural developments only in Arandas, such as the construction of a new highway or paving streets and supporting improved public services. With immigration, San Ignacio's infrastructure has grown rapidly, resulting in new jobs (mainly in construction) and an increase in small businesses. Although Arandas did not receive dollars directly from the immigrants, it was benefiting through its infrastructural developments and through federal and state funds. San Ignacians not only wanted to take control of the funds allocated by the federal and state governments but also sought the freedom to initiate any structural and infrastructural changes to their town without having to go through Arandas, just like the experience they had with the renovation of the plaza and the construction of the *kiosco*.

San Ignacians began their efforts to break away from Arandas and become a separate *municipio* in the early 1990s, but the state's legislature continually turned them down. Historically, because of Mexico's political tendency toward centralization, *municipios* did not have a large role in local development. In the 1980s national authorities seeking to promote decentralization placed new emphasis on the role of the *municipios* as agents of national development.[21] The state of Jalisco resisted this sharing of power, however, and had not created any new *municipios* since 1946. San Ignacio began its advocacy in the 1990s. This made it harder for the citizens of San Ignacio to move toward becoming a new *municipio*.[22]

State authorities imposed several prerequisites for achieving *municipio* status. One was territorial size. According to a study conducted by the University of Guadalajara in 2001, San Ignacio easily met the criteria that the law called for in this respect. The other requirement was sufficient population. San Ignacio had 17,530 residents in 2000, accounting for 0.3 percent of the total population of the state of Jalisco. The University of Guadalajara study found that 45 percent of the 124 municipios in Jalisco had fewer residents than San Ignacio.[23] But San Ignacio was still denied the right to become a *municipio* on the grounds of population and territorial size, although the latter objection was later dismissed. Finally, Jalisco's state congress approved San Ignacio's becoming a *municipio* on December 4, 2003, making San Ignacio the 125th municipality in the state of Jalisco. This congressional approval went into effect in September 2005. The approval was based on meeting requirements for population (including the immigrants in Detroit), territorial size, and the economic ability to develop independently.

As early as 2000 San Ignacians had put forth a new argument. Immigrants living in Detroit who had been active participants in the economy of the *delegación* of Cerro Gordo should be counted toward the population numbers needed to meet the demographic threshold for becoming a *municipio*. As a result of this, San Ignacians living in Detroit began to get actively involved in the effort to promote municipalization.

While I was conducting interviews in San Ignacio from 2001 through 2004, there were several mobilizations of the entire town to promote the *municipio* project. In tandem with patriarchal nationalist political pro-

cesses, however, men were the only representatives of the future govern-
ing body for this San Ignacian *delegación*, thus completely undermining
women's political participation. My research, interviews, and images at-
test to the participation of women during long meetings as well as in the
marches held in Guadalajara. Women, however, were not included in the
Comité para un Nuevo Municipio (Committee for a New *Municipio*).
The committee held meetings at the plaza, using the *kiosco* as a platform.
As a component of this male-dominated regional political resistance
movement, the committee (seeking to get the town involved in the process) hired musicians who played *banda* music on the plaza after some
of the meetings were adjourned. This happened more often during the
months when returning immigrants attended the meetings. Male immigrants were encouraged to participate in political platforms while female
immigrants were associated with subsidizing the church's renovations,
celebrations, and religious economic needs.

Local authorities in San Ignacio, specifically the Committee for a New
Municipio, made the arguments for municipalization in terms that emphasized the immigrants' contributions and the town's enduring link with
Detroit. José, the president of the committee and many townspeople's
favorite to become municipal president in the 2007 elections, commented
on the expected benefits of becoming independent from Arandas:

> The first benefit will be that our people or we, the local authorities,
> will be able to decide the future of our town. Second, we will be able
> to rely on the money that legally belongs to us [he meant indirectly
> dollars from Detroit and state and local allocations] and use it to de-
> velop services to make the town more attractive, such as taking care of
> our environment and strengthening the cultural links with cities in the
> United States . . . When we become a *municipio*, we will create a sister
> city relationship with Detroit.[24]

It is important to emphasize here that José's "we" means San Ignacians in
Detroit and in San Ignacio, but more specifically "we" means men since
there were no women on the committee and no allusions to women becoming members of "the local authorities." It was clear to me that the
nationalist/regional message of becoming an autonomous entity was gendered male, and the expected messiahs for this transnational body were
San Ignacian men residing both in San Ignacio and in Detroit.

Tori, an immigrant businessman living in Detroit, emphasized how
important it was for San Ignacians in Detroit to accomplish the goal of
becoming independent from Arandas:

Now they [the regional authorities] want to take away some of our territory so that we do not qualify [to become a *municipio*]. But we have qualified already, and they can't just take our territory away from us. Arandas is supposed to govern us this year [2004] and the next, but in 2006 we'll begin to elect a municipal president and by 2007 San Ignacio will become completely independent. The reason for breaking away is because Arandas has kept San Ignacio very marginalized. It is estimated that between 26 and 28 million pesos flow annually from here [Detroit] to San Ignacio in remittances. Arandas never gave us anything. Everything went to Arandas and not even to better their public services; it usually went into the pockets of the authorities [in Arandas].[25]

Tori had been living in Detroit since 1970. The owner of a money-transfer business, he had been an active participant in Detroit's economy since he opened the first Mexican *taquería* and ice cream parlor in the early 1990s in Mexican Town. These two small businesses also served as job stepping-stones for new arrivals, particularly women who worked for Tori as waitresses and cooks. Yet more than three decades after moving to the United States, he still used the pronouns "we" and "us" when talking about the town of San Ignacio. Like Tori, many immigrants who have lived for years in Detroit still consider themselves proud citizens of San Ignacio and remain involved in the town's political, economic, and social life.

GENDERED ATTITUDES TOWARD U.S. CITIZENSHIP

Men tended to boast when given the platform to express their understandings about transnational citizenship, placing particular importance and emphasis on their contributions—political, social, and economic—to their community of origin. They proudly pointed to the building of the plaza and their political triumph of becoming a *municipio* in the state of Jalisco. In general, for San Ignacian men, local identity trumped state or national affiliation. Their sociopolitical existence in the United States also brought about a great deal of anxiety, however, as José commented:

It's a place with a lot of opportunity to grow and prosper, but the legal insecurity makes you feel unstable; you can't put down roots. And that was difficult for me as a person. I was in a place where I wanted to prosper but at the same time I did not have the legal right to stay in the country. . . . But I liked it a lot. . . . I didn't feel that I had the possibility to participate as a citizen.[26]

The anxiety about a denied "imagined dual-citizenship" undermined Mexican men's ideologies about citizenship and legality in the United States.

Many women, however, tended to emphasize their interest in civic and political recognition in the receiving community—Detroit and the United States. Their discourses focused on the politics of movement; in other words, women translated "transnational citizenship" into a pseudo-freedom of movement from one nation-state to the other. While women's discourses about citizenship centered on movement and familial dislocations, men's discourses offered a patriarchal gendered male (trans)nationalist participation in "men-only politics" in their community of origin (such as accomplishing independence from Arandas). Vivi (twenty-eight), an undocumented San Ignacian residing in Detroit, expressed her worries about transnational movement, saying that she would never cross through the desert again because the experience had been so frightening and that it would be better for her to stay in Detroit.[27] Vivi had not seen her mother and two younger siblings for four years prior to the interview. Her major worry was that her mother had not met her younger daughter, and she was afraid to think when they would reunite again. The mobility of men, however restricted by their illegal status, is much more fluid than women's. Edna A. Viruell-Fuentes interviewed forty Mexican women from Jalisco residing in the United States and found that "while some women had not visited family—sometimes for years—their husbands had done so with much more regularity, regardless of the husbands' documented status."[28] Thus her findings support the gendered nature of the politics of movement across two generations.

Historically women's movement in public spaces has been restricted by patriarchal systems that believed women should remain in domestic spaces. Working-class women on both sides of the border, however, continuously challenged these regulations. Transnational movement entails a whole new set of sexist ideologies dominated by male hegemony, scrutinizing the general movement of women and in particular their movement from one nation-state to the next.[29] Adelaida R. Del Castillo suggested the repercussions of "state sovereignty in the United States[, which] has been disrupted by the unauthorized practice of social citizenship by illegal immigrant Mexicans, forcing a rethinking of social, political and human rights and nationhood status."[30] The experience of San Ignacians demonstrates that Mexican immigrant women contest definitions of sociopolitical citizenship by their mere existence within and active participation in the receiving nation-state—the United States. Within this framework, San Ignacian women seek to be recognized as sociopolitical citizens in the receiving community in order to be able to travel back and forth and ameliorate some of the emotional and physical hardship that an "illegal" status confers on them. Some of these transnational dislocations include what Pierrette Hondagneu-Sotelo and Ernestine Avila have defined as "transnational motherhood."[31] They point to the emotional and physical stress that Latina immigrants undergo while their families are dislocated and dismembered as an inherent process of the politics of transnational mobility.[32]

My friend Gaby narrated the serious and irreparable repercussions of her experience—both emotional and physical—when she was pregnant with her son, including one of the reasons why she thinks her son was born three months premature with a muscular disease:

> [It] was a combination of many things, only God knows why certain things happened. We had just purchased our home [in Detroit] and I had to clean it all up by myself. The house was very dirty, it was disgusting, and I had to make sure it was clean. At that same time, my brother went to jail and I was very worried because my mother [in San Ignacio] didn't know what was happening and I had to lie to her. We used to tell my mother that my brother had gone to work somewhere else. I was very worried and then we had a tornado advisory in Detroit. So I think that in a way my body just exploded.[33]

Viruell-Fuentes also found that "family needs in Mexico often required that immigrant women in the United States extend their care-taking roles across borders. [They] also bore the brunt of the emotional toil that maintaining these relationships entailed."[34] This emotional toil combined with the sustenance of the social networks that support immigration influenced the way Mexican immigrant women defined themselves as (trans)national "citizens" in relation to their new "home" in the United States.

In part because of their disenfranchised status, experiences of transnational dislocation and hostile environments in the United States, and ideologies about the politics of movement, San Ignacian women in Detroit regard U.S. citizenship as a highly desirable commodity that ultimately will grant them the coveted "holy grail" for an undocumented immigrant. Above all this is perceived to mean freedom of mobility and an acquisition of power and status within the family and the transnational community. Those who are eligible to apply for citizenship have readily done so, although they faced many sociopolitical barriers. Tina recalled:

A great miracle happened to me: I became a U.S. citizen without knowing English. My husband and I applied through a church [in Detroit]. We took the test and submitted our documents. We paid $150 for everything, and all the questions that Immigration is supposed to ask you, they [the church] asked us and we practiced the answers. We got a call from Immigration, and my husband went. They asked him what were the three branches of government and he said, "I don't know." They told him to wait until he had fifteen years of residency status or until he was fifty-five years old to take the exam in Spanish.[35]

Tina pointed out the extreme challenge that applying for citizenship entailed while at the same time devaluing her husband's vain efforts to accomplish the same goal—to become a U.S. citizen. They were separated from their children when they migrated to Detroit. This separation almost drove Tina crazy. Her acquired citizenship status guaranteed that she would never have to risk her life or that of her offspring, because now she could sponsor her children's citizenships as well. She emphasized:

As for me, I got my appointment and I went there on a Monday fasting and putting my fate in the hands of our Lord. "If he wants me to, I'll become a citizen or at the very least be able to stay as a legal permanent resident." I answered their questions and I only missed one word: when I wrote two sentences in English I wrote "lobe" instead of "love." Then the woman from Immigration asked, "Do you believe in the Constitution?" and I answered, "No." And she replied [in disbelief], "What? Listen to me again." So she repeated the question and I said, "Yes, yes, yes!" And she said, "Okay, bye-bye."[36]

Like other San Ignacians in Detroit, Tina considered it important to gain recognition as a citizen of her new country. She was proud of her success in navigating the citizenship exam even though she did not speak much English. She seemed especially pleased that she had prevailed while her husband had been unable to accomplish their mutual goal. Her narrative also shows how Mexicanas took opportunities—albeit small and few—to generate an ideology of gender superiority in an effort to maintain gender dignity. Not only did Mexican women who applied for citizenship frame their discourses as an accomplishment in relation to their mates (as in Tina's case)—they also framed their citizenship as an accomplishment vis-à-vis the state. Doña Luna became a U.S. citizen in 1979, overcoming the barrier of low literacy. She remembered:

I became a citizen and nobody believed me [because I barely know how to read or write]. When we went to get my passport they asked how I could possibly become a citizen without knowing how to read or write and why my certificate of citizenship was not signed. So they investigated. Finally, I made them laugh when I signed with an X.[37]

Doña Luna's pride in having achieved the impossible underscores the importance that Mexican Detroiters attached to being recognized by their adopted community, a recognition that is symbolized by citizenship status.

Yet citizenship could not address all the challenges that women faced. Despite the many economic, social, and cultural contributions that San Ignacians have made to Detroit, their status as aliens has persisted.[38] Moreover, pernicious stereotypes of Mexican inferiority and white superiority are embedded in U.S. culture and politics, and San Ignacians often face hostile attitudes in Detroit. As the alternate consul in Detroit noted, Mexican immigrants must develop self-defense mechanisms to "survive in this society that provides clothing and protection and offers them the opportunity to work but also insults them and discriminates against them."[39] One way that Mexican immigrants react to this feeling of being unwelcome is by maintaining strong ties to San Ignacio as their place of origin. The militarization of the border through projects such as Operation Gatekeeper has made crossing very risky, however, vastly complicating their efforts to live transnational lives.[40]

Ideologies about citizenship are gendered: Mexican immigrant men and Mexican immigrant women experienced sociopolitical and economic disenfranchisement in vastly different ways—for the men it implied political recognition in the community of origin (among other things), while the women sought freedom of movement and familial reunification in their receiving community. San Ignacians in general shared one main preoccupation, however, while experiencing transnationalism: accomplishing a sense of inclusion and a sense of belonging—social recognition through economic participation.

CHALLENGES OF TRANSNATIONAL LIFE IN A DECLINING DETROIT

San Ignacians arriving in Detroit sought to build a community where they could feel a sense of safety and belonging. A key way of gaining this security was by owning their homes. Since the 1970s, when Doña Tita arrived with her family, San Ignacians have been purchasing homes in Mexican Town. Many recall wistfully how inexpensive their houses were when they bought them several decades ago. Tina and Saúl came in the late 1970s. "We arrived in Detroit on a Monday and by Wednesday we had already purchased a house for $15,000 cash. . . . We borrowed half the money and the other half we contributed ourselves."[41]

Don Chuy's son Jaime left for Detroit in 1989 and brought his family a year later. In 1991 Jaime and his wife, Irma, bought their first property. He joked about the low prices they paid: "We bought the house two years after we arrived. It was very expensive [he laughs]. It cost $5,000, there in Mexican Town where all the San Ignacians live." Irma said:

> We bought the house on a Tuesday. We filled out all the paperwork and gave them the money. And on Thursday the house next door burned down. It didn't burn down completely, only the plastic melted. On Friday we urgently needed to move there. Because the other one was burned, and there was danger that it might ignite. So they cleaned up and demolished the burned house and only the lot was left. We bought that lot as well.

Jaime added: "I fixed up the house. It was not very pretty. I bought the lot next door, very expensive as well—I paid $300 [he laughs]. Just a few months ago we had someone from the bank appraise the house and they offered me $70,000."[42]

Housing segregation in Detroit after World War II meant that the immigrants' choices of where to buy were mostly limited to the area now known as Mexican Town. Banks would not provide mortgages to African Americans or Mexicans. Houses in the southwest quadrant were cheap, but the neighborhood was run-down. Banks along with landlords and real estate agents discouraged investment in the sections of the city where African Americans or Mexicans lived, and the city steadily decreased public and social services to minority neighborhoods.[43]

In his 1996 book *The Origins of the Urban Crisis: Race and Inequality in Postwar Detroit*, Thomas Sugrue analyzes the systemic segregation and marginalization of the city's African Americans in the decades following World War II—a process that also affected the smaller Mexican population. He highlights three interrelated trends that began in the 1950s: deindustrialization, racial discrimination in labor markets, and racial segregation in housing.[44] Detroit went from being one of the most important manufacturing cities in the nation to becoming a rust-belt relic, losing more than half its population in a span of fifty years. While Mexican immigrants were buying houses in Detroit, a massive white exodus to the suburbs was underway, leaving behind working-class African Americans and working-class Mexican immigrants in decaying neighborhoods.[45] This shrinking urban population, along with the economic hardships that the city was enduring, led urban authorities to curtail public and social services such as health care, education, maintenance of streets and lighting, police, and garbage collection.[46] Marie Farrell-Donaldson, Detroit's ombudsperson, remarked in 2004: "We have streets with one person living on them, yet you still have to provide streetlights for that street. You still have to provide police protection. You still have to provide fire protection. We should move those people out."[47] Farrell-Donaldson's tone ("move those people out") emphasized the disposability of Mexicans in the minds of local authorities. Despite Mexican immigrants' development of (trans)national attachments to their new "home" in Detroit, they remained foreigners in Euro-Americans' collective imaginary.

The Mexicans who arrived in Detroit in the early 1970s witnessed first-hand the effects of deindustrialization and urban decline. Many were unaware of the general economic situation of the city, however, and tended to blame the slow decay of their neighborhoods on the incoming waves of new Mexican immigrants. Doña Tita commented on the changes she had noticed since her arrival in Detroit:

> Nowadays people play soccer in Patton Park. Clark Park is much closer to us, but since some young people were killed there, now they only play on one side. It's not very safe in that area anymore. In the past it was not so dangerous. Before, when we lived there it was almost all *americanos* [Euro-Americans]. There were not a lot of Mexicans, very few. It was so much prettier back then, the street was very nice. They never discriminated against us; on the contrary they were friendly to us. But then they left, and more Mexicans arrived.[48]

Patton Park is a good example of the city's reluctance to provide public and social services in Mexican Town. The space was not officially recognized as a park by the city of Detroit, which meant that Mexicans who attended soccer games on Sundays in the summer had to provide and pay for garbage collection, portable toilets, and security. Doña Tita's comment emphasized her own class bias toward her fellow townspeople, but it also signaled her internalization of the pejorative stereotypes of Mexicans that pervade the U.S. collective imagination. Unaware of the outside forces driving the slow decay of the inner city, Doña Tita condemned her fellow Mexicans for worsening her neighborhood.

Doña Tita's daughter-in-law Alina (fifty) echoed these sentiments:

> I don't know if we Latinos ourselves are changing [the neighborhood]. I think that our children and young men [she refers to them as *cholos*] are. There is nothing left. It wasn't like today, it was much prettier. There were no burned houses.[49]

Alina emphasized the idea that it was young Mexican men who had made the neighborhood "more dangerous."

San Ignacians are still buying houses in Detroit, but it is not as easy as in years past. Even in Mexican Town houses are much more expensive now. Moreover, Mexican immigrants' social invisibility, especially in the case of undocumented immigrants, makes them easy prey for financial predators. Nena's story is an example:

> Lately we have not had much money because they robbed us here in the house. We bought a house from a [expletive] man and apparently he had taken out several loans on the house, and the bank took the house from us. Something was wrong with the finances of the house from the beginning. It was a fraud, and he stole $35,000 from us. We went to see a lawyer and we are still battling this, but apparently there is not a lot that we can do.[50]

Nena's financial fiasco exemplified how vulnerable undocumented San Ignacians were to social vultures that capitalized on the social and political invisibility of Mexican immigrants.

TRANSNATIONAL IDENTITIES: GENDER AND GENERATIONAL DIFFERENCES

Despite the economic hardships that they experienced in a deindustrializing Detroit, San Ignacian immigrants slowly constructed a dynamic transnational community. In the process they developed a sense of transnational identity and citizenship that reflected strong personal ties to both their sending and their receiving communities. This construction of a strong collective identity helped Mexicanos and Mexicanas endure and resist the negative sides of life in Detroit—the hostility they encountered from other residents and the frustrations of living in a marginal neighborhood with few public and social services. But this identity construction was not without conflict, especially in relation to the dilemma of whether to remain permanently in Detroit or return to San Ignacio.

In 2001, after residing in Detroit for thirty-one years, Doña Tita returned to live permanently in San Ignacio because her health had declined. But she expressed conflicted feelings.

> I really liked being there [Detroit]. If it were up to me I would have stayed there, but my husband and daughters wanted to come back. I was very comfortable there. . . . I even worked here and there cleaning houses and office buildings. I also worked in a restaurant in the kitchen. Now everything is so grand here in San Ignacio because of all the people from here that live in Detroit. . . . Whole families move from here [to Detroit]; even the young women leave and make money and buy a house. The houses in Detroit are much more expensive now than they were back then. I want to go back. I have a daughter-in-law who has told me, "Come and live with me, the house has plenty of bedrooms"—the house that used to be mine. Yes, I think I will go back.[51]

Since the bracero era, the accumulation of capital has radically reshaped Mexican immigrants' identities. In the 1940s and 1950s braceros mostly performed manual labor, similar to what they had done in San Ignacio, and their priority was to send home any surplus earnings to support their families in Mexico. In the 1960s former braceros who moved to Detroit became industrial workers and gained greater purchasing power. With the arrival of Mexicanas in Detroit in the 1970s and 1980s, San Ignacians became active economic participants in their adopted community by purchasing homes in Detroit for their families. By the 1990s many immigrants had accumulated sufficient capital to invest in both San Ignacio and Detroit, becoming heroines and heroes in the eyes of the San Ignacio townspeople for their contributions to the town.

The accumulation of capital also enabled many Detroit San Ignacians to plan for a comfortable retirement in Mexico. Older men from the bracero generation, in particular, expressed a desire to return to San Ignacio permanently in their old age. The Hernández brothers, for example, all went back to live in San Ignacio when they retired. Delfino, Rubén, and Jesús have passed away, but Don Gabriel is still alive and resides in San Ignacio.

> My intention since I left [to work in the United States] was to try to save, to try to earn enough to come back here to rest. . . . I didn't think that I was going to live past fifty, but here I am turning seventy. I say

that life is too short and to work every day until the end of your days is not worth it.[52]

Don Gabriel's comment exemplifies the bracero generation's attitudes toward *el norte*. Their purpose in leaving home was to earn a better living and provide for their families. The United States gave them this opportunity, but their identities remained rooted in their sending communities. Unlike his children, who all reside permanently in Detroit, Don Gabriel envisioned returning to San Ignacio to enjoy the fruits of his labors and the respect of his fellow townspeople. Don Chuy, another pioneer of the transnational community, returned to San Ignacio in 1974 permanently because of ill health. Don Manuel and Don Raúl, also from the bracero generation, have moved back to San Ignacio, even though their descendants all reside in Detroit.

Most of their wives have passed away, but several wives who are still alive and now live in San Ignacio expressed their desire to go back to Detroit. Indeed, gender differences were evident on the question of where to spend their retirement years. Older men tended to regard San Ignacio as the place where they wanted to spend their last years, whereas older women typically wanted to live out their lives in Detroit in order to be near their children and grandchildren. Older men seemed to value their status as regional and hometown heroes and to tie their sense of self-worth to their social position in San Ignacio. Although they had made good lives in Detroit, many never really felt that they belonged there. In San Ignacio, however, they are admired for their success as immigrants, and younger San Ignacians consult them when they plan a journey north. Older women, by contrast, most valued staying with their families in Detroit, where they enjoyed a collective strength that made them feel secure and comfortable. The social networks that sustain the flow of San Ignacian migration were managed and nurtured by women in Detroit, so it is not surprising that Mexicanas preferred to stay there with their families. Nonetheless, these women continued to own *casas solas* even if they decided to retire in Detroit.

Like women of the bracero generation, younger Mexicanas valued being near family members and tended to regard Detroit as their community of choice. Many aspired to own a home in Mexican Town. But there were generational differences in women's attitudes. For older Mexicanas, the presence of Euro-Americans in Mexican Town "made the neighborhood better." They saw the deterioration of the area as the result of too many Mexicans moving in rather than as related to larger forces of deindustrialization and racial segregation. Younger Mexicanas expressed more cynicism about life in Detroit. They recognized the reality of living in a harsh and racist environment in which resources were distributed unfairly and citizenship was narrowly defined. Younger women were acutely aware of the shortage and poor quality of public and social services in Mexican Town.

Gaby, whose child was born with a muscular disorder, was in the process of suing the hospital where her child had been delivered. She remembered how the resident on call had tried to delay the birth, resulting, she believes, in damage to the baby. Gaby and most of her family members are socially invisible "aliens" in Detroit, but this did not stop her from seeking justice. Her determination to seek accountability and provide for her child's future reflects the attitudes of a younger generation of Mexicanas. Women like Gaby are initiating an ideology of accountability for the institutionalized racism embedded in social structures in Detroit.

DEPORTABLE ALIENS OR HOMETOWN HEROES?

While taking me on a tour of the neighborhood, Gaby showed me the local elementary school, where most of the students are of Mexican origin. We joked about the fact that the school proudly displayed by its main entrance the flags of fifteen different countries, but not the Mexican flag. Despite the large population of Mexicans, Chicanas/os, and other Latinas/os in the neighborhood, racialized institutions such as schools continue to discriminate against Mexicans no matter where they were born (the United States or Mexico). This is highlighted by the racist persecution and sociopolitical and economic marginalization of Mexican Americans and Chicanas/os since the U.S. conquest of half of the Mexican territory in 1848.

Continuing on the tour, we passed several burned houses (not uncommon in the neighborhood) and piles of garbage in what used to be front and back yards. I had my video camera on, but Gaby turned to me and said, "No, Luz María, don't tape that!" When I asked why not, she responded, "People who watch the video will think the whole neighborhood is like that." Her reaction underlined her pride in her community, her acknowledgment of the lack of public services, and her rejection of the idea that Mexicans are responsible for the abandonment and deterioration we saw around us. It also emphasized her awareness of the pernicious stereotypes surrounding Mexican immigrants and their desire to take an active role in shaping their own identity and image.

Much of this stereotyping centers on the notion of the immigrant as alien—as a noncitizen who is in the country illegally and is therefore deportable. Nicholas De Genova and Ana Y. Ramos-Zayas write:

> Insofar as the institution of U.S. citizenship is commonly presumed to differentiate subjects in relation to the power of the nation-state, differences, divisions, and inequalities are elaborated in terms of "citizenship" and "immigration": Who is a U.S. citizen? Who is a "foreigner," or an "alien"? Who is eligible for citizenship? Who is deportable? And moreover, who is a "real American"?[53]

In the minds of many Euro-Americans, Mexican Americans, Chicanas/os, and Mexican immigrants will always be deportable aliens, regardless of their actual immigration status. This provides a rationale for denying Mexican immigrants and people of Mexican descent in the United States opportunities, equal access to resources, and even the right to occupy the spaces where they live and work. Moreover, it serves to validate the country's historically racist and oppressive practices against Mexican Americans, Chicanas/os, and Mexican immigrants. These attitudes often are absorbed and internalized by Mexican immigrants and people of Mexican descent. While they are denied citizenship and social recognition in the United States, they continue to strengthen and constantly redefine their self-identification as citizens of their own transnational community.

This social exclusion in the adopted country stands in stark contrast to the immigrants' position in their hometown. San Ignacians living in Detroit become heroes and heroines in the eyes of fellow townspeople in San Ignacio when they invest in their sending community's economy. Contrary to their lowly social position in Detroit, in San Ignacio the immigrants gain upward social mobility when they flaunt their monetary success by parading cars, clothing, jewelry, cell phones, and other consumer goods during visits. One of the most important ways in which immigrants enhance their prestige is by building new and elaborate homes in San Ignacio. Homes built with Detroit dollars now dot the landscape of the town.

The San Ignacian homes built by both working-class female and male immigrants appeared very luxurious. On a walking tour in San Ignacio an older woman showed me her construction site and then two other houses that belonged to her brothers, who were living in the United States. Her brothers' homes were as elegant as hers; and she let me know that both houses stood empty most of the year, since the brothers only came to San Ignacio for the patron saint festivities in January. As I walked along with

One of the many San Ignacian casas solas *cared for by close female relatives of San Ignacian immigrants. This house in particular was replicated from a small advertisement in a real estate magazine from California. The immigrants imported the two palm trees from California as well. Martha, a close relative of the family, gave me a tour of the house while explaining the choices for tile, woodwork, paint colors, and furniture. All of this was supervised directly by her sister, who resided in California at the time.*

her, I realized that what she was doing was showing off her family's immigrant success.

This was my first encounter with what San Ignacians call *las casas solas* (the empty houses). I had heard about these houses when I was in Detroit, listening to Mexican women talk in Patton Park. The houses became symbols of economic success and upward mobility. Mexicanas would compete with each other, boasting about how much money they had spent laying down floors, designing kitchen cabinets, and so forth, while consulting each other on what colors would be best for the different bedrooms and what pictures would look good on the walls.

Investing in the construction of new houses and making renovations to their existing homes in San Ignacio were two of the most important goals of San Ignacian women in Detroit. They would travel back and forth to Mexico in order to supervise the construction or renovation work and to decorate and furnish the new house. Most of these houses were exact replicas of houses in the United States. Immigrants would peruse real estate magazines, choosing pictures of the houses they liked best and then seek out architects in Mexico who could reproduce them. This left San Ignacio with a very eclectic architectural style. The construction of a new home generally involved the whole extended family, with women in San Ignacio acting as caretakers of the *casas solas*. When I walked by the empty houses I got the impression that they were not really *casas solas*, because most of the time the doors were slightly open at certain times, the curtains were drawn open, and the yards and plants were perfectly landscaped and cared for, thus emphasizing the "absence/presence" of the *hijos/as ausentes*.

For the immigrants, their exalted citizenship in the San Ignacio community contrasted with the negation of their citizenship status in the United States. Their economic and social participation in their hometown gave them a sense of belonging that alleviated the pain of their marginalization in Detroit. Moving back and forth between center and periphery, between hero and "illegal alien," Mexicanos and Mexicanas developed different notions of what it means to be a citizen of a transnational community. In their collective imagination, most of them fantasized about returning to San Ignacio to retire in their newly built or renovated homes. The contested terrain in Detroit is seen as integral to laboring for a better future.

Not many San Ignacians have returned to San Ignacio as they planned, however. The *casas solas* remain for the most part uninhabited, except when immigrants return for the *fiestas patronales* during the fall and winter months. These luxurious homes stand as symbols of how San Ignacians have constructed their concepts of citizenship and belonging. Since most Mexicanos and Mexicanas will make arrangements to have their bodies sent back to San Ignacio when they die, these homes in a sense become giant resting places that will house them if not during their lives then at least at the end.

As successive generations of San Ignacians become more firmly rooted in Detroit, they continue going back to San Ignacio to reaffirm their transnational citizenship and celebrate their status as hometown heroines and heroes. The number of *hijas/os ausentes* lined up behind the Aztec dancers for the grand procession to the plaza during the *fiestas patronales* continues to grow. As Gel put it, "Yes, next year we will risk it [crossing the border again for familial reunification and the fiestas]. After all, everybody crosses, come what may."[54] They march with pride and dignity while the band plays in the *kiosco* and their fellow San Ignacians look on respectfully, acknowledging the immigrants' success. It is this recognition that provides San Ignacians both in San Ignacio and in Detroit with a true transnational citizenship that rewards their struggles and their courage in building new lives amid the racism and discrimination in the United States.

CONCLUSIONS

Luis's excitement filled the living room of the small three-bedroom house that Gaby and Gabriel owned in San Ignacio while awaiting the arrival of his father from Detroit. In the five years that I spent doing research in San Ignacio Cerro Gordo and in Detroit I witnessed two familial reunions of loved ones who had been dislocated by immigration. Gaby and her husband immigrated to Detroit permanently in 1997. Gabriel's family had moved to Detroit a few years earlier (they were all documented through their uncle, who had been a bracero); and when Gabriel and Gaby got married they moved to Detroit. After the birth of their son, who was born with a muscular disease, they were forced to travel back and forth from Mexico to the United States because they chose to have surgery for their son in Mexico. Their experience with health institutions in the United States was far from positive; in fact it was a very contested experience (both Gaby and Gabriel feel that the hospital where their child was born was responsible for his physical malady).

Gaby and Gabriel moved to Mexico for two years so that their son would get the best care in Mexico. After six months in Mexico, however, they both decided that Gabriel needed to return to Detroit to work because the retail store that they had opened a couple of months after their arrival in San Ignacio was not doing as well as they thought it would. Gabriel took the trip back to Detroit in order to work and help support the household and cover the high hospital bills.

Within a year Gabriel went back to San Ignacio for a short visit. I waited with Gaby and Luis, who could hardly contain his emotions and was eager to see his father. When Gabriel arrived at their home, it was quite an emotional spectacle. The room was filled with joy, excitement, and the smell of new plastic toys that Gabriel kept pulling out of his luggage. Cousins, friends, neighbors, and other San Ignacian onlookers gathered around the main door, looking at all the consumer goods that Gabriel had acquired for his family to compensate for his absence and to prove that he had been successful.

Two years later I witnessed a completely different reunion. At the end of the two years Gaby and Gabriel were ready to go back "home" to Detroit. Gabriel and Luis (one a green card holder, the other a U.S. citizen) were able to take a plane from Guadalajara to Detroit. Gaby was undocumented, however, so her trip back was a much more obscure venture (she had been waiting to be "legal" for more than five years to get her visa number). She had just arrived from Canada, where she had been arrested for a week. Gaby and a few other Mexicans had been caught hiding in railroad boxcars while trying to cross the U.S.-Canadian border. They were all arrested and imprisoned for a week. She had been humiliated, mistreated, starved, and, sadly, deprived of seeing or hearing about her son's recovery after the long trip from Mexico soon after his surgery. Throughout this week Gabriel and Luis knew nothing of Gaby's whereabouts. She finally crossed the border in Windsor, Canada, and was now being reunited with both her husband and child. Gaby stated that she would not dare cross the border again unless there was a death in the family.

Unlike Gabriel's welcoming in San Ignacio, Gaby's was the complete opposite; the monitoring of undocumented immigrants at the militarized U.S.-Mexico border outlines the gendered nature of transnational mobility. Notwithstanding the immigration status of Mexican immigrants in the United States, working-class Mexican men are more likely to have a less detrimental border-crossing experience than their female counterparts. Families who have been dislocated by the politics of movement suffer the implications of regulatory immigration apparatuses. Despite the general feminization of labor in the 1970s—a consequence of a service-oriented economy—female Mexican immigrants are much more at risk than are their San Ignacian brothers, fathers, male siblings, and male townspeople. This phenomenon illustrates the need to understand the gendered nature of transnational ties across the militarized U.S.-Mexico borderlands. It also points to the complexities and dislocations of transnational life and to the difficulty of the socially constructed meaning—as a diasporic subject—of an imagined "transnational citizenship."

This monograph has traced the lives of working-class Mexican immigrant women and men historically as protagonists of demographic, social, cultural, economic, and political changes in their own histories as they constructed their transnational community in San Ignacio Cerro Gordo and Detroit from 1942 to 2004. I began my study with the inception of the Bracero Program and its effect in initiating the flow of Mexican labor and the first stages of the formation of their transnational community. As Mexicanas from San Ignacio joined the braceros in Detroit, they laid the foundation of what was to become one of the most dynamic transnational communities in the city. I have argued that Mexicanas are the main protagonists in weaving and supporting the social networks that are inherent in the construction of transnational communities. Working-class Mexicanas bear the brunt of nurturing the social networks that sustain immigration. By contributing with both reproductive and paid labor, San Ignacian women construct and maintain a process that facilitates and enables immigration. Mexicanas accepted several townspeople in their homes while they got settled in their receiving community. Furthermore, these women often crossed translocal borders by adopting traditional male roles in the sending community, even becoming heads of households. My study has focused on the intersection of race, gender, class, sexuality, and citizenship that shapes and is shaped by the immigrant experience.

The immigrant experience needs to be analyzed through different lenses that look at the various ways that Mexicanos and Mexicanas construct their lives in their transnational community. In the case of Mexican immigrants and the creation of transnational communities, sexuality has been constantly informed, shaped, and reshaped by the immigrant experience. As gender historians of immigration we need to reconsider the meaning of transnationalism so that the experience of immigrants is not fragmented into two different spaces—their community of origin and the receiving community. I argue that both are integral to their everyday lives and therefore we need to consider them as one. Within this context I have introduced the concept of "transnational sexualities," which emphasizes the social constructions of sexuality informed by both experiences and how these in turn transform understandings of sexuality that apply to Mexicanas' and Mexicanos' everyday lives in San Ignacio and in Detroit. Mexicanas transgress male-dominated mores on "appropriate" dress codes that define women's purity and virtue and appropriate new transnational cultural ways to approach courting rituals that have been affected by immigration.

I argue that it is Mexicanas' productive and reproductive labor that maintains the social networks that are inherent in the sustainability of transnational communities. Through the deconstruction of these networks we can understand how Mexicanas created a community by being exposed to and participating in U.S. social structures such as schools and hospitals, through church-related activities, and through kinship. Kinship systems have been expanded to accommodate the immigrant experience, and thus reconfigurations of family hierarchies and structures have continuously changed and adapted to the needs of the transnational community. Mexicanas challenge traditional gender roles while they navigate within the contested spaces they create despite oppressive and patriarchal systems. Everyday processes affect social networks and gender struggles and tensions that derive from them. These tensions in turn affect notions of "femininity" and "masculinity," "motherhood" and "fatherhood," domesticity, and workers' identities.

Feminist approaches to Mexican and Latin American immigrant communities in the United States have emphasized the gains secured by immigrant women during the process in terms of gender awareness, reproductive rights, and separation from patriarchal structures in the traditional society. These analyses, however, have failed to recognize both the fluid nature of traditional patriarchal structures and the patriarchal nature of U.S. institutions. Moreover, they have failed to recognize that the immigrant experience for Mexican women has been both liberating and repressive. The roots of such misconceptions lay in the uncritical adoption of "zero sum" general approaches toward women immigrants, by which two opposite spaces (sending and receiving communities) struggle for the control and domination in social values and culture among immigrants.

The trajectories of women from San Ignacio prove that gender dynamics expand and create new and complex social spaces where the dominant patriarchal values are permanently renegotiated and readjusted by women's agency. Marriage rituals historically controlled and managed by the Catholic Church are now reconfiguring their structures to serve the immigrant community. The mandatory premarriage counseling sessions illustrate this phenomenon: they are now shorter and faster, providing an "express" version of services that address the immigrant community's needs. Absolution—a primary clause of Catholic religious belief systems—has now been molded to a transnational time-frame. Courting rituals are now explicitly centered around the immigrants' return calendar, and the choices for potential candidates are now enmeshed in the transnational experience. Far from conforming to a "zero sum" model, the immigrant experience multiplies and expands the gender dynamics between men and women to create a new matrix of networks where these two groups interact and bargain.

In deconstructing such interaction, my research suggests that the women's participation in the formation of transnational communities cannot be understood without analyzing the pivotal role of female reproductive labor. As discussed in Chapter 3, the creation of permanent and organic transnational ties between San Ignacio and Detroit has its foundations in the network activated and maintained by women's reproductive labor. New moral and emotional bonds formed among San Ignacians in Detroit as the immigrants stretched the meaning of familial obligation to include people from their hometown in addition to blood relatives. Working-class San Ignacian women positioned themselves (among other roles) as surrogate mothers to all the "guests" they welcomed in their homes. Thus their reproductive labor redefined the parameters of kinship systems in response to the unique imperatives of the immigrant experience. While current scholarship on immigrant women rightfully insists on the ramifications of female incorporation into the productive force, its inability to identify and analyze the effects of reproductive labor on the immigrant experience has had a negative impact on our understanding of transnational communities. These effects include the confrontational feelings that women faced while sustaining large numbers of people in tight accommodations: on the one hand the need to "help" co-nationals, but on the other the emotional and physical burden that this care entails.

The stories of San Ignacian families from the 1940s to the present illustrate the extent to which female reproductive labor has been the key element in the activation of a transnational network and the subsequent formation of a permanent community in Detroit. My study places a new emphasis on the significance of domestic and recreational spaces created by immigrant women in this process and the ways in which they use these so-called traditional areas to create the conditions for a permanent network between San Ignacio and Detroit as well as a permanent life in Detroit with permanent ties to San Ignacio. Patton Park in Detroit illustrates how women appropriated a public leisure space to build a transnational identity and to discuss important issues related to their shared immigrant experience.

Mexicanas gain power to negotiate gender relations by claiming ownership of their domestic space, where they are responsible for the caretaking of not only their immediate family but all the "guests" that might be staying with them. Furthermore, these responsibilities in a sense turned Mexicanas into surrogate mothers, daughters, and sisters of extended family, friends, and *comadres* or *compadres*. By expanding and readapting these "traditional" gender roles, women not only empower themselves in the migrant experience but also create the conditions in which families can better navigate between San Ignacio and Detroit and ultimately between Mexico and the United States.

My research shows that this fluid expansion of gender roles cannot be conceptualized as a "natural" decision to preserve or maintain values from the rural Mexican pueblo. The transition from a rural to an urban environment instead is only understood against the background of San Ignacio women's agency and crucial participation in the immigrant experience.

The analysis of reproductive behavior among San Ignacio immigrant women showcases the complex and vibrant dynamics between gender and immigration. Despite constant moral vigilantism by the religious authorities in both San Ignacio and Detroit, patriarchal behavior displays by San Ignacio men, and the socioeconomic pressures of their incorporation into the U.S. job market, women from San Ignacio have turned their reproductive practices into a highly contested terrain and have managed to find ways to reduce their fertility rates and the number of pregnancies in comparison to previous generations. While women of reproductive age in the 1940s and 1950s traditionally had large families, new generations in the 1980s and 1990s significantly reduced the number of children.[1]

By adopting an eclectic approach, from which they select information from Planned Parenthood programs in Mexico and the U.S. Spanish-language media talk shows, and by choosing not to abide by religious prescriptions, women have found venues to reduce fertility rates while complying with marital expectations. My research data strongly suggest that this considerable negotiating power vis-à-vis the church and the family traditional values and especially vis-à-vis the husband's authority highlights the women's newly enhanced position regarding reproduction and family planning.

This female agency, through which women have successfully renegotiated the implementation of different contraceptive methods (the patch, rhythm, *mi viejo me cuida* [my old man takes care of me]), exemplifies the way in which they have used the immigrant experience to enhance their position in the bed, the household, and the church.

My research shows the ways in which younger women have developed a new ability to negotiate with their partners by manipulating patriarchal power and praising men's notions of masculinity and allowing them to "take care" of women. In contrast, women from the past generations were unable to negotiate such situations, due mostly to the overwhelming patriarchal and ecclesiastic controls as well as the positive value placed on children as potential contributors to family labor.

In the immigrant experience, younger generations of women have created new ways to construct womanhood values that do not necessarily include a large number of children. While motherhood values have been expanded to include surrogate members or "guests," the standards for womanhood are no longer associated with having *los hijos que Dios me mande* (as many children as God sends me). These two elements—expanded motherhood roles and reduced fertility rates—provide defining characteristics of the Mexicanas' transnational sexualities, a crucial feature in our understanding of transnational communities.

Transnational sexualities certainly include premarital sex and new courtship patterns based on strong ideological changes both in Mexico and in the United States and, most importantly, on the circumstances developed within the immigrant experience. Constructed in their everyday lives in San Ignacio and in Detroit, transnational sexualities cannot be separated as two opposing and distinct experiences in the community of origin and in the receiving community; it is a new creation that informs Mexicanas' and Mexicanos' concepts of masculinity and femininity, which in turn inform gender negotiations that shape and are shaped by the immigrant experience. Immigration is not only a social process but a subjective conceptualization of living experiences that include agency and resistance within contested terrains in Mexico and in the United States.

My research shows that women in San Ignacio responded to the immigration trends by creating and reshaping courting rituals that better mirror their mate-choosing expectations and enhance their bargaining power before and during marriage.

Using, but not necessarily staying within, the social spaces created by local church and local authorities to celebrate the immigrant experience, local women have generated new venues to meet and select their potential life partners and accommodate to the time restraints on young male immigrants by Detroit's job market.

Perhaps unintentionally, the church has become an important influence in this process by enhancing and glorifying the return of the immigrants as part of the religious rituals during the *fiestas patronales.* Courting rituals have come a long way from peeking through holes in doors or walls to a more intimate contact and a more elaborate ritual of showing off material possessions to prove a successful immigrant experience. Within this context both men and women have expanded their range of choices in selecting either partners for temporary pleasure or potential marriage candidates.

While Mexicanas' transnational sexualities no longer attach a positive value to virginity or a negative value to premarital pregnancy, there is still a strong identification between love and marriage and between sexual intercourse and lifetime commitment. Nonetheless, self-awareness and body exploration of sexual identities are certainly becoming more important issues for younger generations.

Transnational sexualities not only have reshaped the life cycle of young women in San Ignacio but, no less importantly, also have had a profound impact on the local institutions. Local church officials, for instance, no longer refuse to marry pregnant women (for not attending premarital talks) or chastise them from the pulpit. The traditional stigmatization of single mothers, according to older women, has also loosened up, while local officials have recently started to marry people in the civil court to expedite the process, curbing the ecclesiastic hegemony on marriage.

The life around the *kiosco* during the immigrants' seasonal return has become a new central feature of local courtship rituals, replacing the traditional *serenatas* and summer working-class dating practices. Moreover, the church has reshaped the traditional festivities calendar to accommodate the schedule of returning immigrants while allowing "marriageable" young women to use the celebration to showcase their attributes and charm. Although December 12 is a national holiday in Mexico, celebrating the birth of the Virgin of Guadalupe, San Ignacians wait to celebrate her birthday the last week of January, when they celebrate their *fiestas patronales*.

Traditional festivities associated with harvest and civic celebrations have been challenged and in some cases replaced by "American-style" female beauty contests, where physical attributes, current U.S. fashion styles, and truck platform carnival parades are common currency. Women's beauty becomes a precious commodity that allows men to satisfy rivalries among nearby towns that intertwine with economic success due to immigrants' monetary contributions (both in the form of remittances and in the increase of small businesses). Towns such as San Ignacio historically have followed the tradition of crowning women in parades or processions, although these young women represented the spring or a successful harvest. Cultural influences from the United States have turned these parades or processions into beauty pageants. For the immigrants in San Ignacio, the beauty pageants are intrinsically a part of the January religious festivities. As women display their femininity via these pageants, they in turn acknowledge the importance of possible empowerment. San Ignacio's young queen for the January festivities in 2004 was born and raised in Detroit, making her participation in the pageant an important symbol of second-generation San Ignacians' adherence to their traditional cultural and social mores.

Young immigrant women are constantly bombarded by critiques of their sexualities by elderly women and church officials (who claim that the immigrant experience tends to "loosen" women if they are not watched

The Beauty Queen Pageant for the 2003 celebrations in San Ignacio. Many San Ignacians have assimilated social rituals from Euro-American culture and integrated these into their own socioreligious rituals for their annual festivities. The title of Miss San Ignacio Cerro Gordo carries a lot of prestige for the family as well as for the young woman who is selected to represent the town.

closely by their parents). But their bodies have come to represent the progress of the town, the success of the immigrant community in Detroit, and the new era of prosperity that separates (at least in local eyes) San Ignacio from the rest of Mexico. Female beauty has become synonymous with a successful immigrant experience. In particular, San Ignacio as a political entity also competes with neighboring *municipios* and *delegaciones* that have been transformed by the large numbers of immigrants. Female beauty thus is the point of departure to claim regional pride.

The construction of a transnational community includes the formation of a transnational set of values and principles regarding memory, identity, and citizenship. As the process of creating translocal and transnational ties between San Ignacio and Detroit (and between Mexico and the United States) has accelerated in the last decades of the twentieth century, new ways of constructing civic values, ethnic identities, and translocal concepts of citizenship have emerged.

Civic memory provides an example of the realignment of traditional values in the new framework set by the immigrant experience. San Ignacio as an independent *municipio* (autonomous from Arandas) was only possible because of the Detroit immigrant community's active involvement in local political affairs. As Detroit's San Ignacians achieve a new prominent status in the village, and as the *delegación política* (political delegation) increases its connections with the Michigan immigrants' group, the association between success abroad and "local pride" seems more consolidated. This political scenario delineates the gender dynamics that center on male-dominated political arenas. The more success the "children of San Ignacio" experienced in Detroit, the stronger the chances for a viable and autonomous political entity for San Ignacians in Jalisco.

It would be a mistake, however, to identify local pride sponsored by Detroit immigrants as the only source of San Ignacian identity in both Mexico and the United States. For the participants in the immigrant network, regional and national identification as San Ignacians, Jaliscans, and Mexicans is also the result of their interactions in the United States with other groups from Jalisco, other Mexican states, and, especially, other non-Mexican groups in the Detroit area. As long as the urban conditions of the Mexican community in Detroit continue to reflect a pattern of political disenfranchisement, racial segregation, police brutality, and economic exploitation, the incentives to "become American" and forge a new "American" identity will be outweighed by the "Mexicanness" provided by or constructed against the background of the immigrant experience.

Transnational citizenship is a concept that mirrors both the conditions of identification with San Ignacio as successful immigrants and the conditions of struggle against oppression by other groups in Detroit. As discussed in Chapter 4, older men find satisfaction in identifying with their "hero" status in San Ignacio, thus choosing it as their final destination. Contrary to this decision-making process, women find their strength in their collective transnational citizenship in Detroit. Women of the younger generation, however, align themselves with older women by seeing themselves as both San Ignacians and Mexican-Detroiters.

Political life in San Ignacio centers on men as protagonists, unlike Detroit, where women establish transnational families and thus create a community where they can consolidate their role as the dynamic leaders of culture, tradition, and family union. In tandem with the work of Adelaida R. Del Castillo, my research also supports the statement that "future conceptualizations of citizenship will have to consider more seriously supranational phenomena such as the growth of international migration, the intervention of international organizations, and the moral weight of universal human rights advocacy."[2] As my research attests, however, we must always give priority to the voices of the women who are the focus of the study. A feminist perspective needs to come from the bottom up and represent the "silenced." Inasmuch as transnational studies have grown exponentially in the last three decades, the need for female narratives as an integral methodology in analyzing the transnational phenomenon is still great. The immigrant experience is embedded in transnational circuits and underpins the historicity of transnational working-class Mexican communities in the United States.

The immigrant experience and the transnational identities generated along gender lines can be visualized as some of the protagonists of the Fiestas of the Absent Children parades in the January celebrations. The Aztec dancers in intricate costumes as the reminders of a proud heritage walk side by side with the Mexicanas in Miss Universe–style fashions and the elaborate procession of immigrants behind them, representing the present successes and interchangeable identities of a promising future.

NOTES

INTRODUCTION

1. The approval for San Ignacio to become an independent municipality went into effect in 2005. The first elections were held in 2007.

2. Dennis N. Valdes, *Al Norte;* Juan R. García, *Mexicans in the Midwest, 1900–1932;* Zaragosa Vargas, *Proletarians of the North.*

3. Vicky L. Ruiz, *From Out of the Shadows.*

4. Deena J. González, *Refusing the Favor.*

5. Antonia Castañeda, "Women of Color and the Rewriting of Western History."

6. Douglas S. Massey, Rafael Alarcón, Jorge Durand, and Humberto González, *Return to Aztlan.*

7. Gabriela Arredondo, *Mexican Chicago.*

8. Among them, Rhacel Salazar Parreñas, *Servants of Globalization;* and Gloria González-López, "De madres a hijas."

9. Pierrette Hondagneu-Sotelo, *Gender and U.S. Immigration* and *Gendered Transitions.* In "Strategic Instantiations of Gendering in the Global Economy," Saskia Sassen points to the creation of global cities as a consequence of today's global economy. She adds that "we are seeing the return in all the global cities around the world of the so-called serving classes, made up largely of immigrant and migrant women." In Hondagneu-Sotelo, *Gender and U.S. Immigration,* 45. See also Saskia Sassen, "U.S. Immigration Policy toward Mexico in a Global Economy," 213–227; and Roger Rouse, "Mexican Migration and the Social Space of Postmodernism," 247–263.

10. Pierrette Hondagneu-Sotelo, *Doméstica.*

11. Salazar-Parreñas, *Servants of Globalization,* 3.

12. Emma Pérez, *The Decolonial Imaginary,* 77.

13. Juan Javier Pescador, *"¡Vamos Taximaroa!"*

14. Juan Javier Pescador, *The New World inside a Basque Village.*

15. José Alamillo, *Making Lemonade Out of Lemons.*

16. Catholic influence is strong in the area around San Ignacio. Los Altos de Jalisco and Michoacán were the core of the Cristero Revolt of 1926–1929. Because of their strong religious beliefs and their attachment to traditional modes of land

ownership centered on the *ejido* (community-owned land), people in the western part of Mexico rose in arms when the new centralized government (driven by anticlerical sentiments and agrarian reform objectives) threatened to dispossess the church of its landholdings and to reform land distribution through privatization. For more information on the Cristero Revolt, see Jennie Purnell, *Popular Movements and State Formation in Revolutionary Mexico.*

17. Writing in 1930, Manuel Gamio (*Mexican Immigration to the United States*) noted significant numbers of Mexican immigrants and Mexican Americans in Illinois, Indiana, Michigan, Ohio, and New York as well as larger populations in Texas, New Mexico, Arizona, and California. He focused his research in Mexico on the states of Michoacán, Guanajuato, and Jalisco. Also see Paul S. Taylor, *A Spanish-Mexican Peasant Community.* For more on early Mexican migration to the Midwest, see García, *Mexicans in the Midwest, 1900–1932;* Vargas, *Proletarians of the North;* and Dionicio Nodín Valdés, *Barrios Norteños.*

18. Thomas J. Sugrue, *The Origins of the Urban Crisis,* 3.

19. W-76-3, AHGE.

20. Edna A. Viruell-Fuentes, "'My Heart Is Always There,'" 337.

21. Olga Nájera-Ramírez, "Unruly Passions," 461.

22. Pérez, *The Decolonial Imaginary,* 6.

23. Ibid.

24. My six years of field research from 2000 through 2005 included an initial short stay of two weeks and a longer six-month stay in San Ignacio, several short trips to Detroit over three years, and then a two-month stay in Detroit. I conducted a total of fifty-four open-ended, in-depth interviews in both research sites. These interviews, which were videotaped, lasted from two hours to more than sixteen hours, typically starting in the morning with breakfast and ending at night with a *merienda* (snack). I used a short list of questions for all the interviews; but since the conversations were open-ended the questions served more as prompts than as markers for the narrative. The interviews were conducted with individuals, couples, and in two cases a whole family. The interviewees included twenty-nine women and twenty-eight men, ranging in age from thirteen to eighty-three. Of the fifty-seven interviews, ten were conducted in Detroit, one in Arandas, and forty-six in San Ignacio; however, some of the people I interviewed in San Ignacio were there on visits and lived most of the year in Detroit. I also conducted more than two hundred informal interviews at religious and civic events such as weddings, *fiestas patronales,* birthdays, local carnivals, baptisms, and high school graduations and made many informal social visits to several people who became close friends over the six years.

25. Many of my male subjects began working as agricultural laborers for the Bracero Program in the 1950s then moved to Detroit to take industrial jobs during the 1960s and 1970s. Those who were still working typically had moved into jobs in construction and landscaping, where most Mexican men in Detroit are now employed. Mexicanas worked as waitresses and in factory jobs. In addition to

ordinary San Ignacian families, I also interviewed the local priest, the municipal president of Arandas, the Mexican alternate consul in Detroit, and the representative of the *delegación* in San Ignacio Cerro Gordo.

I have changed most of the names of the people who participated in this project in order to protect their privacy. A few individuals who have already been profiled in the media or who are prominent in their community are identified by their real names, with their permission. Some did not provide their ages. All the interviews were conducted in Spanish, and I had all the interviews transcribed and transferred onto DVDs for easier management. All translations, unless otherwise noted, are my own.

In addition to the interviews, I drew on supplemental sources ranging from primary documents to popular songs. I collected background data from local, regional, and national archives, including the National Archives in Mexico City, the Hemeroteca Nacional (the newspaper library at the Universidad Nacional Autónoma de México), the archives of the Secretaría de Relaciones Exteriores (Ministry of Foreign Relations) in Mexico City, the regional archives of the U.S. Immigration and Naturalization Service in Chicago, the archives of the Mexican newspaper *El Arandense*, the regional archives in San Miguel el Alto in the state of Jalisco, San Ignacio's archive of property records, and the U.S. census.

CHAPTER ONE

1. "Aquí el patrono es San Ignacio de Loyola, pero curiosamente como que no lo queremos. La virgen como que le dijo, 'Hazte que ahí te voy.' La Virgen de Guadalupe, entonces ni siquiera el día 12 nos esforzamos para hacer algo, es como que la virgen dice, 'Yo me voy a esperar para enero para que me hagan toda la fiesta.' Y es cuando la peregrinación es decir las mañanitas y cuetes y lo que se puedan como primeras comuniones y también viene el señor obispo para enero."

2. "Entonces era cuando nos íbamos de aquí a Tijuana y de ahí nos contrataban y nos metían para dentro." Don Chuy (seventy-three), interview in San Ignacio, November 2001.

3. Douglas S. Massey, Jorge Durand, and Nolan J. Malone, *Beyond Smoke and Mirrors*, 39.

4. Ibid., 36–38.

5. TM-309, ARE, Fondo de Braceros: Contratación de Trabajadores Agrícolas en Estados Unidos.

6. For more on the Bracero Program, see Massey, Durand, and Malone, *Beyond Smoke and Mirrors*; Manuel García y Griego, "The Importation of Mexican Contract Laborers to the United States, 1942–1964," 45; Erasmo Gamboa, *Mexican Labor and World War II*; Richard Craig, *The Bracero Program*; and Ernesto Galarza, *Merchants of Labor*.

7. In 1945 a group of "concerned citizens" in Mexico City sent a memorandum to the president of Mexico, saying: "In the past, braceros would return to

Mexico. Today it is common for them to remain outside the country, and when they acquire more resources they arrange the migration of their families as well. So what was the loss of one man becomes for Mexico the loss of an entire family. In our current situation we don't have a surplus of population but rather a deficiency. Even if it might seem inhumane, we need to deny any protection to those who choose to leave their country so that we begin to stem this growing migration to the United States" (IV-657–63, AHGE). Mexico's position regarding emigration and the loss of workers to the United States was also outlined in a conference held in Mexico City on July 16, 1951, to address the question "How can Mexico fulfill the demand for labor in the United States without affecting Mexico's economy?" (TM-1-1, ARE, Fondo de Braceros: Contratación de Trabajadores Agrícolas en Estados Unidos).

8. Justin Akers Chacón and Mike Davis, *No One Is Illegal*, 192–193.

9. Letter from braceros to Secretaría de Relaciones Exteriores, November 19, 1951 (TM-3-1, ARE, Acuerdo Básico Internacional).

10. 27-3-117, ARE, Fondo de Braceros, Contratación de Trabajadores Agrícolas en Estados Unidos.

11. Norman Daymond Humphrey, "The Housing and Household Practices of Detroit Mexicans," 433.

12. David E. Hayes-Bautista, *La Nueva California*, 53.

13. "Y es por ello que le suplicamos muy encarecidamente a Ud. Sr. Presidente, en el nuevo convenio remediar en algo nuestra raquítica situación, tocante a salarios y alojamientos que también se encuentran en pésimas condiciones así como los servicios médicos que también no son nada eficaces porque toda clase de enfermedad quieren eliminarla con puras pastillas, cuando hay otras enfermedades que requieren diferente tratamiento, y no lo hacen" (vol. 718, Exp 546.6/287, AGN).

14. A memorandum from Relaciones Exteriores dated February 25, 1956, underscores the responsibility of the Mexican consulates to protect the rights of Mexican workers in the United States. "The movement of approximately 400,000 braceros a year to the United States; their geographic distribution in places of employment; the period renewal of their work contracts; and above all the protection provided to them under the terms of the International Agreement in force require the continuous and timely intervention of our consulates in that country" (TM-1-3, 186, ARE).

15. Consul Miguel G. Calderón, in a letter to Relaciones Exteriores dated October 30, 1952, reported the "cancellation of contracts" and attached a complaint about "Mexican workers deserting because of their living conditions" (TM-3-5, ARE, Cancelación de Contratos).

16. In 1952 a bracero sent a letter of complaint to Relaciones Exteriores in Mexico City, which followed up with the Mexican Embassy in Washington, D.C. The Mexican ambassador, Rafael de la Colina, wrote to the subsecretary of for-

eign relations, Manuel Tello Baurraud, commenting on several complaints filed by braceros working for the Royal Parking Company in Salinas, California. "One of our workers was supported by a member of the National Agricultural Workers Union, which had opposed the hiring of Mexican agricultural workers. He only interfered to persuade Mexicans to join the union. This worker, Francisco Cano Hernández, spoke for three thousand workers, who paid his expenses so that he could make the trip to Washington, D.C., in order to complain to the embassy. Their major complaint was against the Royal Parking Company in Salinas, California, where room and board were bad and they were charged $1.75 per day. They also complained that the work was not consistent and sometimes they only worked three hours and they were charged $0.65 a thousand for the barbed wire used to tie the lettuces together and sometimes they weren't given it at all. And they were given a blanket for $6 or $7 that they had to leave behind when their contracts expired; they had to pay $3 monthly for health services that do not exist; they had complained numerous times to the Mexican consul in Fresno, and he had done nothing. According to the workers, when they complained to the work authorities and the contractor's representative they were deported in reprisal" (TM-3-6, ARE, Documentos sobre la alimentación de trabajadores).

17. IV-1066-14, ARE, Fondo de Braceros, Contratación de Trabajadores Agrícolas en EU.

18. Zaragosa Vargas, *Proletarians of the North*.

19. "Me llevó a mí cuando fui la primera vez en donde trabajaba. Un ruidazo, un ruidazo y no se ponían ni tapones. No se como aguantaba. . . . Muy grande [la fábrica de acero] y como muy sucia, como lleno de aceite. Las partes venían como en un cinturón que se mueve." Doña Chavelita (sixty-nine), interview in San Ignacio, November 2002.

20. "En Detroit pasamos una pena muy grande porque uno de mis hijos se le cortó una mano. En una máquina. Le pasó a Gerardo en una máquina." Doña Luna (seventy-two), interview in San Ignacio, November 2001.

21. TM-3-6, ARE, Fomento de Braceros, Contratación de Trabajadores Agrícolas en Estados Unidos.

22. "Una vez tratando yo después de haberme ido de alambre en el 51, me fui de bracero pero solo por cuarenta días y no me gusto." Don Antonio (seventy-eight), interview in San Ignacio, November 2002.

23. "De todos modos estoy lejos de mis padres, de mi familia, pues me voy de una vez hasta allá, y me anime y me fui." Don Chuy, November 2001.

24. "Varios de aquí del pueblo se fueron a arreglar sus pasaportes ahí [Ciudad Juárez]. Y entonces vino mi esposo: 'Ya arregle ya me voy.' La primera vez se fué a Stockton y luego estuvo en Salinas como cocinero de los braceros. Trabajó primero en el campo y de ahí lo agarró un señor y le dijo, 'Tu sabes hacer de comer, vente a la cocina.'" Doña Chavelita, November 2002.

25. "El venía a verme, el se fué a estudiar al seminario. El estuvo en el semina-

rio de Guadalajara como cuatro años. Y como al segundo año nos volvimos a ver y entonces el quería que volviéramos a ser novios. Yo le dije, 'No, porque tú estás en el seminario y yo no te quiero quitar tu vocación.' [Dijo:] 'Pero yo ya no tengo ganas de estar en el seminario,' y así estuvimos hasta que se salió del seminario." Doña Chavelita, November 2002.

26. "Cuando el estuvo trabajando ganaba más o menos bien y aparte a él le daban chance de vender a los braceros. Les vendía que rastrillos, que cigarros, y cosas que ocupaban ellos como jabón. Ellos iban al pueblo a comprar cosas y se ganaban sus centavitos." Doña Chavelita, November 2002.

27. "Me mandaba cheques casi cada mes. Me mandaba primero $40 y después $80, pero mientras tanto yo criaba veinte puercos aquí embarazada. Yo hacía todo lo de mi casa, lavaba, planchaba . . . le digo yo la juventud es hermosa, no te cansas, descansas en la noche te levantas con nuevos bríos y con niños. A uno le daba el biberón y al otro, entonces no había pañales desechables, era lavar y planchar porque éramos tontas y hasta los pañales planchaba, que tonta fui. Ahora se quejan con dos." Doña Ana (sixty-two), interview in San Ignacio, January 2003.

28. "[Cuando el no estaba] yo cuidaba a mi hija. Pues sola bien con trabajos no crea que bien. Yo sola los gobernaba lo que hacía con ellos, mano dura y los mandaba a la escuela." Doña Minerva (sixty-seven), interview in San Ignacio, December 2001.

29. Vol. 593, Exp. 546.6/1–15, AGN.

30. IV-826–29, ARE, Fondo de Braceros, Contratación de Trabajadores Agrícolas en Estados Unidos.

31. "A veces mu cuñado Nacho se venía a ayudarme. Otras veces mi cuñada Celia o otra de mis cuñadas. Yo crié a mis hijos sola." Doña Ana, January 2003.

32. "Yo digo que los muchachos que les ayudan a sus mujeres. Jorge y Raúl son buenos para cocinar. Cuando no trabajaba Raúl, Nena se iba a trabajar y cuando regresaba Nena él ya le tenía su comida echa. Sí, se enseñaron pues anduvieron mucho tiempo allá solos. ¡A mi se me hace bien! Si mi otro hijo también le ayuda a Ana. Y se pone y hace tortillas en la máquina pero le ayuda. Antes había mucho machismo pero ahorita yo veo que les ayudan a las mujeres allá. Aquí todavía hay mucho machismo en San Ignacio; yo no veo que les ayudan." Doña Minerva, December 2001.

33. Vargas, *Proletarians of the North*, 3.

34. Ibid., 134.

35. "Entre a la construcción. Una suerte que me toco tan buena, llegué un domingo, el 21 era domingo. Y ahí en el parque Clark me senté como unas dos horas. Ahí en una banca pero entonces era una cosa pacífica. Ahí dormía uno en el parque. Ya eran como las tres de la tarde, '¿A donde pudo ir a buscar?' Pues a ver quién habla español. Ya esa Sra. hablaba español, era Cubana. Una Sra. Cubana tenía una tiendita ahí en frente. Y dice, '¿Oye, señor, a quién andas buscando tú?' 'Pues a nadie pero usted habla español.' 'Pues mi esposo también somos Cubanos,

ahí tenemos esa tienda. ¿No tiene ganas de comer?' 'Pues si,' dije, 'traigo dinero con que comer pero no se donde venden y ando como perdido pues no conozco aquí el pueblo, la ciudad.' 'Vente para acá.' Y ella me llevo a su tienda y me acuerdo que me ofreció un plato de cocido." Don Chuy, November 2001.

36. Vargas, *Proletarians of the North*, 1.

37. Ibid., 124.

38. Juan R. García, *Mexicans in the Midwest, 1900–1932*, 244.

39. Dionicio Nodín Valdés, *Barrios Norteños*, 142.

40. "The Mexican population of Michigan was scattered more widely than in neighboring states, a consequence of the dispersion of automobile factories, foundries, and parts plants. Growth was more rapid in the industrial suburbs than in Detroit, particularly its downriver neighbors of Ecorse, Wyandotte, and River Rouge, where foundries had begun recruiting workers directly from Texas during World War II. In Detroit, the aging barrio was disrupted by an expanding central business district and new warehouses, factories, and shops, and later it was divided by the John C. Lodge and Fisher Freeways. New construction destroyed hundreds of homes, caused a sharp increase in noise and air pollution, displaced thousands of residents, and shifted the heart of the barrio toward the Southwest, from Bagley and Porter to the Clark Street district." Ibid., 140.

41. "Mi esposo [Rubén Hernández] y ellos vivían juntos en una casa con sus hermanos y Chuy y Luis Mercado. Se juntaban puros hombres y bien para los gastos. Pero él era el trabajador, mi marido, porque él era al aseado. Decía, 'Cabrones huevones, llego y los trastes así.' Porque él se ponía y dejaba la cocina limpísima." Doña Ana, January 2003.

42. Valdés, *Barrios Norteños*, 27.

43. Ibid., 144.

44. "Nosotros nos fuimos a viaje de bodas a México, y de México a Tulancingo, Hidalgo, allá tenía él una tía. . . . Luego nos venimos con otra tía a Guadalajara y de ahí nos venimos aquí." Doña Tita (seventy-three), interview in San Ignacio, December 2001.

45. "La primera vez me fui por Laredo y luego de Laredo, no me fui en camion, me fui en unas camionetitas que hechan viajes a Chicago. El Sr. chófer se compadeció porque ellos iban a Chicago y nada más. Yo entonces tenía que irme en un camión hasta Detroit. Había un Sr. que iba también a Detroit, y mis dos hijos Pepe Luis y Javier y los dos chiquillos. Entonces Pepe Luis, él le dijo al chófer, 'Oiga, ¿por cuanto nos lleva hasta Detroit para no transbordar?' Se me hace que en 40 dólares, y él nos llevo hasta Detroit, una mañana muy temprano llegamos a la casa. Pues no crea que me gusto mucho [Detroit] y la casita no me gusto mucho tampoco, pero yo estaba contenta porque yo tenía a toda mi familia y mi esposo. Entonces uno es feliz porque tiene a su familia. Digo ahora que ya he pasado más experiencia yo me sentía feliz y además estaban sus hermanos de él y otros dos amigos de él [los hermanos Mercado]." Doña Tita, December 2001.

46. "A lo mejor me llevó porque me quería mucho, porque la mayoría de los señores no. Bueno no se es que yo un día le dije, 'Porque no me arreglas un turista, anda vamos a Guadalajara, vamos al consulado.' . . . Y porque no mejor le arreglas un residencial, así tú puedes ir y venir cuando quieras. Entonces todos los demás hijos, dijeron: 'Papá, para qué está mi mama allá, mejor que este acá con todos juntos al cabo entre todos nos mantenemos.'" Doña Tita, December 2001.

47. "Yo no tenía ganas de irme para allá con tanto niño y mi mamá enferma. Y mi esposo decía que allá [Detroit] se le hacía que había mucho libertinaje y que no quería que mis hijos se criaran allá." Doña Chavelita, November 2002.

48. Denise A. Segura and Patricia Zavella, eds., *Women and Migration in the U.S.-Mexico Borderlands*, 3.

49. "[Hablando de Detroit] Pues muy feo, tenía nieve. . . . Pues *ahora* donde quiera me vengo [a San Ignacio] con pesar, por los hijos [todos residen en Detroit]." Doña Minerva, December 2001.

50. "Pero yo no hallaba como vivir y mantener a tanto allá verdad. Decía pues como vamos a caber todos en la casa, porque para esto ya habían unos hermanos de mi esposo y mis hijos y los hijos de mis cuñados y para comprar otra casa no había dinero. Se me hacía muy duro, pues ahí encerrados porque no podíamos salir y el invierno pues bien duro. Hasta que él le daban vacaciones me traía aquí y nos estábamos otra temporada aquí y se llevaba a otros y así estábamos." Doña Chavelita, November 2002.

51. Vargas, *Proletarians of the North*, 127.

52. Thomas J. Sugrue, *The Origins of the Urban Crisis*, 259.

53. "Compramos casa, verdad, hija, a los dos años. Que me costó re cara [se ríe] sí me costó $5,000. Ahí en Mexican Town donde estamos todos los de San Ignacio. En ese tiempo casi regalaban las casas. Es que era el barrio . . . Había mucho Cubano donde el *Mariel* . . . pero ahorita éramos puro Mexicano y del otro lado de la calle puro Moreno." Jaime (forty), interview in San Ignacio, February 2003.

54. For more information on white flight and the deindustrialization of Detroit, see Sugrue, *The Origins of the Urban Crisis*.

55. "Y él compro casa y estuvimos bien. . . . Cuando se fueron [a Detroit] llegaron a una casa de asistencia de una persona de por acá que era de ahí de Santiaguito de un pueblo que esta cerca de Arandas." Doña Tita, December 2001.

56. "Conocí a una señora que se llamaba Lupita y era de Chihuahua. Ella luego luego se hizo mi amiga y me dio protección o sea me ayudó para que entraran mis cuatro hijos que llevaba a la escuela, Héctor, Martín, Gustavo y Graciela a si y Lorena. Me ayudó el padre Francisco para que entraran a la escuela del Holy Redeemer, porque ahí se tenía que pagar y ya era tiempo de que entraran y yo necesitaba ayuda de alguien porque tenía que pagar desde antes la colegiatura. Tenía otra amiga de por acá, se llamaba Raquel Fonseca de Atotonilco, y Lupita Anaya de Chihuahua. [Si se enfermaban los niños] ellas me orientaron. Raquel estaba desde que se casó. Ellas eran mayores que yo." Doña Tita, December 2001.

57. Vicky L. Ruiz, *From Out of the Shadows*, 31–32.

58. Ibid., 32.

59. Jennie Purnell, *Popular Movements and State Formation in Revolutionary Mexico*, 2.

60. "Pues de bueno no la entendía pero yo de todos modos iba, ya que la hicieron en Español pues ya más bonita." Doña Minerva, December 2001.

61. "Hazte que ahí te voy." Father Ignacio Ramos Puga, interview in San Ignacio, November 2001.

62. Patricia Arias and Jorge Durand, *La enferma eterna*, 23.

63. Ibid., 116.

64. "En el mes de octubre de 1858 habiendo benido aun negosio Luz Garcia a Tepatitlan se incorporo con los federales y la madre en union de hijo lo encomendaron al Sr. de la Misericordia biniendo desde Silao en busca de . . . Garcia el cual tenía separado de la madre un año y siete meses que por milagro de este Si hubo." Ibid., 216 (original spelling).

65. "Doy gracias a la Sma. Virgen de Tlalpa por haberme traido a mi hijo de los Estados Unidos que duro mucho tiempo, empece a resar su novena y aun no la terminaba cuando regreso. ¡Gracias madre mia!" Ibid., 220 (original spelling and punctuation).

66. "Uf, era un pueblito chiquitito con 100 casas. . . . La iglesia la han ampliado más, pero el estilo de afuera no le han cambiado nada." Doña Ana, January 2003.

67. "Un radio traje la primera vez nada más de Arkansas. También luego me traje otro. No pues aquí de todos modos en esta parte fue en el '57 muy buen radio. Si ese radio lo vendí yo y le saqué 1,000 pesos en ese tiempo" [I only brought a radio from Arkansas the first time. I later brought another one. Well here, in this place in 1957, it was a good radio. Yes, that radio I sold it, and I made $1,000 pesos back then]. Don Cosme Martínez (eighty-three), interview in San Ignacio, December 2001.

68. Purnell, *Popular Movements and State Formation in Revolutionary Mexico*, 276.

69. "Cuando me case fue Raúl Cortés. Pero el que más a cambiado es el que esta ahorita. O si este cambió todo el pueblo. Las fiestas las planeo y todo. Pero ahora estamos muy tristes porque lo acaban de cambiar. Me acabó de enterar, anteayer mi hermana me dijo. Se me hace muy triste porque él duró quince años. Las fiestas el las hacía muy bonitas. A ver él que va a llegar que va a hacer por el pueblo." Alina (fifty), interview in Detroit, June 2004.

70. Arias and Durand, *La enferma eterna*, 119.

71. Ibid., 214.

72. Ecclesiastical authorities looked the other way when transnational women exercised a degree of power by violating traditional social mores, such as wearing revealing clothing to highlight their successful immigrant experience.

CHAPTER TWO

1. Paul S. Taylor, *Mexican Labor in the United States*, 197.

2. "En mi opinión no importa si vienen de allá o de acá, pero el problema es que aquí los hombres son muy celosos. . . . Te aseguro que la mayoría de las mujeres de aquí [San Ignacio] tienen novios en los Estados Unidos."

3. Kathy Peiss, "Charity Girls and City Pleasures," 301.

4. Edna A. Viruell-Fuentes, "'My Heart Is Always There,'" 356.

5. Denise A. Segura and Patricia Zavella, eds., *Women and Migration in the U.S.-Mexico Borderlands*, 3.

6. Gabriela F. Arredondo, *Mexican Chicago*, 94.

7. Robert McKee Irwin, Edward J. McCaughan, and Michelle Rocío Nasser, *The Famous 41*, 155.

8. Peiss, "Charity Girls and City Pleasures," 299.

9. Olivia M. Espín, "'Race,' Racism, and Sexuality in the Life Narratives of Immigrant Women," 172.

10. "Lo conocí un día antes de mi cumpleaños aquí en la plaza, gracias a un amigo que se llama Ramón y ya fue donde me habló. . . . Se llama Alonso, lo conocí aquí en las fiestas. El vive aquí pero se fue a Detroit. Como allá están sus papás, se fue a trabajar." Mónica (fifteen), interview in San Ignacio, January 2003.

11. Ramón Goyas Mejía, "Elementos históricos para la conformación cultural del ranchero en los Altos de Jalisco," 175.

12. "Estas diversiones estaban íntimamente relacionadas con la iglesia y la respetabilidad de las muchachas no se perdía con esta extraña simbiosis. Antes de la plaza y las serenatas, la misa, el rosario, la procesión." Ibid.

13. "[La serenata] a mí no me gusta porque ahora no nomás te agarran el pelo sino una pompi. Tu sabes todo eso, pero eso viene de muchos años y no se porque." Alma (eighteen), interview in San Ignacio, 2003.

14. "Vivíamos en ranchos cercanos. El pasaba por ahí por mi casa, pasaba a vender leche, así nos conocimos. Yo tenia quince años cuando empezamos a platicar. Platicábamos por un hoyito en la pared." Tina (forty-seven), interview in San Ignacio, January 2003.

15. "No podía salir con él, no, tenía que platicar ahí en la puerta de la casa y de repente en alguna serenata. Ahí en la plaza era donde nos veíamos, nada más." María (fifty), interview in Detroit, June 2004.

16. "Teníamos que platicar con la puerta cerrada, y por una hendedurita de la madera de la puerta nos veíamos así [hace la mímica] un ojo y el otro y así no veíamos." Doña Chavelita (sixty-nine), interview in San Ignacio, November 2002.

17. "Con su cachuchita se veía bien guapo. Traía cachucha de la que antes se usaban, los chóferes. No cachuchas de las de ahorita. De otro modo, tenían su placa de chófer. . . . Tenía una hermana en el rancho y nos juntábamos dos o tres y nos íbamos con él . . . y ahí platicábamos un ratito en el camino." Doña Chavelita, November 2002.

18. "A las cinco o seis de la tarde me metía mi mamá y ya él se iba a su casa, y así, así fue nuestro noviazgo; no había que un baile, que había la serenata pero no siempre nos dejaban, la serenata que había en la plaza para dar la vuelta. Desde mi mamá existía la serenata. . . . Desde mi mamá es la tradición de la serenata, pero mi mamá dice que, ya vez que avientan papelitos, confeti se llama, a mi mamá le aventaban unas cosas serpentines que se las embonaban en todo el cuerpo" [At five or six in the evening, my mother would call me in and he [her boyfriend] would go home. And that's how our courtship happened. There were no dances; we had *la serenata*, but we weren't always allowed to go, *la serenata* in the plaza, where we would go in circles. *La serenata* existed even when my mother was young, but my mother says—you know how they throw confetti nowadays?—she says that back then they would throw *serpentines* that would get entangled all over her body." Alma, 2003.

19. The Immigration and Reform and Control Act (IRCA) of 1986 allocated $400 million to the Border Patrol for hiring more officers and allegedly penalized employers who hired undocumented workers. As compensation to wealthy growers who had become dependent upon Mexican labor, IRCA also granted amnesty to 2.3 million undocumented Mexican workers. Four years later the Immigration Act of 1990 authorized the Border Patrol to hire 1,000 additional agents, tightened sanctions against employers who hired undocumented workers, and systematized deportation procedures. A number of anti-immigrant initiatives also passed at the state level in the 1980s, most notably California's Proposition 187, which denied undocumented immigrants access to social services, including health services and public education.

The 1990s, however, marked the history of immigration legislation, because of the alarming increase in immigrant deaths after the implementation of Operation Gatekeeper (1994) and its offspring. Operation Safeguard (1995), in Nogales, Arizona; Operation Hold the Line (1997); and Operation Rio Grande (1997) consolidated the militarization of the U.S.-Mexico border.

20. See Jennifer S. Hirsch, *A Courtship after Marriage;* and Katherine Elaine Bliss, "The Sexual Revolution in Mexican Studies." The historiography on courting rituals during the colonial period is more abundant: for example, Asunción Lavrin, ed., *Sexuality and Marriage in Colonial Latin America;* Noemí Quezada, *Sexualidad, amor y erotismo;* Silvia Marina Arrom, *The Women of Mexico City, 1790–1857;* and Juan Javier Pescador, *De bautizados a fieles difuntos.*

21. Rubén Martínez, "The Undocumented Virgin," 99.

22. Espín, "'Race,' Racism, and Sexuality in the Life Narratives of Immigrant Women," 172.

23. "Pienso que son mas abiertos allá como que, no les interesa como aquí. Por ejemplo un tatuaje y ya, ya trae un tatuaje y allá te lo pones, andas con shorts y como si nada. Y aquí te pones algo así y ay ya son esto y lo otro y como, bueno las muchachas se van allá y vienen aquí y pues allá siempre andan normal con sus shorts y todo y llegan aquí y la gente casi se muere. . . . Pues se distingue la gente,

porque son como más frescos, mas acá, es gente más popis." Elena (fourteen), interview in San Ignacio, January 2003.

24. Michael Nelson Miller, *Red, White, and Green,* 164.

25. "Muchos, la mayoría [de inmigrantes], piensan, 'Ay me voy a ir para comprarme un carro y traerlo para presumirlo.'" Elena, January 2003.

26. "Normal, que junto su dinerito y se compró su carro." Reyna (fifteen), interview in San Ignacio, January 2003.

27. "[Esto significa que] fue porque no se fue a andar de vago y que le echo ganas y fue y lo trajo." Elena, January 2003.

28. "Al principio sí voy a trabajar en el restaurant pero esa no es mi aspiración ser una mesera. No, quiero hacer algo después de un tiempo. Tengo que aprender inglés y todo y luego encontrar un buen trabajo." Alma, January 2003.

29. "Ay dios, pues que mal se han de sentir. A mí me da tristeza por esa discriminación que si nuestro Señor es el único que nos tiene que castigar y yo no quisiera que el señor cura, no me gusta, yo opino eso. Digo yo que comprendiendo que al matrimonio se va puro y con vestido blanco significa verdad, la pureza y todo, yo lo único que diría es que no se casaran de blanco, pero a la hora que quisieran y cuando quisieran. Si ellas mismas deben decir, 'Pues agarro mi vestido un color hueso, un rosita que la fregada, si ya toda la gente sabía que vivía con el otro o con lo que sea, pues no me pongo blanco, ya no voy pura al sacramento.' Pero que las casen a la hora que quieran. Se me hace muy feo que tienen que ser en sábado a las siete de la mañana." Doña Chavelita, November 2002.

30. "Como tienen aquí sus novias sus pretendientes entonces quieren venir y en caliente rápido a quererse casar. . . . Saben que no son las pláticas sino que es todo un año que tienen sus pláticas cada mes o cada quince días. . . . Tienen sus retiros con catequistas." Father Ignacio Ramos Puga, interview in San Ignacio, November 2001.

31. Hirsch, *A Courtship after Marriage,* 62.

32. Rosa Linda Fregoso, "Re-imagining Chicana Urban Identities in the Public Sphere, Cool Chuca Style," 75.

33. In the 1960s the rural population grew at a rate of 1.6 percent annually, while the urban population increased by 5.4 percent. Lorenzo Meyer, "La encrucijada," 1342.

34. Ibid.

35. "Central to my discussion is the recognition that the media in Mexico, and particularly television, are having unprecedented impact in shaping views about sexuality and gender. . . . Via exposure to the media, attitudes about couple's relations, family, work, sexuality, and other forms of everyday interactions are shaped by argumentative forms of culture and morality and less by the authority of tradition." Héctor Carrillo, *The Night Is Young,* 155–156.

36. "No me gustaría que después de que estuviera casada mi esposo me dijera, o que tuviera problemas, 'No, ya no eres virgen, y quién sabe con cuantos anduviste.'" Elena, January 2003.

37. Gloria González-López, "*De madres a hijas*," 234.

38. "[Yo sabía del sexo] porque yo tenía amigas y todo de que pues a lo mejor ya habían tenido sexo, o algo, nada más te decían, 'Ay, de lo que te pierdes, tonta.' Y tú pues, tenías una idea pero no sabías que onda. Pero a mí me daba pena andar platicando de eso o pues así, y yo tuve sexo con mi esposo [antes de casarse] ahora que pues hace unos cinco años. Tenía veinte años, así que para mí fue algo nuevo, ¡ay padre!" Nena (twenty-six), interview in Detroit, June 2004.

39. "Yo pienso que ahorita que tengo a mi pareja todo estable, yo pienso que tienes que conocerte en todos sentidos y el sexo es bien importante en una pareja, yo creo que entenderte en este sentido es bien importante. Yo pienso que no es tan importante ser virgen, o no antes del matrimonio. Aunque algunos hombres son sexistas, no solamente los de San Ignacio, sino todos los hombres en general." Vivi (twenty-eight), interview in Detroit, June 2004.

40. "En veces le dice mi hermana a mi mama, 'Ay, ustedes porque nunca dijeron que íbamos a sufrir tanto para tener hijos y todo, para no haberse metido.' Mi mama nomás nos dice, 'Pues ¿quién las manda?' Pero nunca nos platicaba, mi papá tampoco, nadie, sola te diste cuenta, sola, sola." Nena, June 2004.

41. Carrillo, *The Night Is Young*, 132.

42. "Estaba yo embarazada de Galan, del niño más grande, entonces Polo [su esposo] se iba a venir y yo le dije que pos que se viniera y yo le dije que estaba embarazada y dijo no pues nos vamos juntos y por eso decidimos por estar embarazada, no me podía estar en mi casa, el se iba a venir." Gela (twenty-five), interview in Detroit, June 2004.

43. Peiss, "Charity Girls and City Pleasures," 303.

44. Gloria González-López, *Erotic Journeys*, 38.

45. "Yo era enfermera y me mandaron aquí en el 59 . . . era una campaña contra la diarrea." Doña Ana (sixty-two), interview in San Ignacio, January 2003.

46. María Eugenia Zavala de Cosio, "Políticas de población en México," 18.

47. Carlos Monsiváis, "La familia, lo familiar," *El Universal*, Sunday, April 11, 2004 (http://www2.eluniversal.com.mx/pls/impreso/version_imprimir.html ?id_nota=21321&tabla=editoriales).

48. "Aquí se morían de parto y decían, morir en la raya." Doña Ana, January 2003.

49. Rickie Solinger, *Pregnancy and Power*, 137.

50. Zavala de Cosio, "Políticas de población en México," 18.

51. Ibid., 19.

52. "Sí, cuando el empezó a arreglar papeles, incluso nosotros no estábamos casados por el civil, porque antes lo que importaba era la iglesia y más aquí que era un pueblo de Cristeros. Y me dijo mi esposo, 'Mañana vamos a ir a la presidencia a casarnos por el civil,' a no, yo no. En mi pueblo la que se va a la presidencia es la que se va con el novio. Así que yo no voy a quedar mal, a que sepan en mi pueblo que fui a casarme, van a decir que me case mal, y no nos casamos." Doña Ana, January 2003.

53. Miller, *Red, White, and Green*, 165. See also Aurelio de los Reyes, *Medio siglo de cine mexicano (1896–1947)*.

54. Ibid.

55. "Yo los empecé a usar por prescripción médica, porque de otro modo no, aquí se morían de parto y decían 'morir en la raya.' Yo decía, 'Yo no me quiero morir.' Y fui con un ginecólogo en Guadalajara y me dijo, 'Me vas a tomar esto y ya no mas hijos.' ¡Y todavía me eché dos! Mi suegra decía que ella ni siquiera se quejaba cuando nacían. ¡Yo sí! grito y pataleo mientras sale." Doña Ana, January 2003.

56. "No menos en aquellos tiempos no sabíamos, uno atrás del otro, ni siquiera sabíamos como los vamos a educar ni como los vamos a mantener. No pensábamos en nada de eso, solo Dios de vivir para delante." Doña Toña (sixty-one), interview in San Ignacio, November 2002.

57. "La clínica que había aquí en San Ignacio, entonces, improvisada, era simplemente un cuarto grande, una galera, y ya hicieron separaciones como para consultorios, sala de espera y eso, eso era todo. Fue duro porque tuve que educar a la gente se puede decir, aquí había mucha mosca, mucha insalubridad. No había baños, tuvimos que enseñarlos a hacer las letrinas. Y lo de aconsejarles casa por casa sobre como hirvieran el agua como se trataba a los parásitos porque todo el mundo tenía parásitos. Y era una campaña contra la diarrea, les dábamos medicina y les hacíamos análisis." Doña Ana, January 2003.

58. "Cuando yo tenía diez yo empecé a saber a oír, 'Mira, que cuídate que esto y que lo otro.' Pero y no a mí, no me valía. No podía tomar medicamento porque me hacía daño para la cabeza, me ponía muy nerviosa y no había otra cosa." Doña Toña, November 2002.

59. Lara V. Marks, *Sexual Chemistry*, 131.

60. "Mientras que se cuiden, que no vayan en contra de la iglesia y que no les haga daño a su salud, ¿verdad? Yo cuando estuve yendo con un siquiatra porque estuve yendo a la de los nervios, vi muchas señoras encerradas y me dijeron que así todas eran porque habían tomado pastillas anticonceptivas y que les caía mal y se ponían medio trastornadas de la mente. Y les dije yo eso, les hace daño mis hijas, ustedes sabrán, pero ahora hay métodos que les han servido muchísimo, el método natural, Billings." Doña Chavelita, November 2002.

61. "Podemos decir de echo la misa tiene este sentido hacerles ver [a los inmigrantes] que no pierdan sus valores morales cristianos, que no pierdan sus tradiciones, sus costumbres, y eso nos toca a sus mismas familias y al sacerdote y a las personas que están aquí en el pueblo." Father Ignacio Ramos Puga, November 2001.

62. "Detroit Archbishop Edward Moody (1937–1958) initiated a conscious and public effort to repress Mexican culture. Early in his tenure, he presided over the closing of Nuestra Señora de Guadalupe [Catholic Church], and despite frequent pleas he refused to permit parishioners to construct another national church or

to engage in any Mexican religious or cultural functions under church auspices, claiming that such activities would impede Americanization. Furthermore, the archbishop demanded that no racial or nationality distinction be made toward the Mexican. He absolutely forbids the priests giving any encouragement to the idea of a church especially for Mexicans, and this applies to other organizations, religious or otherwise." Dionicio Nodín Valdés, *Barrios Norteños*, 114–128. For more information on Americanization programs in the Midwest, see Juan R. García, *Mexicans in the Midwest, 1900–1932*, 141–145, 176–178, 215–221.

63. Arikia Millikan, "A Dark Medical History," *Michigan Daily*, February 12, 2008 (http://www.michigandaily.com/content/arikia-millikan-dark-medical-history).

64. Ibid. On sterilization laws and the state's approach to the reproduction of women of color, see also Mark A. Largent, *Breeding Contempt*.

65. In her work on Mexican women in the twentieth century, Vicky Ruiz introduces her concept of "cultural coalescence," whereby Mexican immigrants and their children "pick, borrow, retain, and create distinctive cultural forms." Ruiz begins to unpack certain understandings of transnationalism, but in her work Chicanas take center stage, limiting the analysis of Mexican immigrant women. Nevertheless, Ruiz emphasizes subjectivity and agency and shows how Euro-American institutions were obsessed with managing and disciplining Mexican immigrants' lives. Vicki L. Ruiz, *From Out of the Shadows*, xvi.

66. Solinger, *Pregnancy and Power*, 148.

67. "[Los inmigrantes] si también han sido influenciados por esa costumbre de que allá [Detroit] es muy fácil, muy cómodo [tener menos hijos]. Y si tu quieres hasta moralmente y hasta se promueve el 'No seas tonta, nada mas ten dos hijos,' cuando que sus costumbres sus tradiciones acá en su pueblo son familias de diez o doce. Y allá pues esa muchachita que pertenece a una familia de doce pues pierde todo eso. No necesariamente tienen que ser de ocho, nueve, o diez, pero tiene que ser lo que llamamos una paternidad responsable que es de pareja y que es conciencia delante de Dios en cuanto al tiempo y las circunstancias que estamos viviendo. Pues hay que organizarse, hay que planificar su familia conforme a las normas de la iglesia católica y ellos allá [Detroit] pues no se guían por la iglesia católica." Father Ignacio Ramos Puga, November 2001.

68. "Pues ahora como están los tiempos, se ponen a pensar y ya hay muchos medios de que se pueden evitar eso [embarazo]. En mis tiempos no se usó eso. Yo tuve diecisiete hijos. Yo aprendí sobre eso [anticonceptivos] en Detroit, con mis amigas y mis hijas. Yo les platico a mis hijas y a mis nueras también para que quieren tantos hijos, ahorita ya por lo difícil que es, por la manutención y la educación. Yo les digo que se cuiden." Doña Luna (seventy-two), interview in San Ignacio, November 2001.

69. "Fíjese, si me viera el señor cura se enoja." Doña Luna, November 2001.

70. "Entonces en esos tiempos se cuidaba uno lo posible, verdad, y decía uno pos seguro va a tener uno los que sean y no había nada. Ni sus padres le dijeran a

uno, 'has esto o has lo otro.' Entonces eran los que Dios le dieran a uno. Así pasara uno los trabajos que pasara uno. Porque si nos vimos batallando." Doña Luna, November 2001.

71. "Te diré una cosa o dos. Hay que usar anticonceptivos aunque en mi experiencia pues tuve a toda mi familia y las mujeres entonces tenían familias numerosas." Doña Luna, November 2001.

72. "Con la inyección Depro cada tres meses pero como estoy mala de los nervios a mí me cayó mal y tenía bien tenso el cuello y bien nerviosa que me puse. Entonces el doctor aquí me dijo que yo no podía cuidarme con nada porque pues tenía un problema de los nervios pues todo me iba a afectar y el dolor de cabeza y eso." Gela, June 2004.

73. "Yo no quería tener otro pero estoy embarazada de dos meses. Mi viejo me estaba cuidando según él pero no. Use pastillas pero me estaban cayendo mal y ya no, me sentía mal, las use por un año, las estaba tomando y las deje como en octubre pasado y pues ya pasaron como siete meses y salí embarazada." Nena, June 2004.

74. Although this chapter focuses on heterosexual couples, transnational sexualities encompass the diverse range of sexual identities expressed by Mexican immigrants in the United States. For studies on immigration and sexualities, see Eithne Luibhéid, *Entry Denied*. See also Eithne Lubhéid and Lionel Cantú, Jr., eds., *Queer Migrations;* and Eithne Luibhéid, "Looking Like a Lesbian."

CHAPTER THREE

1. "No, yo ya no regreso allá [a México] por el desierto. No, porque yo tenía miedo de ir por el desierto. Pero pues pasamos bien pero ya no. Mejor me quedo aquí."

2. Programs were implemented in the United States to "repatriate" Mexicans who were believed to be the cause of many social ills. A large sector of U.S. society blamed Mexican immigrants and Mexican Americans for depleting the meager welfare resources available to civil society during the Depression. Many Euro-Americans felt that they were the only ones entitled to public assistance. The repatriation programs were launched during the Great Depression throughout the United States but concentrated in places where Mexican population numbers were higher, like California and certain areas of the Midwest, such as Detroit. Mexican consulates and welfare officials collaborated to "convince" Mexicans and Mexican Americans to return "home." Approximately five hundred thousand Mexicans were repatriated from 1929 to 1939. These programs were unorganized and inhumane; according to Norman Daymond Humphrey of Detroit, "even families of naturalized citizens were urged to repatriate, and the rights of American-born children to citizenship in their native lands were explicitly denied or not taken into account." Rodolfo Acuña, *Occupied America*, 222. For more on the relationships

between Euro-American institutions and Mexican consulates during the Depression, see also Francisco E. Balderrama, *In Defense of La Raza.*

3. Zaragosa Vargas, *Proletarians of the North,* 175.

4. Ibid., 189.

5. George J. Sánchez, *Becoming Mexican American,* 12.

6. Dionicio Nodín Valdés, *Barrios Norteños,* 134–142.

7. Ibid., 140.

8. Ibid., 215. On economic displacement and dislocations of Chicanas from Texas, forcing them to migrate "transregionally" to different states for work, see also Antonia Castañeda, *"Que Se Pudieran Defender* (So You Could Defend Yourselves)."

9. Louis Aguilar, "Mexicans Bolster a Corner of Detroit," *Detroit News,* March 6, 2005. The 2000 U.S. Census reported 47,167 "people of Spanish Language" in Detroit, 33,143 of whom were Mexicans. If the estimate of 15,000 San Ignacians is accurate, then about 45 percent of Mexicans in the city would be from that town. All these numbers, however, are probably too low, given that thousands of Mexicans are rendered socially invisible by their undocumented status. Members of the community sometimes cite much higher numbers. A *New York Times* article from 2000 quotes María Elena Rodríguez, president of the Mexican Town Community Development Corporation and a longtime resident of Detroit, saying that "more than 40,000 of the people that live in southwest Detroit are either from Jalisco [state] or have relatives there." Nichole M. Christian, "Detroit Journal: Mexican Immigrants Lead a Revival," *New York Times,* May 21, 2000. In 2006 the U.S. Census Bureau's American Community Survey reported 39,885 Mexicans in Detroit. It is likely that a substantial proportion of them are from San Ignacio, but exact numbers are not available.

10. "No crea que me gusto mucho, y la casita no me gusto tampoco. Pero yo estaba contenta porque yo tenía toda mi familia y mi esposo allá." Doña Tita (seventy-three), interview in San Ignacio, December 2001.

11. "Cuando llegue empecé a ir a templo de Santa Ana porque ellos [su esposo Delfino y sus hermanos] ya habían empezado a ir al Santa Ana. El templo es más acogedor [que el Holy Redeemer]. Uno se reúne, hay un lugar donde hacen café, da dinero y hay una persona que hace café y pan dulce y entonces la gente se va al café y al pan y entonces cada quién se hace bolitas a platicar con sus familiares o con sus amigos. Ahí había de todo—no había gente de San Ignacio cuando yo llegue, pero había gente de Santiaguito [un pueblo cerca de San Ignacio]. Había gente puertorriqueña, había de Cuba. Yo me hice amistades de todo, como yo tenía muchos hijos ya grandes y luego no están tan feos, muy vanidosa yo. [Se ríe.] Entonces yo me hice de muchas amistades porque las personas aquellas les gustaban mis hijos para sus hijas entonces a mi me hacían amistades." Doña Tita, December 2001.

12. "Me gusta estar allá [Detroit] y que las personas de allá que son de aquí, nos

vemos también con mucho gusto. Cuando nos encontramos en las tiendas, en la misa, en donde quiera nos prestamos algún servicio, alguna cosa." Doña Chavelita (sixty-nine), interview in San Ignacio, November 2002.

13. Adelaida R. Del Castillo, "Illegal Status and Social Citizenship," 98. See also Vicky L. Ruiz, *From Out of the Shadows*, 32: "Confronting 'America' often meant confronting the labor contractor, the boss, the landlord, or *la migra*. It could also involve negotiating the settlement house, the grammar school, and the health clinic."

14. "Sí, Delfino se llevo a toda la familia para allá, pero eso nos sirvió de experiencia, porque los hijos como que se le rebelaron. Delfino les arreglo a los hijos más grandesitos y luego a la señora y a todos también. Fueron trece de familia. Pero como que los hijos se le empezaron a rebelar a Delfino y eso nos sirvió de experiencia para Rubén, que dijo, 'No, yo por eso, los míos no.'" Doña Ana (sixty-two), interview in San Ignacio, January 2003.

15. Ruiz, *From Out of the Shadows*, 64–65.

16. "Me hice amigo de un vecino, se llamaba Santiago, era de aquí del pueblo. Tenía dos muchachitas, una de dieciséis y otra de dieciocho, y un día me dice, 'Don Jesús, venga a platicarme, no tengo con quién cabrones, me siento muy solo.' . . . Cuando en eso llegan las muchachas con los novios las traían bien borrachas, que no se podían ni parar . . . y se fue pa' dentro y les puso una mula [paliza] que quién sabe si harían caso o no. . . . En la mañana pague la multa. . . . Salimos de ahí al parque los echo [documentos] ahí en un bote y les prendió fuego, me dijo, 'Que chingen a su madre me las llevo para México y jamás vuelvo.' A mi no me gusto eso y por eso no me lleve a mi familia" [I befriended a neighbor, his name was Santiago and he was from here, from the town. He had two daughters, sixteen and eighteen. And one day he said to me: "Don Jesús, come talk to me, fuck! I don't have anyone, I feel lonely." When suddenly his daughters came back with their boyfriends and they were so drunk that they could hardly stand. So he went inside and beat them so hard that I don't know if they learned their lesson or not. In the morning I paid his bail, we left there (jail) and went to the park. He then threw them (immigration documents from his family) in a garbage can and set them on fire. He said to me, "Fuck them! I'm taking them back to Mexico and I'm never coming back!" I didn't like that, that's why I never took my family (to Detroit)]. Don Chuy (seventy-three), interview in San Ignacio, November 2001.

17. Ruiz, *From Out of the Shadows*, 64–65.

18. Raymond Williams comments on the different ideologies that have been created surrounding the conceptualization of country versus city: "On the country has gathered the idea of a natural way of life: of peace, innocence, and simple virtue. On the city has gathered the idea of an achieved centre: of learning, communication, light. Powerful hostile associations have also developed: on the city as a place of noise, worldliness and ambition; on the country as a place of backwardness, ignorance, and limitation. A contrast between country and city, as fun-

damental ways of life, reaches back into classical times." Raymond Williams, *The Country and the City*, 1.

19. "Yo les hacía sopa, ensalada y carne al horno y ya cuando venían de trabajar ya estaba todo porque lo hacía antes. Me levantaba temprano y les hacía lunches. ¡Fíjese! nomás y llegaron a estar diecisiete personas en mi casa! Porque los muchachos llevaban más amigos de San Ignacio. Dormían en el basement apilados hasta que les dije ya no puedo tenerlos. . . . Pero mis muchachos y mi esposo no decían nada." Doña Tita, December 2001.

20. "Ahí se hacían muchos relajos, cantaban y hacíamos fiestas. Cumpleaños hacíamos de todo en mi casa porque era grande y yo no era delicada. . . . Porque decía yo si no recibo a mi gente para andar (ay que no me pisen aquí que no me pisen allá), pues las personas no se sienten a gusto, como si estuvieran en su casa." Doña Tita, December 2001.

21. Aguilar, "Mexicans Bolster a Corner of Detroit."

22. "In the period 1940 through 1963, Detroit was the greatest manufacturing city in the world, unmatched in real physical productivity. But during the period 1964–2004, Detroit became synonymous with blight and decay beyond imagination." Richard Freeman, "Death of Detroit," 1.

23. Dionicio Nodín Valdés points out that Mexicans in Detroit were only 13 percent of Mexicans in Michigan in 1990 according to the census and by the late 1990s Mexicans were still only 3 percent of Detroit's population. Nodín Valdés. *Barrios Norteños*, 223. Urban studies of Detroit, such as Thomas J. Sugrue's *The Origins of the Urban Crisis*, focus on African Americans and say little about the less numerous groups such as Mexicans. Nonetheless, even this relatively small population of Mexican immigrants had an impact on the economic life of the city that should be taken into account.

24. Aguilar, "Mexicans Bolster a Corner of Detroit."

25. For more information on coyotes in the early twentieth century, see Manuel Gamio's work on Mexican immigrants in 1926–1927. "The real forces which move illegal immigration are, first of all, the smugglers or *coyotes* who facilitate illegal entrance to Mexican immigrants, and the contractors or *enganchistas* who provide them with jobs. The smuggler and the contractor are an intimate and powerful alliance from Calexico to Brownsville." Manuel Gamio, *Mexican Immigration to the United States*, 11. Coyotes in this period provided a range of services: smuggling Mexicans across the border was the most important, but they also worked with contractors (*enganchistas*) who hired Mexicans and sent them directly to the fields. These two figures in essence worked as a labor recruitment agency.

26. Luz María Gordillo, "The Bracero, the Wetback and the Terrorist: Mexican Immigration, Legislation, and National Security," in *A New Kind of Containment*, edited by Carmen R. Lugo-Lugo and Mary K. Bloodsworth-Lugo, 158.

27. See Chapter 2 for a discussion of how Mexicanas approach the expres-

sion of transnational sexualities. Even though Mexicanas do experience the use of contraceptives through more information and availability both in Detroit and in Mexico, many continue to rely on withdrawal (*mi viejo me cuida* [my old man takes care of me]). Mexicanas' fertility rates have dropped, however, both in the United States and in Mexico, showing that Mexican immigrants want to have smaller families.

28. See Douglas S. Massey et al., *Return to Aztlan.* In this work, immigrant women are reduced to appendages (the wives or dependents) of immigrant men. The analysis does not take into account women's labor (even their reproductive labor).

29. "No, ella se dedicaba a la casa, yo la mantenía." Don Antonio (seventy-eight), interview in San Ignacio, November 2002.

30. "¡No, ella nunca trabajó, ni un minuto!" Don Gabriel (seventy), interview in San Ignacio, December 2001. "A trabajar en la casa pues ella era una mujer muy activa o sea yo creo que lo mismo, bueno diferente porque las casas allá no son tan grandes y no trapeaba todos los días porque teníamos alfombra. Yo creo que era más liviano." Sergio Hernández (forty-six), interview in San Ignacio, December 2001.

31. "Pues es que allá estábamos toda su familia y no trabajaba tanto en la casa como aquí. Allá, solo una recogidita a la casa. Toda la alfombra nosotros se la limpiábamos y le ayudábamos. Allá estábamos todos y pues estaba contenta." Benjamín (fifty-eight), interview in San Ignacio, December 2001. "Compramos una casa porque el apartamento era muy chiquito; luego la mujer empezó era medio delicadona porque llegaban otras gentes ahí de San Ignacio y yo los tenía a ellos para ayudarlos. Y les dije pues mejor vamos a comprar una casa, yo pensaba durar más años, ¿verdad?, porque en realidad si me gustaba. Entonces me dio la idea de comprarme una casa y a los cuatro años compre otra que puse muchos apartamentos para rentar." Don Raúl (seventy-eight), interview in San Ignacio, December 2001.

32. "Se vinieron todos sus hermanos [de su esposo]. Ya habían arreglado también a algunos de sus hijos. Pero vivían todos en una casa, vivíamos todos bien apilados y mi viejo [su esposo], todo el que llegaba iba a dar ahí hasta que encontraba trabajo y no le cobraba comida, no les cobraba nada. . . . Todos me ayudaban a hacer el quehacer yo con mis chiquillos ahí revueltos con todos, se me hacía rete feo a mí pues yo no estaba impuesta a eso. Al poco tiempo compramos una casa." Doña Chavelita, November 2002.

33. See Table 3.1.

34. "No me gusto el trabajo primero, era bien trabajoso y cuando salí embarazada de Fabiola me salí. Pero después volví a entrar cuando tuve a mi hija Araceli. Cocía lonas con máquinas industriales. Empecé a trabajar ahí porque mi comadre fue la que me metió. Entonces entre yo y luego después entró Aurora, que en paz descanse, ella duró muchos años, como veintisiete años. Después luego empezó a llegar más gente. Primero éramos muy poquitas, nada más Lola y Aurora; Elia

llegó después que yo. Nos juntábamos, nos visitábamos mucho porque éramos las únicas. Yo corría para allá con Lola, que viene siendo mi tía, en las tardes para no estar sola." Alina (fifty), interview in Detroit, June 2004.

35. "Yo me sentía bien aquí con todos porque no estaba sola, hace treinta y uno años no había gente de San Ignacio como ahora." Alina, June 2004.

36. "Nos podríamos mantener con lo que él gana. Con lo que yo gano lo uso como para cosas que no son [necesidades] . . . para vestirnos, para salir, para guardar. Lo que yo gano es para lo que yo quiera." Gela (twenty-five), interview in Detroit, June 2004.

37. "Si el hombre atiende a sus obligaciones mejor, que las mujeres ni trabajen, que atiendan a su familia. Pero si no cumplen, sí, están mejor allá porque aquí no hay mucho trabajo para las mujeres." Tina (forty-seven), interview in San Ignacio, January 2003.

38. Emma Pérez, *The Decolonial Imaginary*, 6.

39. "Sí, primero fue difícil pero ahora me gusta, a gusto. No tienes nada de que preocuparte." Tina, January 2003.

40. "Tengo muchas amigas. Apenas tiene una año que cerró [la fábrica] todavía nos hablamos y ahora estamos yendo a las clases de inglés." Tina, January 2003.

41. "No puedo, es mi hermano." Gaby (twenty-two), interview in San Ignacio, December 2007.

42. "Hey, deberíamos de comprar otra para mi sobrina. Y bueno, ¿debería de comprar dos más para las niñitas de la señora? No, a la chingada, no soy responsable por las otras dos niñas, ¿verdad?" Gaby, interview in Detroit, June 2004.

43. "Habemos muchas personas que nos dan la mano, eso es lo importante, que llegues y haya una persona que te de la mano. Yo conozco a muchas personas que no tienen a donde llegar, que no conocen a nadie, que no tienen un lugar ni siguiera para dormir que hasta que tengas trabajo no tienes que comer. Yo gracias a Dios a mí me toco la suerte que yo tenía aquí a mi hermana. Pues es bien bonito, así te da mas ánimo poderte venir cuando tienes así un lugar en donde llegar que tu sabes que no es tan fácil aquí la vida. Si no trabajas pues esta más duro, pero así está bien que tengas familia y gracias a Dios como te digo que uno pueda ayudar a otra gente porque tu ya sabes porque tu viniste lo que tu pasaste, todos venimos a lo mismo, todos." Vivi (twenty-eight), interview in Detroit, June 2004.

44. "Y se hace muy bonito estarles dando allá a mi hijos también. ¡Yo se que me quieren mucho y yo a ellos y donde quiera me ocupan pues son tantos! Sucede que ya estoy tan enferma de reumatismo del corazón y todo eso, que no puedo soportar penas grandes ni trabajar mucho porque ya me dieron infartos." Doña Chavelita, November 2002.

45. "Ahorita ya no trabajo. Ya estamos a gusto aquí. Por allá solo hago algún remiendo, eso hago pero ya no trabajo." Luis Mercado (seventy-one), interview in San Ignacio, December 2001. "Allá vamos y venimos duramos un tiempo allá y acá. Pues ahora donde quiera me vengo [a San Ignacio] con pesar, por los hijos." Doña Minerva (sixty-seven), interview in San Ignacio, December 2001.

46. "Me fui yo con él. Me lleve al más chiquito, tenía siete meses, y deje a los otros cuatro con mi familia." Tina, January 2003.

47. "A los tres meses que llegue empecé a trabajar en un hotel de *housekeeping* y juntando dinero para traer a los otros cuatro niños. Y ya teníamos el dinero y no hayábamos [encontrábamos] quién nos los llevara de San Ignacio a Tijuana. Entonces mis parientes que están retirados, les pagamos el boleto para San Ignacio para que nos llevará a los niños de San Ignacio a Tijuana. Con coyote pasaron. Pero duramos seis meses sin verlos. Yo ya me estaba volviendo loca, dios mió, yo le decía a Saúl si no nos los traemos yo me voy. En las noches sin dormir yo me salía a chillar, y hasta que pensamos quién nos los trajera. En cuanto llegaron los inscribí en la escuela y empezamos a hacer una vida." Tina, January 2003.

48. The experience of border crossing needs more attention, considering the hundreds of undocumented Mexican immigrants who die trying to cross, but this subject is beyond the scope of my investigation.

49. "Ya habló tu papá que está bien. Con ese dinero voy a ir a hacerte unos análisis para ver porque no te viene tu regla." Mari (thirty-nine), interview in San Ignacio, January 2003.

50. "Yo le dije, 'Ay que barabara, ¿porque te esperaste a que tu padre se fuera, porque no nos dijiste ahora que el estaba aquí?' Yo le pedí a nuestro Señor que nadie le fuera a decir, si no antes decirle yo. Y ya sucede que a los ocho días habla, y ya le digo, 'Sabes que se me descompuso la camioneta, se me quebró un fierro.' Entonces el se enojo mucho porque no la había recogido de donde se me descompuso y ya me dice, 'Pero como que no la han recogido que por ahí los vagos que le van a quebrar los vidrios,' y que quién sabe que. Le pedí a Dios que me ponga las palabras, y yo le dije, 'Uy mijo si todo parara en fierros que bueno sería,' y ya fue donde le dije que Lily estaba embarazada. El se agarro llorando y golpeaba en la pared." Mari, January 2003.

CHAPTER FOUR

1. "[Speaking of Detroit] Pues muy feo, tenía nieve. . . . Pues ahora donde quiera me vengo [a San Ignacio] con pesar, por los hijos [todos residen en Detroit]."

2. This song, composed by Chucho Monje, was interpreted by the popular Mexican singer Jorge Negrete on his compact disc *México lindo y querido* (New York: Bertelsmann de México, S.A., distributed by BMG Music, 1991), first released in 1959.

3. Rosa Linda Fregoso, "Re-imagining Chicana Urban Identities in the Public Sphere, Cool Chuca Style," 77.

4. See, for example, Manuel Gamio, *Mexican Immigration to the United States;* and Paul S. Taylor, *A Spanish-Mexican Peasant Community.*

5. Recruitment of immigrant labor has at times included measures that seem to be "illegal" under U.S. law. In the late 1940s the U.S. workforce could not

meet the demand for agricultural labor, and growers began to hire undocumented Mexican workers. "In doing so, they incurred no liability under U.S. immigration law: the well-known 'Texas Proviso' (named for the congressional delegation that originally wrote it) had explicitly prohibited the prosecution of employers for hiring undocumented workers." Douglas S. Massey, Jorge Durand, and Nolan J. Malone, *Beyond Smoke and Mirrors*, 36.

By the 1950s U.S. agriculture became so dependent on Mexican labor that in 1954, while the Immigration and Naturalization Service deported thousands of Mexicans under Operation Wetback, "the U.S. Department of Labor . . . promptly processed them as braceros and retransported them back to the very fields where they had been arrested in the first place!" Ibid., 36–37.

6. Luz María Gordillo, "The Bracero, the Wetback, and the Terrorist: Mexican Immigration, Legislation, and National Security," in *A New Kind of Containment*, edited by Carmen R. Lugo-Lugo and Mary K. Bloodsworth-Lugo.

7. Ongoing legislative changes were affecting immigration flows, as severe militarization and implementation of border restrictions claimed the lives of Mexican immigrants forced to cross deadly "border traps"—the Sonora Desert and the Tecate Mountains, among others. In 1993 Operation Blockade took place in El Paso, Texas, and in 1994 the Immigration and Naturalization Service (INS) launched Operation Gatekeeper in the San Diego border region, which "installed high-density floodlights to illuminate the border day and night, as well as an eight foot steel fence along fourteen miles of border from the Pacific Ocean to the foothills of the Coast Ranges." Massey, Durand, and Malone, *Beyond Smoke and Mirrors*, 94. The INS launched Operation Safeguard in Nogales, Arizona, in 1995; in 1997 Operation Hold-the-Line was extended into New Mexico, while Operation Rio Grande was implemented along thirty-six miles of the border in southeast Texas.

8. Maxine Molyneux, "Twentieth-Century State Formations in Latin America," in *Hidden Histories of Gender and the State in Latin America*, edited by Maxine Molyneux and Elizabeth Dore, 35.

9. Ibid.

10. "[Nos hizo una plaza] tipo de allá, Europea pues que no hacía contraste con el templo, entonces la gente no estábamos de acuerdo." Gustavo (fifty-one), interview in San Ignacio, January 2003.

11. "El kiosco que está ahí afuera tiene su historia porque yo lo tumbé, yo me lleve de aquí en el '82 una máquina para escavar. Y como el kiosco estaba muy feo y la plaza muy abandonada, muy fea, y por órdenes de las autoridades de Arandas yo lo tumbé. Entonces fui a ver al patronato de las fiestas patrias y juntamos $6,000. [Arandas] se pusieron a hacer una placita y nos enseñaron un proyecto muy bonito y todo el pueblo aceptó. Y cuando se nos acabó el dinero nos hicieron para un lado e hicieron una plaza muy diferente de la que nos prometieron, muy fea. Y a través tres o cuatro años se tumbó y por medio del Señor Patiño y la gente de aquí [Detroit] se renovó la plaza" [The kiosk that is outside has its history. I tore it down; in 1982 I took a bulldozer. And because the kiosk was very ugly and the

plaza very abandoned, the Arandan authorities asked me to tear it down. So I went to see the *patronato* for the *fiestas patrias* (committee that organizes the regional celebrations) and we put together 6,000 pesos. They (Arandas) started to build a *placita* and showed us very pretty sketches for the project, and the whole town (San Ignacio) accepted. When we ran out of money they ignored us and built a very different plaza from the one they had promised us; it was very ugly. In a matter of three or four years we tore it down again, and thanks to Mr. Patiño and our people here (in Detroit) the plaza was renovated]. Tori (fifty-seven), interview in Detroit, June 2004.

12. "Empezamos a hacer borlote para tumbarla y sí nos dieron permiso de tumbarla. Entonces yo antes de tumbarla fui con Don Alfonso Patiño y le dije que si nos podía ayudar en algo. Y cuando vio las fotos dijo, 'Esa plaza no es para mi pueblo.' . . . Al día siguiente nos pusimos a tumbar el kiosco y la plaza. Y luego luego me tocó ir a Irapuato con el Don Alfonso y el primer cheque que nos dio fue de 11,700,000 pesos, para que empezáramos, y luego nos dio 50 millones de pesos para el kiosco. . . . El kiosco que tenemos es una réplica del kiosco de Chapala, buscamos la forma de que se hiciera la plaza bonita. Yo pienso que logramos lo que queríamos." Gustavo, January 2003.

13. "Lo de los arcos no es obra de ningún ayuntamiento, ningún ayuntamiento puede decir de que 'en nuestro tiempo nosotros hicimos esos arcos.' Nadie lo puede evitar el pueblo es testigo de que esos arcos de entrada se hicieron con un peso que daba la gente de aquí y de Detroit. El que me quiera dar un ladrillo, un costal de cal, una semana de trabajo, así hicimos esos arcos. Y el camellón pues era un arroyo entonces dijimos cale la pena hacer una avenida y hicieron esa avenida. . . . Lo mismo el adoquín y así siguió pues con algunas otras calles." Father Ignacio Ramos Puga, interview in San Ignacio, November 2001.

14. David G. Gutiérrez and Pierrette Hondagneu-Sotelo, "Introduction."

15. Paul S. Taylor, *A Spanish Mexican Peasant Community.*

16. María Basilia Valenzuela Varela and Claudia Mónica Sánchez Bernal, "Aportes para la formación del municipio San Ignacio Cerro Gordo."

17. Ibid.

18. Roberto González Amador, "Las remesas están financiando el desarrollo de México: encuesta," *La Jornada*, February 2, 2007. For more recent information on remittance totals, see Anthony Harrup, "Remesas a México cayeron 20 percent en mayo," *Wall Street Journal*, July 1, 2009; and Joel Millman and Anthony Harrup, "Remittances to Mexico Fall More Than Forecast," http://online.wsj.com/article/SB123310695110822547.html.

19. Taylor, *A Spanish Mexican Peasant Community*, 41.

20. María Basilia Valenzuela Varela, "Municipalización, ciudadanía y migración en los Altos de Jalisco," 240.

21. This was initiated in 1983 by a change in article 115 of the Mexican Constitution, which recognized "the importance of the *municipio* as an agent of local

change." Valenzuela Varela and Sánchez Bernal, "Aportes para la formación del municipio San Ignacio Cerro Gordo," 40.

22. Ibid., 41.

23. Ibid.

24. "El primer beneficio será que ya nuestras gentes o nosotros podemos decidir el futuro del pueblo. En segundo lugar contar con ese presupuesto que legalmente corresponde y desarrollarlo en servicios para que tenga más atractivos para cuidar la ecología y para tener más vínculos culturales con ciudades en Estados Unidos. . . . Si somos municipio vamos a emprender una ciudad hermana con Detroit." José (forty-seven), president of the Committee for a New *Municipio*, interview in San Ignacio, January 2003. José did not run for municipal president, but he is still involved in political and social matters in the town. He owns a very successful *maderería* (wood furniture shop) in town.

25. "Ahora quieren quitar territorio para que no califique San Ignacio, pero ya esta calificado, ya no pueden quitarlo. Arandas todavía nos gobierna este año y el que sigue y ya el 2006 empezamos a votar para un presidente municipal y en el 2007 ya San Ignacio se independiza. Se logro porque Arandas nos ha tenido muy marginados. Se cree que son 26 a 28 millones de pesos lo que debe entrar a San Ignacio de aquí, cuando no nos daban nada. Todo para Arandas y desgraciadamente no era para servicios públicos en Arandas. El dineral que agarra se lo echa a la bolsa el gobierno, los mandamases." Tori, June 2004.

26. "Es un lugar donde da mucha oportunidad para crecer para prosperar, pero la inseguridad legal lo hace sentir a usted de una forma instable, no crea una raíz. Y eso para mi propia persona estar en un lugar donde yo quería prosperar pero a la vez no tenía la legalidad para permanecer en ese país. . . . Pero sí me gusto muchísimo. . . . No me sentía con posibilidad de participar como ciudadano." José, January 2003.

27. "No, yo ya no regreso allá [a México] por el desierto. No, porque yo tenía miedo de ir por el desierto. Pero pues pasamos bien pero ya no. Mejor me quedo aquí." Vivi (twenty-eight), interview in Detroit, June 2004.

28. Edna A. Viruell-Fuentes, "'My Heart Is Always There,'" 353.

29. In her essay "Cruzando la Línea," Yolanda Chávez-Leyva depicts the historically strict and aggressive management of Mexican children and women when crossing the U.S.-Mexico border through immigration law; one example is the Immigration Act of 1917, which "specifically banned women and girls entering the U.S. for 'immoral purposes' and made it possible to deport women who 'acted in immoral ways after arrival,' even decades after their entry" (73). The historical scrutiny of women's bodies at the border is clearly mapped out in the history of immigration law. In the nineteenth century the United States passed anti-Chinese laws, one of which (the Page Law of 1875) exclusively banned the entrance of Chinese women. Eithne Luibhéid has documented the systematic discrimination against lesbian bodies at the border. See, for example, her book *Entry Denied*.

30. Adelaida R. Del Castillo, "Illegal Status and Social Citizenship," 102.

31. Pierrette Hondagneu-Sotelo and Ernestine Avila, "'I'm Here, But I'm There,'" 388.

32. See note 7 above.

33. "Tuvo que ver muchas cosas, solo Dios sabe porque hace las cosas. Pero cuando habíamos comprado la casa, entonces tuve que limpiarla toda. Porque estaba bien sucia, bien mugrosa, estaba asquerosa. O sea que tuve que limpiar todo. Y luego metieron a mi hermano a la cárcel y pues estaba bien preocupada. Porque mi mamá no sabía nada, tenía que echarle mentiras. A mi mamá le decíamos que se iba a trabajar a otra parte. Yo estaba con mucha preocupación y luego pasó lo del tornado. Entonces has de cuenta que yo pienso que exploto no se que . . . mi cuerpo." Gaby (twenty-two), interview in Detroit, June 2004.

34. Viruell-Fuentes, "'My Heart Is Always There,'" 354.

35. "Un milagro grande me pasó, me hice ciudadana sin saber inglés. Metimos la aplicación por una iglesia, dimos el test y metimos los papeles. Pagamos $150 por todo y todas las preguntas que hacen en migración nos las hicieron ahí, las contestamos. Y nos llamaron de migración, fue mi esposo y le preguntaron cuales son las tres ramas y el dijo, 'I don't know.' Y le dijeron que se esperara hasta quince años de residencia para hacer el examen en español o hasta que tuviera cincuenta y cinco años." Tina (forty-seven), interview in San Ignacio, January 2003.

36. "Yo me fui el lunes en ayunas, poniéndome en las manos del señor. 'Si quiere me vuelvo ciudadana si no residente.' Contesté, sí, solo una no supe, puse dos oraciones en inglés y las escribí me equivoque una sola letra, puse 'lobe' en vez de 'love.' Y la de la migra me preguntó, 'Do you believe in the Constitution?' y yo dije que no. Y me dijo, '¿Qué? Escúcheme,' y repitió la pregunta y yo le dije, 'Yes, yes, yes!' Y ella me dijo, 'Okay, bye-bye.'" Tina, January 2003.

37. "Le digo algo, que me hice ciudadana y hasta ni lo creen porque ahí mismo me dijeron ahora que cuando fuimos a sacar el pasaporte dijeron que cómo era posible que me hubiera hecho ciudadana sin saber leer ni escribir, porque no estaba firmado el papel, y hasta investigaron. Y no pues ahí los hice reír pues puse la cruz." Doña Luna (seventy-two), interview in San Ignacio, November 2001.

38. "Mexican migrants are very commonly the implied if not overt focus of mass-mediated, journalistic, as well as scholarly discussions of 'illegal aliens.' . . . The figure of the 'illegal alien' itself has emerged as a mass-mediated sociopolitical category that is saturated with racialized difference, and, moreover, serves as a constitutive feature of the specific racialized inscription of 'Mexicans' in general, regardless of their immigration status in the United States or even U.S. citizenship." Nicholas De Genova and Ana Y. Ramos-Zayas, *Latino Crossings*, 3.

39. "[Los Mexicanos a su vez usan un mecanismo de seguridad] para poder sobrevivir en esta sociedad que los arropa y los protege y les ofrece la oportunidad de trabajo, pero que también los agrede y los discrimina." Oscar Antonio de la Torre Amezcua (forty-nine), interview in Detroit, June 2004.

40. Since the implementation of Operation Gatekeeper and the other deter-

rent operations along the Mexico-U.S. border, an estimated 300 Mexican nationals have died every year trying to cross the border. The California Rural Legal Assistance Foundation reported that 1,186 migrants died while crossing from 1998 to 2000. The most common causes of death are hypothermia, heatstroke, drowning, accident, and homicide. In August 2006 the United States Government Accountability Office (in its Report to the Honorable Bill Frist, Majority Leader, U.S. Senate, entitled "Illegal Immigration: Border-Crossing Deaths Have Doubled since 1995; Border Patrol's Efforts to Prevent Deaths Have Not Been Fully Evaluated") concluded that the number of border crossing deaths more than doubled from the late 1990s through 2005. The report may be found at http://www.gao.gov/new.items/do6770.pdf.

41. "Llegamos a Detroit un lunes y para el miércoles ya habíamos comprado una casa en $15,000 al contado. . . . Conseguimos la mitad del dinero y la otra mitad la llevábamos nosotros." Tina, January 2003.

42. Jaime: "Compramos casa, verdad, hija, a los dos años. Que me costó re cara [se ríe], sí me costó $5,000. Ahí en Mexican Town donde estamos todos los de San Ignacio." Irma: "Compramos la casa un martes, llenamos los papeles y dimos el dinero. Y el jueves se quemó, la del otro lado no se quemó toda nada más se derritió todo el plástico. Eso fue el jueves y el viernes nos fuimos de emergencia a vivir ahí. Porque la otra quedó quemada y había mucho peligro de que prendieran la casa quemada. Y quitaron todo, derrumbaron la casa y quedo el terreno y él lo compró." Jaime: "Y la arreglé las casa, no estaba muy bonita. Compré el terreno de al lado bien carísimo también—$300 [se ríe]. Y ahora que fui me hicieron un abaluo en el banco y me ofrecieron $70,000 por la casa." Irma and Jaime (forty-seven and forty, respectively), interview in San Ignacio, February 2003.

43. In 1946 sociologist Norman Daymond Humphrey published "The Housing and Household Practices of Detroit Mexicans," in which he made numerous racist statements about the way Mexicans lived in Detroit. He ignored their lack of access to basic resources and the housing segregation that affected both African Americans and Mexicans. Humphrey instead argued that Mexicans chose to live in deplorable conditions because it was in their nature: "One segment of the Mexican population is found living in basement apartments which, in being lightless and airless, approximate the adobe huts of the peasant village. The likeness of this dwelling to that in Mexico accounts for the persistence with which it is retained by the least assimilated migrants." His views may be seen as typical of Euro-American attitudes in the period.

44. Thomas J. Sugrue, *The Origins of the Urban Crisis.*

45. In 1950 Detroit's population was 1.85 million people, but by 2000 the population had decreased to 951,270 (49 percent below the 1950 level). The same period saw white flight to the suburbs, so that by 2000 about 82 percent of the city's population was African American. Richard Freeman, "Death of Detroit," 9.

46. "The process of close-down of hospitals, and insufficient beds to treat people, has been exacerbated in Detroit. . . . [In a three-year period] Samaritan

Hospital, Holy Cross Hospital, and Saratoga Hospital, all located on Detroit's East Side, have closed down." Ibid., 12.

47. Farrell-Donaldson is quoted in ibid.

48. "Ahora juegan football en Patton Park porque el Clark, que le dicen esta más cerquita de la casa, pero como ahí mataron a unos muchachos ya ahora nada más se ponen de un lado. No es muy recomendable. Antes no, antes no era tanto. Antes que nosotros vivíamos casi había pura gente americana, no había muchos Mexicanos, muy pocos. Y estaba más bonito por la calle, donde estaba más bonito, nunca nos hicieron discriminación más bien se hacían amistad con nosotros. Pero después se fueron muchos y llegaron más Mexicanos." Doña Tita (seventy-three), interview in San Ignacio, December 2001.

49. "Yo no se si los Latinos nosotros mismos lo estamos cambiando [el barrio]. Yo pienso que sí, lo hijos, los muchachos [los cholos]. No había lo que hay ahora, estaba más bonito. No habían casas quemadas." Alina (fifty), interview in Detroit, June 2004.

50. "No hemos tenido dinero, nos robaron aquí en la casa. Compramos una casa de un [g] buey y el la hipotecó o no se que, y nos la quitó el banco, porque no estaba, no pues estaba mal esa casa desde un principio. Nos hizo un fraude. Nos robó como $35,000. Fuimos a un abogado y todavía estamos en eso pero parece que no podemos hacer mucho." Nena (twenty-six), interview in Detroit, June 2004.

51. "Pues a mí sí me gustaba estar allá [Detroit] y si no se hubieran venido mi esposo y mis hijas yo no me hubiera venido. Yo ya estaba bien ubicada hasta trabajaba. . . . Yo trabajé limpiando casas y oficinas. Trabajé también en un restaurant en la cocina. Ya está todo muy grande aquí en San Ignacio porque la cantidad de gente que hay en Detroit de aquí. . . . Se van familias enteras de aquí y también muchachas se van y ya se quedan y compran casa y bueno carísimas de baratas que estaban. Yo me quiero ir. Tengo una nuera que me ha dicho, 'Véngase conmigo, hay muchos cuartos en la casa,' que era mía. Y sí yo creo que me voy a ir ahí, sí voy." Doña Tita, December 2001.

52. "Mi intención desde que me fui, tratar de ahorrar, tratar de ganar lo suficiente para venirme a descansar. . . . Yo no pensaba durar más de los cincuenta años pero ya ando en los setenta. Y digo la vida es muy corta y trabajar todos los días, hasta el ultimo día, no tiene caso, no tiene caso." Don Gabriel (seventy), interview in San Ignacio, November 2001.

53. De Genova and Ramos-Zayas, *Latino Crossings*, 2.

54. "Sí, y así para el otro año sí nos aventuramos también. Al cabo todo el mundo pasa oye sea como sea." Gela (twenty-five), interview in Detroit, June 2004.

CONCLUSIONS

1. See Tables 2.2 and 2.3.

2. Adelaida R. Del Castillo, "Illegal Status and Social Citizenship," 94.

BIBLIOGRAPHY

ARCHIVES

Archivo de Relaciones Exteriores (ARE), Mexico City
  Acuerdo Básico Internacional: Departamento de Contrataciones
  Fondo de Braceros: Contratación de Trabajadores Agrícolas en Estados
    Unidos
Archivo General de la Nación (AGN), Mexico City
  Fondo Lázaro Cárdenas
Archivo Histórico Genaro Estrada (AHGE), Mexico City
  Departamento de Archivo de Concentración
National Archives of the United States (NARA)
  RG 184, Railroad Retirement Board (re: braceros)
    RG 184 re: Bracero Program
    (923296), box 1:
      Claims for Annuities and Death Benefits in Mexico, March 1, 1944
      Distribution of Pamphlets, July 5, 1944
    (923297), box 2:
      Mexican Contract Laborers, August 24, 1944
      Mexican Importation: State Department of Translation of Draft, Bene-
        fits under the RA of 1937, August 25, 1944
      Mexican Importation Program, October 4, 1945
      Mexican Payroll, October 15, 1945
    (919738), box 13:
      Validation Study of Mexican Proofs Conducted by SSA, August 3, 1973
    (919752), box 17:
      Mexican Nationals re: Retirement Benefits, June 14, 1978
    (923303), box 19:
      Proposed Refund to Mexican Nationals, June 19, 1953
      RG 202, National War Labor Board
      RG 211, War Manpower Commission, Region 5
      RG 211 re: Bracero Program
      RG 228, Fair Employment Practice Committee
      Naturalization Records, 1837–1998
      Declarations of Intention, 1856–1989

NEWSPAPERS AND LOCAL PAMPHLETS

El Arandense (Arandas, Jalisco, Mexico)
Boletín Municipalista (San Ignacio Cerro Gordo, Jalisco, Mexico)
Detroit News (Detroit, Michigan)
La Expresión de la Palabra: Panorama Alteño (San Ignacio Cerro Gordo, Jalisco, Mexico)
El Informador (Guadalajara, Jalisco, Mexico)
Michigan Daily (Detroit, Michigan)
Noti-Arandas (Arandas, Jalisco, Mexico)
Noticias Notimex (Mexico City)

INTERVIEWS

Alejandro (thirty-four), San Ignacio, December
Alex (thirty), San Ignacio, February 2003
Alina (fifty), Detroit, June 2004
Alma (eighteen), San Ignacio, January 2003
Ana, Doña (sixty-two), San Ignacio, January 2003
Andrés, Don (seventy-four), San Ignacio, November 2001
Angeles (twenty-nine), Detroit, June 2004
Antonio, Don (seventy-eight), San Ignacio, November 2002
Armando (thirty-four), San Ignacio, January 2003
Benjamín (fifty-eight), San Ignacio, December 2001
Bianca (thirteen), San Ignacio, January 2003
Camilo (early twenties), San Ignacio, February 2003
Carmen (early twenties), San Ignacio, January 2003
Chavelita, Doña (sixty-nine), San Ignacio, November 2002
Chemo (fifty-two), San Ignacio, February 2003
Chuy, Don (Jesús Mercado) (seventy-three), San Ignacio, November 2001
Cosme, Don (eighty-three), San Ignacio, December 2001
El Cantor (sixty-five), San Ignacio, January 2003
Elena (fourteen), San Ignacio, January 2003
Elodia, San Ignacio, November 2001
Francisco (forty-four), Detroit, June 2004
Gabriel (twenty-eight), San Ignacio, December 2002; Detroit, June 2004
Gabriel, Don (seventy), San Ignacio, November 2001
Gaby (twenty-two), San Ignacio, December 2002; Detroit, June 2004
Gela (twenty-five), Detroit, June 2004
Gilberto Arias (twenty-six), *delegado* of San Ignacio Cerro Gordo, San Ignacio, January 2003
Gustavo (fifty-one), San Ignacio, January 2003
Ignacio Ramos Puga, Priest, San Ignacio, November 2001

Irma (forty-seven), San Ignacio, February 2003
Jacinto, Don (sixty-six), San Ignacio, November 2002
Jaime (forty), San Ignacio, February 2003
Jorge Díaz Pérez, *presidente municipal* of Arandas, Arandas, January 2003
José (forty-seven), president of the Committee for a New *Municipio*, San Ignacio,
    January 2003
Karla (fifty-four), San Ignacio, January 2003
Lidia (fifty), Detroit, July 2004
Liliana (fourteen), San Ignacio, February 2003
Lily (late teens), San Ignacio, February 2003
Luis Mercado (seventy-one), San Ignacio, December 2001
Luna, Doña (seventy-two), San Ignacio, November 2001
Magda (fifty-three), San Ignacio, February 2003
Mari (thirty-nine), San Ignacio, January 2003
María (fifty), Detroit, June 2004
Mercedes (forty-nine), San Ignacio, January 2003
Minerva, Doña (sixty-seven), San Ignacio, December 2001
Mónica (fifteen), San Ignacio, January 2003
Nena (twenty-six), Detroit, June 2004
Oscar Antonio de la Torre Amezcua (forty-nine), Detroit, June 2004
Raúl, Don (seventy-eight), San Ignacio, December 2001
Reyna (fifteen), San Ignacio, January 2003
Ricky (fifteen), San Ignacio, February 2003
Roger (fifty-five), San Ignacio, February 2003
Rosi (thirty-one), San Ignacio, January 2003
Saúl (fifty-two), San Ignacio, January 2003
Sergio (forty-six), San Ignacio, November 2001
Sonia (forty-three), Detroit, June 2004
Tina (forty-seven), San Ignacio, January 2003
Tita, Doña (seventy-three), San Ignacio, December 2001
Toña, Doña (sixty-one), San Ignacio, November 2002
Tori (fifty-seven), Detroit, June 2004
Vivi (twenty-eight), Detroit, June 2004

BOOKS AND ARTICLES

Acuña, Rodolfo. *Occupied America: A History of Chicanos.* 4th ed. New York: Addison Wesley Longman, Inc., 2000.
Aguilar, Louis. "Mexicans Bolster a Corner of Detroit." *Detroit News,* March 6, 2005.
Alamillo, José M. *Making Lemonade Out of Lemons: Mexican American Labor and Leisure in a California Town, 1880–1960.* Urbana: University of Illinois Press, 2006.

Altman, Ida, Sarah Cline, and Juan Javier Pescador. *The Early History of Greater Mexico*. Upper Saddle River, N.J.: Prentice Hall, 2003.

Anzaldúa, Gloria. *Borderlands/La Frontera: The New Mestiza*. San Francisco: Aunt Lute Books, 1987.

Arias, Patricia, and Jorge Durand. *La enferma eterna: Mujer y exvoto en México, siglos XIX y XX*. Guadalajara: Universidad de Guadalajara/San Luis Potosí: El Colegio de San Luis, 2002.

Arredondo, Gabriela F. *Mexican Chicago: Race, Identity, and Nation, 1916–39*. Urbana: University of Illinois Press, 2008.

Arrom, Silvia Marina. *The Women of Mexico City, 1790–1857*. Stanford, Calif.: Stanford University Press, 1985.

Baca Zinn, Maxine, Pierrette Hondagneu-Sotelo, and Michael A. Messner, eds. *Gender through the Prism of Difference*. Boston: Allyn and Bacon, 2000.

Balderrama, Francisco E. *In Defense of La Raza: The Los Angeles Mexican Consulate and the Mexican Community, 1929–1936*. Tucson: University of Arizona Press, 1982.

Behar, Ruth. *Translated Woman: Crossing the Border with Esperanza's Story*. Boston: Beacon Press, 1993.

Berlant, Lauren. *Intimacy*. Chicago: University of Chicago Press, 2000.

Blea, Irene I. *La Chicana and the Intersection of Race, Class, and Gender*. New York: Praeger, 1992.

Bliss, Katherine Elaine. *Compromised Positions: Prostitution, Public Health, and Gender Politics in Revolutionary Mexico City*. University Park: Pennsylvania State University Press, 1968.

———. "The Sexual Revolution in Mexican Studies: New Perspectives on Gender, Sexuality, and Culture in Modern Mexico." *Latin American Research Review* 36, no. 1 (2001): 247–268.

Burkholder, Mark A. *Colonial Latin America*. New York: Oxford University Press, 1998.

Butalia, Urvashi. *The Other Side of Silence: Voices from the Partition of India*. Durham, N.C.: Duke University Press, 2000.

Carrillo, Héctor. *The Night Is Young: Sexuality in Mexico in the Time of AIDS*. Chicago: University of Chicago Press, 2002.

Castañeda, Antonia I. "*Que Se Pudieran Defender* (So You Could Defend Yourselves)." *Frontiers* 22, no. 3 (2001): 116–142.

———. "Sexual Violence in the Politics and Policies of Conquest: Amerindian Women and the Spanish Conquest of Alta California." In *Building with Our Own Hands: New Directions in Chicana Scholarship*, edited by Beatríz Pesquera and Adela de la Torre, 15–33. Berkeley: University of California Press, 1991.

———. "Women of Color and the Rewriting of Western History: The Discourse, Politics, and Decolonization of History." *Pacific Historical Review* 61, no. 4 (November 1992): 501–533.

Castillo, Ana. *Massacre of the Dreamers: Essays on Xicanisma.* Albuquerque: University of New Mexico Press, 1994.

Castles, Stephen, and Mark J. Miller. *The Age of Migration: International Population Movements in the Modern World.* New York: Guilford Press, 1993.

Caulfield, Sueann. *In Defense of Honor: Sexual Morality, Modernity, and Nation in Early Twentieth-Century Brazil.* Durham: Duke University Press, 2000.

Chacón, Justin Akers, and Mike Davis. *No One Is Illegal: Fighting Racism and State Violence on the U.S.-Mexico Border.* Chicago: Haymarket Books, 2006.

Chávez-Leyva, Yolanda. "Cruzando la Línea: Engendering the History of Border Mexican Children during the Early Twentieth Century." In *Memories and Migration: Mapping Boricua and Chicana Histories,* edited by Vicky Ruiz and John R. Chávez, 71–92. Urbana: University of Illinois Press, 2008.

Christian, Nichole M. "Detroit Journal: Mexican Immigrants Lead a Revival." *New York Times,* May 21, 2000.

Corwin, Arthur F. "Mexican Emigration History, 1900–1970: Literature Research." *Latin American Research Review* 8, no. 2 (Summer 1973): 3–24.

Cotera, Martha P. "Diosa y Hembra: The History and Heritage of Chicanas in the United States." Dissertation, Austin, University of Texas Mexican American Library Project, 1976.

Craig, Richard. *The Bracero Program: Interest Groups and Foreign Policy.* Austin: University of Texas Press, 1971.

Davalos, Karen Mary. "Ethnic Identity among Mexican and Mexican American Women in Chicago, 1920–1991." Dissertation, University of Michigan, 1995.

De Genova, Nicholas, and Ana Y. Ramos-Zayas. *Latino Crossings: Mexicans, Puerto Ricans, and the Politics of Race and Citizenship.* New York: Routledge, 2003.

Del Castillo, Adelaida R. "Illegal Status and Social Citizenship: Thoughts on Mexican Immigrants in a Postnational World." In *Women and Migration in the U.S.-Mexico Borderlands: A Reader,* edited by Denise A. Segura and Patricia Zavella, 92–105. Durham: Duke University Press, 2007.

De León, Arnoldo. *They Called Them Greasers: Anglo Attitudes toward Mexicans in Texas, 1821–1900.* Austin: University of Texas Press, 1983.

Denton, Nancy A., and Douglas S. Massey. "Racial Identity among Caribbean Hispanics: The Effect of Double Minority Status on Residential Segregation." *American Sociological Review* 54, no. 5 (October 1989): 790–808.

Deutsch, Sarah. *No Separate Refuge: Culture, Class and Gender on an Anglo-Hispanic Frontier in the American Southwest, 1880–1940.* New York: Oxford University Press, 1987.

Durand, Jorge, and Patricia Arias. *La experiencia migrante: Iconografía de la migración México–Estados Unidos.* Mexico City: Altexto, 2000.

Durand, Jorge, and Douglas S. Massey. "Mexican Migration to the United States: A Critical Review." *Latin American Research Review* 27, no. 2 (1992): 3–42.

Ehrenreich, Barbara, and Arlie Russell Hochschild, eds. *Global Woman: Nannies,*

Maids, and Sex Workers in the New Economy. New York: Henry Holt and Company, 2002.

Espín, Olivia M. "'Race,' Racism, and Sexuality in the Life Narratives of Immigrant Women." In *Latina Realities: Essays on Healing, Migration and Sexuality,* 171–185. Boulder, Colo.: Westview Press, 1997.

Fernández-Kelly, María Patricia. *For We Are Sold, I and My People: Women and Industry in Mexico's Frontier.* Albany: State University of New York Press, 1983.

Foucault, Michel. *The History of Sexuality: An Introduction, Volume 1.* New York: Vintage Books, 1978.

Freeman, Richard. "Death of Detroit: Harbinger of Collapse of Deindustrialized America." *Executive Intelligence Review* (April 23, 2004): 21–35.

Fregoso, Rosa Linda. "Re-imagining Chicana Urban Identities in the Public Sphere, Cool Chuca Style." In *Between Woman and Nation: Nationalisms, Transnational Feminisms, and the State,* edited by Caren Kaplan, Norma Alarcón, and Minoo Moallem, 72–91. Durham: Duke University Press, 1999.

Gabaccia, Donna R. "Liberty, Coercion, and the Making of Immigration Historians." *Journal of American History* 84, no. 2 (September 1997): 570–575.

Galarza, Ernesto. *Merchants of Labor: The Mexican Bracero Program Story—An Account of the Managed Migration of Mexican Farm Workers in California, 1942–1960.* Santa Barbara, Calif.: McNally and Loftin, 1964.

Gamboa, Erasmo. *Mexican Labor and World War II: Braceros in the Pacific Northwest, 1942–1947.* Austin: University of Texas Press, 1990.

Gamio, Manuel. *The Mexican Immigrant: His Life Story.* Chicago: University of Chicago Press, 1982.

———. *Mexican Immigration to the United States: A Study of Human Migration and Adjustment.* Chicago: University of Chicago Press, 1930.

Garcia, John A. "Political Integration of Mexican Immigrants: Explorations into the Naturalization Process." *International Migration Review* 15, no. 4 (Winter 1981): 608–625.

García, Juan R. *Mexicans in the Midwest, 1900–1932.* Tucson: University of Arizona Press, 1996.

García y Griego, Manuel. "The Importation of Mexican Contract Laborers to the United States, 1942–1964." In *Between Two Worlds: Mexican Immigrants in the United States,* edited by David G. Gutiérrez, 45–85. Wilmington, Del.: Scholarly Resources, 1996.

Gaspar de Alba, Alicia. *Chicano Art Inside/Outside the Master's House: Cultural Politics and the CARA Exhibition.* Austin: University of Texas Press, 1998.

Gilmore, David D. *Manhood in the Making: Cultural Concepts of Masculinity.* New Haven: Yale University Press, 1990.

Gluck, Sherna Berger, and Daphne Patai, eds. *Women's Worlds: The Feminist Practice of Oral History.* London: Routledge, Chapman and Hall, Inc., 1991.

González, Deena J. *Refusing the Favor: The Spanish-Mexican Women of Santa Fe, 1820–1880.* New York: Oxford University Press, 1999.

González, Juan. *Harvest of Empire: A History of Latinos in America*. New York, Penguin Group, 2000.

González, Soledad, Olivia Ruiz, Laura Velasco, and Ofelia Woo. *Mujeres, migración y maquila en la frontera norte*. Mexico City: El Colegio de La Frontera Norte y El Colegio de México, 1995.

González Gutiérrez, Carlos. "Fostering Identities: Mexico's Relations with Its Diaspora." *Journal of American History* 86, no. 2 (September 1999): 545–567.

González-López, Gloria. "*De madres a hijas*: Gendered Lessons on Virginity across Generations of Mexican Immigrant Women." In *Gender and U.S. Immigration: Contemporary Trends*, edited by Pierrette Hondagneu-Sotelo, 217–240. Berkeley: University of California Press, 1999.

———. *Erotic Journeys: Mexican Immigrants and Their Sex Lives*. Berkeley: University of California Press, 2005.

Goyas Mejía, Ramón. "Elementos históricos para la conformación cultural del ranchero en los Altos de Jalisco: Un estudio histórico." Thesis, Universidad Autónoma Chapingo, 1999.

Griswold, Daniel T. "Willing Workers: Fixing the Problem of Illegal Mexican Migration to the United States." *Executive Summary*, Cato Institute No. 19 (October 15, 2002): 1–26.

Gutiérrez, David G. *Walls and Mirrors: Mexican Americans, Mexican Immigrants, and the Politics of Ethnicity*. Berkeley: University of California Press, 1995.

———, ed. *Between Two Worlds: Mexican Immigrants in the United States*. Washington, Del.: Scholarly Resources, 1996.

Gutiérrez, David G., and Pierrette Hondagneu-Sotelo. "Introduction: Nation and Migration." *American Quarterly* 60, no. 3 (September 2008): 503–521.

Gutmann, Matthew C. *The Meanings of Macho: Being a Man in Mexico City*. Berkeley: University of California Press, 1996.

Hartshorne, Richard. "Racial Maps of the United States." *Geographical Review* 28, no. 2 (April 1938): 276–288.

Harzig, Christiane, ed. *Peasant Maids: City Women from the European Countryside to Urban America*. Ithaca: Cornell University Press, 1997.

Hayes-Bautista, David E. *La Nueva California: Latinos in the Golden State*. Berkeley: University of California Press, 2004.

Hernández Alvarez, José. "A Demographic Profile of the Mexican Immigration to the United States, 1910–1950." *Journal of Inter-American Studies* 8, no. 3 (July 1966): 471–496.

Hirsch, Jennifer S. *A Courtship after Marriage: Sexuality and Love in Mexican Transnational Families*. Berkeley: University of California Press, 2003.

Hondagneu-Sotelo, Pierrette. *Doméstica: Immigrant Workers Cleaning and Caring in the Shadows of Affluence*. Berkeley: University of California Press, 2001.

———. *Gendered Transitions: Mexican Experiences of Immigration*. Berkeley: University of California Press, 1994.

———. "Overcoming Patriarchal Constraints: The Reconstruction of Gender

Relations among Mexican Immigrant Women and Men." *Gender and Society* 6, no. 3 (September 1992): 393–415.

———, ed. *Gender and U.S. Immigration: Contemporary Trends.* Berkeley: University of California Press, 1999.

Hondagneu-Sotelo, Pierrette, and Ernestine Avila. "'I'm Here, But I'm There': The Meanings of Latina Transnational Motherhood." In *Women and Migration in the U.S.-Mexico Borderlands*, edited by Denise A. Segura and Patricia Zavella, 388–414. Durham: Duke University Press, 2007.

Humphrey, Norman Daymond. "The Changing Structure of the Detroit Mexican Family: An Index of Acculturation." *American Sociological Review* 9 (December 1944): 622–626.

———. "The Detroit Mexican Immigrant and Naturalization." *Social Forces* 22 (March 1944): 332–335.

———. "The Education and Language of Detroit Mexicans." *Journal of Educational Sociology* 17 (May 1944): 534–542.

———. "Employment Patterns of Mexicans in Detroit." *Monthly Labor Review* 68 (November 1945): 913–924.

———. "Ethnic Images and Stereotypes of Mexicans and Americans." *American Journal of Economics and Sociology* 14 (April 1955): 305–313.

———. "The Housing and Household Practices of Detroit Mexicans." *Social Forces* 24, no. 4 (May 1946): 433–437.

———. "The Integration of the Detroit Mexican Colony." *American Journal of Economics and Sociology* 3 (January 1944): 155–166.

———. "The Mexican Peasant in Detroit." Ph.D dissertation, University of Michigan, 1943.

———. "Mexican Repatriation from Michigan: Public Assistance in Historical Perspective." *Social Service Review* 15 (September 1941): 497–513.

———. "The Migration and Settlement of Detroit Mexicans." *Economic Geography* 19 (July 1943): 357–361.

———. "Some Marriage Problems of Detroit Mexicans." *Applied Anthropology* 3 (December 1943): 13–15.

———. "The Stereotype and Social Types of Mexican-American Youths." *Journal of Social Psychology* 22 (1945): 69–78.

Irwin, Robert McKee, Edward J. McCaughan, and Michelle Rocío Nasser. *The Famous 41: Sexuality and Social Control in Mexico, 1901.* Macmillan: Palgrave, 2003.

Joseph, Gilbert, Anne Rubenstein, and Eric Zolov, eds. *Fragments of a Golden Age: The Politics of Culture in Mexico since 1940.* Durham: Duke University Press, 2001.

Kerr, Louise Año Nuevo. "Chicano Settlements in Chicago: A Brief History." *Journal of Ethnic Studies* 2, no. 4 (Winter 1975): 22–32.

Largent, Mark A. *Breeding Contempt: The History of Coerced Sterilization in the United States.* London: Rutgers University Press, 2008.

Lavrin, Asunción, ed. *Sexuality and Marriage in Colonial Latin America.* Lincoln: University of Nebraska Press, 1989.

Lugo-Lugo, Carmen R., and Mary K. Bloodsworth-Lugo, eds. *A New Kind of Containment: "The War on Terror," Sexuality and Race.* New York: Rodopi Press, 2009.

Luibhéid, Eithne. *Entry Denied: Controlling Sexuality at the Border.* Minneapolis: University of Minnesota Press, 2002.

———. "Looking Like a Lesbian: The Organization of Sexual Monitoring at the United States–Mexico Border." In *Women and Migration in the U.S.-Mexico Borderlands,* edited by Denise A. Segura and Patricia Zavella, 106–133. Durham: Duke University Press, 2007.

Luibhéid, Eithne, and Lionel Cantú, Jr., eds. *Queer Migrations: Sexuality, U.S. Citizenship, and Border Crossings.* Minneapolis: University of Minnesota Press, 2005.

Malkin, Victoria. "Reproduction of Gender Relations in the Mexican Immigrant Community of New Rochelle, New York." In *Women and Migration in the U.S.-Mexico Borderlands,* edited by Denise A. Segura and Patricia Zavella, 415–437. Durham: Duke University Press, 2007.

Marks, Lara V. *Sexual Chemistry: A History of the Contraceptive Pill.* New Haven: Yale University Press, 2001.

Martin, Patricia Preciado. *Songs My Mother Sang to Me: An Oral History of Mexican American Women.* Tucson: University of Arizona Press, 1992.

Martínez, Rubén. *Crossing Over: A Mexican Family on the Migrant Trail.* New York: Henry Holt and Company, 2001.

———. "The Undocumented Virgin." In *Goddess of the Americas: Writings on the Virgin of Guadalupe,* ed. Ana Castillo, 98–112. New York: Fieverhead Books, 1996.

Massey, Douglas S. "Understanding Mexican Migration to the United States." *American Journal of Sociology* 92, no. 6 (May 1987): 1372–1403.

Massey, Douglas S., Rafael Alarcón, Jorge Durand, and Humberto González. *Return to Aztlan: The Social Process of International Migration from Western Mexico.* Berkeley: University of California Press, 1987.

Massey, Douglas S., Jorge Durand, and Nolan J. Malone. *Beyond Smoke and Mirrors: Mexican Immigration in an Era of Economic Integration.* New York: Russell Sage Foundation, 2002.

Massey, Douglas S., Luin Goldring, and Jorge Durand. "Continuities in Transnational Migration: An Analysis of Nineteen Mexican Communities." *American Journal of Sociology* 99, no. 6 (May 1994): 1492–1533.

McWilliams, Carey. *North from Mexico: The Spanish-Speaking People of the United States.* New York: Praeger, 1990.

Meyer, Lorenzo. "La encrucijada." In *Historia general de México 2,* 1273–1373. Mexico City: El Colegio de México y Harla, S.A. de C.V., 1988.

Miller, Michael Nelson. *Red, White and Green: The Maturing of Mexicanidad, 1940–1946*. El Paso: University of Texas Press, 1998.

Molyneux, Maxine, and Elizabeth Dore, eds. *Hidden Histories of Gender and the State in Latin America*. Durham: Duke University Press, 2000.

Nájera-Ramírez, Olga. "Unruly Passions: Poetics, Performance, and Gender in the Ranchera Song." In *Women and Migration in the U.S.-Mexico Borderlands*, edited by Denise A. Segura and Patricia Zavella, 456–476. Durham: Duke University Press, 2007.

Nakano Glen, Evelyn. *Issei, Nisei, War Bride: Three Generations of Japanese American Women in Domestic Service*. Philadelphia: Temple University Press, 1986.

Nodín Valdés, Dionicio. *Barrios Norteños: St. Paul and Midwestern Mexican Communities in the Twentieth Century*. Austin: University of Texas Press, 2000.

Nye, Robert A., ed. *Sexuality*. Oxford: Oxford University Press, 1999.

Ong Hing, Bill. *Defining America through Immigration Policy*. Philadelphia: Temple University Press, 2004.

———. *Deporting Our Souls: Values, Morality, and Immigration Policy*. Cambridge: Cambridge University Press, 2006.

Orozco Orozco, José Zócimo. *San Ignacio Cerro Gordo: Un pueblo de Jalisco, con su hacienda, su gente y su historia*. Mexico City: Universidad de Guadalajara, 1983.

Pedraza, Silvia. "Women and Migration: The Social Consequences of Gender." *Annual Review of Sociology* 17 (1991): 303–325.

Peiss, Kathy. "Charity Girls and City Pleasures." In *Major Problems in the History of American Sexuality*, 288–298. Boston: Houghton Mifflin Company, 2002.

Pérez, Emma. *The Decolonial Imaginary: Writing Chicanas into History*. Bloomington: Indiana University Press, 1999.

———. "Speaking from the Margin: Uninvited Discourse on Sexuality and Power." In *Building with Our Own Hands: New Directions in Chicana Scholarship*, edited by Beatríz Pesquera and Adela de la Torre, 57–74. Berkeley: University of California Press, 1991.

Pescador, Juan Javier. *De bautizados a fieles difuntos: Familia y mentalidades en una parroquia urbana, Santa Catarina de México, 1568–1820*. Mexico City: Colegio de México and Centro para Estudios de Demografía y de Desarrollo Urbano, 1992.

———. *The New World Inside a Basque Village: The Oiartzun Valley and Its Atlantic Emigrants, 1550–1800*. Reno: University of Nevada Press, 2004.

———. *"¡Vamos Taximaroa!* Mexican/Chicano Soccer Associations and Transnational/Translocal Communities, 1967–2002." *Latino Studies* 2, no. 3 (December 2004): 352–376.

Pesquera, Beatríz, and Adela de la Torre, eds. *Building with Our Own Hands: New Directions in Chicana Scholarship*. Berkeley: University of California Press, 1991.

Phillips, Kim M., and Barry Reay. *A Reader: Sexualities in History*. New York: Routledge. 2002.

Pilcher, Jeffrey M. *¡Que vivan los tamales! Food and the Making of Mexican Identity.* Albuquerque: University of New Mexico Press, 1998.

Pinzón, Dulce. Super Heroes Photographic Series. http://www.dulcepinzon.com/en_projects_superhero.htm.

Purnell, Jennie. *Popular Movements and State Formation in Revolutionary Mexico: The Agraristas and Cristeros of Michoacán.* Durham: Duke University Press, 1999.

Quezada, Noemí. *Sexualidad, amor y erotismo: México prehispánico y México colonial.* Mexico City: Universidad Nacional Autónoma de México y Plaza y Valdés Editores, 1996.

Reimers, David M. *Unwelcome Strangers: American Identity and the Turn against Immigration.* New York: Columbia University Press, 1998.

Reyes, Aurelio de los. *Medio siglo de cine mexicano (1896–1947).* Mexico City: Editorial Trillas, S.A. de C.V., 1987.

Rouse, Roger. "Mexican Migration and the Social Space of Postmodernism." In *Between Two Worlds: Mexican Immigrants in the United States,* edited by David G. Gutiérrez, 247–263. Washington, Del.: Scholarly Resources, Inc., 1996.

Ruiz, Vicki L. *From Out of the Shadows: Mexican Women in Twentieth-Century America.* New York: Oxford University Press, 1998.

Ruiz, Vicki L., and Ellen Carol DuBois, eds. *Unequal Sisters: A Multicultural Reader in U.S. Women's History.* New York: Routledge, 2000.

Ruiz, Vicki L., and Susan Tiano, eds. *Women on the U.S.-Mexico Border: Responses to Change.* Boston: Allen and Unwin, 1987.

Salazar-Parreñas, Rhacel. *Servants of Globalization: Women, Migration, and Domestic Work.* Stanford, Calif.: Stanford University Press, 2001.

Saldívar-Hull, Sonia. *Feminism on the Border: Chicana Gender Politics and Literature.* Berkeley: University of California Press, 2000.

Sánchez, George J. *Becoming Mexican American: Ethnicity, Culture, and Identity in Chicano Los Angeles, 1900–1945.* New York: Oxford University Press, 1993.

Sánchez Susarrey, Jaime, and Ignacio Medina Sánchez. *Jalisco: Desde la revolución, 1940–1975.* Guadalajara: Gobierno del Estado de Jalisco/Universidad de Guadalajara, 1987.

Sassen, Saskia. *Globalization and Its Discontents: Essays on the New Mobility of People and Money.* New York: New Press, 1998.

———. "U.S. Immigration Policy toward Mexico in a Global Economy." In *Between Two Worlds: Mexican Immigrants in the United States,* edited by David G. Gutiérrez, 213–227. Washington, Del.: Scholarly Resources, Inc., 1996.

Segura, Denise A., and Patricia Zavella, eds. *Women and Migration in the U.S.-Mexico Borderlands: A Reader.* Durham: Duke University Press, 2007.

Siems, Larry. *Between the Lines: Letters between Undocumented Mexican and Central American Immigrants and Their Families and Friends.* Tucson and London: University of Arizona Press, 1992.

Solinger, Rickie. *Pregnancy and Power: A Short History of Reproductive Politics in America*. New York: New York University Press, 2005.

Suárez Findlay, Eileen J. *Imposing Decency: The Politics of Sexuality and Race in Puerto Rico, 1870–1920*. Durham: Duke University Press, 1999.

Suárez-Orozco, Marcelo, and Mariela Páez, eds. *Latinos: Remaking America*. Berkeley: University of California Press, 2002.

Sugrue, Thomas J. *The Origins of the Urban Crisis: Race and Inequality in Postwar Detroit*. Princeton, N.J.: Princeton University Press, 1996.

Taylor, Paul S. *Mexican Labor in the United States: Chicago and the Calumet Region*. University of California Publications in Economics, Vol. 7, No. 2. Berkeley: University of California Press, 1932.

———. *A Spanish-Mexican Peasant Community: Arandas in Jalisco, Mexico*. Berkeley: University of California Press, 1933.

Thelen, David. "Rethinking History and the Nation-State: Mexico and the United States." *Journal of American History* 86, no. 2 (September 1999): 438–452.

Twinam, Ann. *Public Lives, Private Secrets: Gender, Honor, Sexuality, and Illegitimacy in Colonial Spanish America*. Stanford, Calif.: Stanford University Press, 1999.

Urrea, Luis Alberto, *The Devil's Highway: A True Story*. New York: Little, Brown and Company, 2004.

Valdes, Dennis N. *Al Norte: Agricultural Workers in the Great Lakes Region*. Austin: University of Texas Press, 1991.

Valenzuela Varela, María Basilia. *Experiencias municipales de ámbito institucional*. Edited by Antonio Sánchez Bernal. Guadalajara: Universidad de Guadalajara, 2002.

———. "Municipalización, ciudadanía y migración en los Altos de Jalisco." In *Experiencias municipales de ámbito institucional*, edited by Antonio Sánchez Bernal, 211–277. Guadalajara: Universidad de Guadalajara, 2002.

Valenzuela Varela, María Basilia, and Claudia Mónica Sánchez Bernal. "Aportes para la formación del municipio San Ignacio Cerro Gordo: Una experiencia de vinculación." *De Vinci* (Universidad de Guadalajara) 3, no. 6 (April 2001): 40–55.

Vargas, Zaragosa. *Proletarians of the North: A History of Mexican Industrial Workers in Detroit and the Midwest, 1917–1933*. Berkeley: University of California Press, 1993.

———, ed. *Major Problems in Mexican American History*. Boston: Houghton Mifflin Company, 1999.

Viruell-Fuentes, Edna A. "'My Heart Is Always There': The Transnational Practices of First-Generation Mexican Immigrant and Second-Generation Mexican American Women." *Identities: Global Studies in Power and Culture* 13, no. 3 (July–September 2006): 335–362.

Wasserman, Mark. *Everyday Life and Politics in Nineteenth Century Mexico: Men, Women, and War*. Albuquerque: University of New Mexico Press, 2000.

Williams, Raymond. *The Country and the City.* New York: Oxford University Press, 1973.

Woo Morales, Ofelia. *Las mujeres también nos vamos al norte.* Guadalajara: Universidad de Guadalajara, 2001.

Zavala de Cosio, María Eugenia. "Políticas de población en México." *Revista Mexicana de Sociología* 52, no. 1 (January–March 1990): 15–32.

INDEX

Page numbers in boldface indicate illustrations.